One Man's Way

One Man's Way

The Story and Message of
NORMAN VINCENT PEALE
Minister to Millions

❧

A BIOGRAPHY BY
Arthur Gordon

NEWLY REVISED
MEMBERS EDITION

FOUNDATION FOR CHRISTIAN LIVING
PAWLING, NEW YORK 12564

ONE MAN'S WAY
NORMAN VINCENT PEALE:
Minister to Millions

Originally published by Prentice-Hall, Inc. under the title NORMAN VINCENT PEALE: *Minister to Millions*.

Revised and published by the Foundation for Christian Living, Pawling, New York 12564.

© 1972, 1958 by
Arthur Gordon

Printed in the United States of America

Contents

❧⚙❧

Say to them that are of a fearful heart,
Be strong, fear not.

—Isaiah 35:4

CHAPTER I

Sweet Land of Liberty

1898

❧

All over Ohio, all over the nation, the scene was being enacted. The Memorial Day ritual varied from place to place, but the essence of it was the same: a gathering at the town hall or the fire station or some central church. Then the parade to the cemetery on the edge of town.

In the cemetery, grassy and quiet and old, the graves of former soldiers had already been decorated by members of the Ladies Volunteer Group. The flowers made bright splashes of color against the weathered stones; the little flags stirred in the breeze. Back in a grove of trees, picnic tables were set up. After the ceremonies, people would want to relax, gossip, eat the lunches brought in buggies or farm-wagons, sometimes from miles away.

Local dignitaries led the parade: the mayor, if there was one, or perhaps some Grand Marshal appointed for the occasion. Then came the band, sunlight glinting on the cornets and tubas, small barefoot boys scampering ecstatically alongside. Behind the band came the military. It was more than thirty years since Appomattox, now, but in Ohio the blue coats of the Grand Army of the Republic still made a brave showing. The G.A.R., the Republican Party, the Methodist Church, and the Anti-Saloon League—these were the forces to reckon with in Ohio as the nineteenth century moved to its close.

This Memorial Day had an unusual solemnity—the country was at war. The war seemed far from Ohio, but, all the same, men were fighting and dying. No one had the slightest doubt as to the eventual outcome. The Spaniards would be licked. It was just a matter of time.

In the cemetery of the little town of Bowersville, the last notes of taps died away. The minister of the Baptist church offered a prayer. An agitated youth, winner of a recent elocution contest, recited the Gettysburg Address—with gestures. The *Star-Spangled Banner* was rendered, solo, by the band's trumpeter, a triple-tongued artist of local renown. It was then announced that after the band had played *Marching Through Georgia* and *Tenting Tonight,* the oration of the day would be delivered by the Reverend Charles Clifford Peale, of the Methodist church.

In the attentive crowd, a sunburned farmer nudged his wife. "Brother Peale looks a little nervous, don't he? Maybe he hasn't had time to figger out what he's going to say."

His wife gave him a scornful glance. "Brother Peale's got more on his mind than just makin' a speech!"

On the bunting-covered platform, young Brother Peale took out a handkerchief and wiped his broad forehead. From where he sat he could see the entrance to the cemetery, and part of the dirt road leading back to town. He had made Anna promise to send word the moment she felt anything like a real labor pain. This first baby, he knew, would probably take its time about arriving and give plenty of warning. Still, he had hated to leave her there, rocking placidly on the porch of the little frame house with her sewing in her lap. In what was left of her lap!

Anna, he thought, with a sudden irrational surge of apprehension. Dear Lord, don't let anything go wrong, let her have an easy time. . . .

Unbidden, there rose up in his mind a recollection of the first time he had seen Anna. He had been standing in his father's store in Lynchburg, and across the street he had glimpsed a girl hurrying along, blue-eyed, blonde, with such an eagerness, such a vitality about her that he had whistled with amazement and delight. "Who on earth is *that?*" he had asked. "That? Oh, that's Andrew DeLaney's daughter," somebody said. "Fine, church-going girl. Pretty as a picture, too." "Well," he had said, "I'll let you in on something. That's the girl I'm going to marry."

They thought he was joking, of course, and maybe he was. But in the end, he had married her. Three years ago, not long after he had made the most important decision of his life— the decision to leave the practice of medicine for the ministry —he had married Anna DeLaney. Married her in Lynchburg and carried her off in triumph to his first church in the tiny farming community of Sugar Tree Ridge. He could see the old buggy yet, loaded with all their possessions, a large tin washtub balanced precariously on top, and the old horse plodding along the dusty road, and all of their lives stretching out invisibly ahead of them.

Those three years in Sugar Tree Ridge had been happy ones. Not much money—in fact, almost none at all. But you didn't need much money in Sugar Tree Ridge. Food was no problem —not with a congregation of farmers who tilled some of the richest land the good Lord ever put at the disposal of His servants. Baskets of apples, bushels of corn, sides of bacon, chickens, eggs, hams—sometimes the donor did not even wait to be thanked, just left them on the doorstep and vanished.

The three years had passed quickly. Now they were in Bowersville, larger than Sugar Tree Ridge, but essentially much the same. Everyone had welcomed them, seemed to like them. Anna's warmth and vitality and sense of humor made friends for her instantly. As for himself, he was no youngster, but a mature man of twenty-eight who had been a successful physician, Health Commissioner of the city of Milwaukee, no less, before he was old enough to vote. . . .

With a clash of cymbals that shivered the warm air, the band completed its stampede through Georgia. Applause burst forth, then was stilled as the conductor raised his baton again. Surreptitiously, the young minister eased out his watch, opened the gold case that covered its face. Eleven fifteen. He would be lucky to escape by noon. One thing he was sure of: today's oration was going to be considerably shorter than usual.

He smiled suddenly, remembering the breath-taking event of a previous Fourth of July. On that occasion the orator of the day, a tall, gloomy man who was a Congressional candidate, had chosen to give a dramatic reading of the Declaration of Independence. At one climactic moment his false teeth had jumped completely out of his mouth. While the audience sat spellbound, he reached out a long arm, caught them neatly in mid-air, and went right on as if nothing had happened. Anna had been convulsed. The episode reminded her, she said, of the old colored cook her family had had back in Kentucky. This cook made beautiful pies with elaborately scalloped crusts. When asked how she achieved such symmetrical patterns, she beamed and brandished *her* false teeth. "Wif dese!" she said happily. The consumption of pies in the DeLaney family was never the same again.

Now the band was playing *Tenting Tonight*. In their blue uniforms, the remnants of the Grand Army of the Republic stood at parade rest, their faces far-away and a little sad. This present war meant little to them. For them that other titanic struggle was far more real: Bull Run, Antietam, Chancellorsville, Gettysburg. As a boy Clifford Peale had listened, spellbound, to the stories told around the pot-bellied stove in his father's store. His father, that gentle man, had fought with a regiment of Ohio volunteers, then had turned—not too successfully—to storekeeping. His mother, Laura Peale—she was the strong-minded one, the one who had prayed over him during his almost fatal illness, who had helped him decide, when he finally recovered, to dedicate his life to the Lord.

The young minister stared blankly ahead of him. Had his mother helped him decide, or had she decided for him? He had wondered often about that, and had come to the conclusion, finally, that it made little difference. He missed the practice of medicine, there was no denying that. He missed the excitement, the intimate contact with the ultimate realities of life and death. And yet, a minister's role was not unlike a doctor's. There was a closer connection than most people realized between diseases of the body and disorders of the soul and of the mind.

Old Grandfather Fulton had taught him that. Robert Fulton, M.D., descendant of the steamboat inventor, who came from Baltimore to Ohio, married Mary Morgan when he was thirty, lived happily with her for fifty-five years, fathered eleven children, and died at eighty-nine after a long and vigorous and useful life. He was a Methodist Local Preacher and an ardent prohibitionist, as well as a doctor. He was just as likely to prescribe prayer for a patient as medicine, and he often said that sugar-and-water pills frequently were just as effective as the latest drugs—so long as the patient didn't know they were only sugar-and-water. "I tell you, Cliff," he used to say, "most of these people aren't really sick in their bodies; they're sick in their minds."

A great doctor, a grand old man . . .

Abruptly, like a cloud passing over the sun, an unwelcome thought slid into his mind. This doctor who was attending

Anna—a good man, a kind man, thoroughly competent, no doubt. He had delivered dozens of babies—hundreds, perhaps. But in this case . . . in this case . . .

He noticed, suddenly, that the palms of his hands were wet. He took out his handkerchief again, dried them, squinted up at the sun, trying to look relaxed and unconcerned. If all went well, if it turned out to be a perfectly normal delivery, there was nothing to worry about. Nature would take care of everything. But if there were any complications, if anything went wrong . . .

He stuffed the handkerchief back into his pocket. Nothing would go wrong. Anna had had a normal pregnancy, she was a strong, healthy girl. And yet . . .

And yet he felt that he himself, by training and experience and temperament, was better equipped to cope with a crisis than any rural doctor was likely to be. It was four years, true, since he had actively practiced medicine, four years since he had renounced the profession he loved to devote the rest of his years to the service of the Lord. But the obstetrical techniques he had learned at the Medical College of Ohio and had perfected in Milwaukee were far ahead of anything this local man—beloved as he was—had been trained in.

This wasn't pride, this wasn't arrogance. This, he felt, was a fact.

He shifted his feet uneasily, staring at the sea of faces. What would be the reaction of these people, of his own congregation, if it became known that the pastor of the Methodist church—apparently pondering his Memorial Day oration—was actually contemplating the possibility of excluding the local physician and delivering his own wife of their first-born child? Most of these people didn't know that he had ever been a doctor. And even if they did know, chances were . . .

The music died away. In the sudden hush that followed, he heard his own name announced. A ripple of applause greeted him as he stood up. Then an expectant silence.

He spoke without notes, as he always did. He knew his audience, and he knew their mood. They were solid people: clean, decent, honest, conservative, and proud. They believed without question in the rightness of their own ideas, their own moral standards, their own way of life. The richness of the rolling countryside supported them, heightened their optimism, strengthened their faith in a just and bounteous God. They believed in the perfectability of man and the inevitability of progress. They were convinced that the United States of America, founded upon religious principles by religious men, was directly under the guiding hand of the Almighty—and that Ohio was the garden spot of the U.S.A.

They were uncompromising people. Black was black and white was white; right was right and wrong was wrong. There was no middle ground, no hesitant shades of gray. A man who did not pay his debts was a thief; for a woman who made a misstep, even one, they had a short and ugly word. The greatest enemy of mankind, many of them felt, was the Demon Rum . . . and a couple of steps behind the Demon came the Democrats.

They were shrewd traders when they had to be, canny businessmen. They were only two or three generations away from the eastern seaboard—the thriftiness of the Yankee was still in them (tightfistedness, a Virginian or a Georgian might have called it), and some of the religious fervor of the Puritans, and the industry of the Pennsylvania Dutch.

The young minister knew his audience because he was a part of it. He knew, instinctively, that the war in Cuba did not touch them deeply, and so at first he spoke of other things: of the debt they owed to the men who had died to bring the nation into being, who had fought for more than a hundred years to safeguard its liberties. War itself, he said, was evil, but there were times when it was the lesser of evils; he hoped the day would never come when, rather than resort to war, Americans would submit to tyranny.

He forgot about his own problems. The mesmeric spell of communication with other minds took hold of him and he spoke earnestly, eloquently for twenty minutes while the sun blazed down and the clouds grazed peacefully across the sky like fat white sheep and the horses tethered outside the cemetery sneezed and snorted and stamped their feet.

At the end he tried to give them a little of the sense of gratitude that he himself felt for life, for living, a word of encouragement and optimism for them to take home if they so desired.

"Never forget," he said, "what a great country this is! Never forget how lucky we are to live in it! We are at war, it's true. But life is still good. It's good because here is the old flag, and over there is the old church, and here we stand among our friends and the graves of the loved ones who have gone before. Troubles may beset us—they come to all of us at times—but they will pass. Every morning the sun will rise, and the stars come nightly to the sky. Soon victory will be ours, and the flags will burst out, and thousands will be singing the old marching song of freedom. Then we shall move into a new era that will tax our intelligence and our faith, but will give us the thrill known to generation after generation of Americans—the thrill of building a new world on a foundation of religion and democracy and freedom!

"So take courage; be of good cheer! And give thanks unto the Lord, for He is very good!"

He sat down, perspiring and wilted, but buoyed up by the elation he always felt when he knew he had reached an audience. That, at least, was one advantage a minister had over a doctor. While the applause continued, he glanced anxiously toward the cemetery gate. Still no message from Anna. Everything must be quiet at home.

The ceremonies were concluded quickly. People came forward to shake his hand and say pleasant things about his speech. One broad-hipped farmer's wife offered him a share of her family's picnic. "We've got more than enough, Brother Peale. Be mighty glad if you'd join us."

"Thanks," he said. "I'd like to, but I've got to get home. If I don't hurry, the stork may arrive before I do."

Walking quickly through the center of town, he wondered what the stork would bring. Boy or girl, it made no difference, really. In either case, he hoped this would be the first of several visits from that overworked bird. When there was only one child in a family, parental attention and affection had a tendency to become too concentrated.

Take his own mother's desire to have him become a preacher, for instance. He had resisted it, apparently rejected it altogether. And yet it must have had its effect. She was a strong-minded woman, deeply devout. The Lord Himself no doubt listened with considerable attention to her prayers. And one of her prayers had always been that her son—Cliffie, she always called him—would become a man of God.

His conversion from the practice of medicine had been a curious thing, really. Medicine had fascinated him, he had been good at it, he had had almost instantaneous success. It was true that a doctor saw a good deal of the seamy side of life, and a Public Health Commissioner even more than an ordinary practitioner. Some latent idealism in him had always shied away from this. But the distaste was not strong enough to have changed his life entirely.

No, it had been something deeper than that, some basic dissatisfaction with himself that made itself known from time to time. The time, for instance, when he went to church in Hamilton, Ohio, and heard a sermon by a brilliant Methodist clergyman named Gillette. The preacher said that most human beings were like men working all day in a coal mine, coming up only at night. What a world they would see, the minister cried, if they could come to the surface at high noon, with the sun shining brightly. What color, what vividness, what joy, what a *difference!* And sitting there listening, he—the rising young Dr. Peale—had found himself greatly moved. He felt almost as if Somebody was standing beside him, saying quietly, "He is talking about *you*. You must change your life. You must come up out of the coal mine of materialism and live in the radiance of the spiritual life."

It had been a profoundly moving experience. Afterwards the thought came to him clearly that it was God, calling him into the ministry. But he decided not to yield. He had studied medicine and he intended to practice medicine. And for a while he did.

But then his health, never too strong, broke down. An operation became necessary, a dangerous and painful one. He survived, but it left him weak, drained, half dead.

They took him home, to Lynchburg, where his mother nursed him night and day. And when at last it was apparent that he was not going to die after all, that he would recover, she said to him, "Cliffie, the Lord has spared your life. I think He had His reasons. What do you think?"

He found that the answer came easily, as if somehow the whole thing had been planned and settled long ago. "I think so too," he said. "I owe my life to the Lord. I'll give it to Him. I'll stop being a doctor. I'll be a minister."

His mother wept.

It had been a tremendous decision. He could not honestly say that he had never regretted it; there were times when he yearned to use the skill and knowledge so painfully acquired. But these twinges of regret were few. He had a new life; he had been born again. What he was doing now was part of a divine plan; he was sure of it. And part of the plan, the best part of all, was Anna.

She was so much more than just a pretty girl. On the one hand she had all the gaiety and humor of her Irish father. Andrew DeLaney had left the old country at the ripe old age of seven, had stowed away on a ship bound for America. He had escaped detection, so the story went, by hiding under a

sympathetic lady's great hoopskirts, had found his way eventually to Kentucky where he became a cooper, a barrel-maker.

Most barrels in those days were designed to contain just one
thing: whiskey. Consequently when Irish Andrew fell in love
with a stanchly Methodist, rigidly moral young lady named
Potts, something had to give. Andy did. He gave up his
whiskey-barrel making, allowed himself to be converted, married the girl, and carried her off to Lynchburg, Ohio, where
they lived happily ever after, battling constantly to put the
town's distillery out of business and raising five children, of
whom Anna was by general consent the liveliest and brightest.

From her DeLaney father she got her love of music and
poetry, her quicksilver moods of optimism and discouragement, her fondness for good conversation, for the mystery and
wonder and romance of living. From the Potts, her solid Dutch
ancestors, she drew her practicality, her frugality, the per-
fectionism that demanded high performance from herself and
everyone else. Her husband was constantly amazed at the
scope and quality of her mind. She had enormous powers of
concentration and a memory bordering on total recall. She
could glance at a printed page, close the book, and recite the
gist of it almost word for word. There were times when the
young minister wondered what his wife would do with these
unusual endowments, whether perhaps they were not wasted
in her role of small-town parson's wife. He had mentioned this
more than once, but Anna always laughed at him. "If the Lord
has something for me to do," she said, "He'll let me know what
it is in His own good time."

The little frame house came into view. Anna was not on the
porch. He quickened his pace, feeling a little chill wind of
apprehension blow down his spine. As he reached the steps, the
front door opened and one of their neighbors came out. Her
broad face reflected nothing but pleased satisfaction, and he
felt the knotted fist inside of him relax. "Everything all right,
Mrs. Morgan?"

She beamed at him, delighted to be the bearer of news. "Anna had her first pain just a little while ago. I told her to go and lie down. I was just going over to let Mrs. Muller know. We'll both be right here, in case you want or need anything. . . ."

"Thanks, Mrs. Morgan." He moved past her quickly, through the small living-room, into the ground floor bedroom. Anna was lying on the big bed, propped up against the pillows. She looked unconcerned, relaxed and happy. "How was it?" she said eagerly. "How did it go?"

He stared at her blankly. "How did what go?"

"The oration, silly! Your speech! Did they like it?"

"Oh, the speech! Sure, it went all right. At least, I think it did. What about you?"

"I had a pain. Not a big one. But maybe he's on his way at last."

"He?"

"It's a boy," she said. "I know it is." She wrinkled her nose and twisted her shoulders suddenly. "Here comes another pain. Still not a very big one. What do we do now?"

He sat down on the side of the bed and put his hand over hers. "Nothing for quite a while, I imagine. We just wait."

"It must be a strange and wonderful thing," she said, "when a woman and her doctor are alone in a room like this, at a time like this. Just the two of them. And all of a sudden, instead of two people, there are three. It must be wonderful when a new life begins, just *is*, all at once."

He nodded. "It's miraculous."

"You must have seen it, many times."

"I have. And it's always miraculous."

They waited. The afternoon ebbed away. The neighbors came, Mrs. Morgan and Mrs. Muller. They sat in the living room, bustled around Anna, made it clear that they considered this no place for a husband. They hinted, more than once, that the doctor ought to be called, or at least notified. He put them off.

The long twilight faded into night. He sat by Anna's bed, told her stories, held her hand. Everything seemed to be progressing normally, there was no hint of complications. And yet the curious intuition remained with him, the conviction that before the night was over his wife or perhaps the baby would need more help than an easy-going country doctor could give.

Near midnight, Mrs. Muller told him bluntly that he should send for the doctor. He looked at her disapproving face, her set lips, and reminded himself that her concern was only natural. Over her shoulder he could see Mrs. Morgan looking equally grim. "You ladies must be tired," he said. "Why don't you go home and get some sleep? I'll call you if I need you."

They looked at each other, then back at him, outrage in their faces. "Very well," said Mrs. Muller. "*Very* well! It's your wife, and your responsibility. But mark my words, Brother Peale, if anything goes wrong you'll have it on your conscience for the rest of your life." She opened the front door. "Come on, Laura. There's nothing more we can do here!"

From the porch he watched them go, backs rigid with condemnation. He looked across the road to the cottage of John and Nant Young, John's old wagon standing in front of the house with its empty shafts resting on the ground. He wished that he could talk with them; they were close friends who would understand. But the house stood dark and silent. It would not be fair to disturb them.

He looked up at the indifferent stars, feeling a sudden weakening of his resolution. Maybe this assumption of superior medical skill was pure arrogance on his part. He had practiced no medicine for four years. Even if he had, this was no ordinary patient about whom he could be cool, impersonal, objective. This was Anna. This was their child. . . .

He walked down the three steps, and hesitated. The doctor's house was not two hundred yards away. It would be easy to rouse him, bring him over, put all responsibility into his hands. Suppose he failed to do this and something *did* go wrong? How would he ever forgive himself?

What, he thought suddenly, would old Grandfather Fulton have done in a situation like this?

The answer to that was not difficult: he would have prayed for guidance and then acted as he felt guided.

He closed his eyes, said a short prayer, waited. Above him the night breeze stirred the trees. It was warm and heavy with the smells of summer: the clean scent of grass, the earthy aroma of somebody's cow barn. And suddenly he found himself thinking, not of grandfather Fulton, but of his other grandfather, old Thomas Peale. Squire Peale, they called him, partly because he was the owner of four farms, partly because he was a man of great dignity, tall and erect, a stately old gentleman.

The smell of the cow barn, doubtless, had triggered the association. Many times, as a small boy, he had tagged at his grandfather's heels as the old man inspected his properties. He hired farmers to do the work, but he always supervised them closely. He knew how to get the most out of men, and out of the land, too. Sometimes he would give his grandson a small sickle and have him cradle around old foundations or in fence corners to garner the grain that the mower had missed.

But his most vivid recollection of his grandfather Peale went back to the day when he and his father and his Uncle Wilson had been sitting around the old stove in the Lynchburg store. Suddenly the door opened, and in stepped Squire Peale. After the death of his second wife, the old man—now almost eighty —had hired a housekeeper, a Miss Eliza Lemon, to run his home for him. Now he walked up to the stove and surveyed his two sons and his grandson, "Wilson and Sammy," he said, "Eliza and I have decided to get married."

There was a stunned silence. Nobody said a word. Nobody dared to say a word, although it was obvious from the expression on their faces that his father and his Uncle Wilson would have liked to say a good deal.

"Well," said Squire Peale finally, "I've said what I came to say. I guess I might as well be going."

He went, and then the storm broke. "Ridiculous! At his age!" "All she wants is his money!" "Well, she's got him now!" And so forth, and so on.

But he had taken no part in the discussion because, young though he was, he had secretly admired his grandfather who did proceed to marry Miss Eliza Lemon, and lived with her happily until he died at the age of eighty-three.

And what was it, he asked himself now, that he had admired? Wasn't it the old man's courage to act as he thought right in the face of certain disapproval? And wasn't that chiefly what was giving him pause now, this very moment—fear of the disapproval he had seen in the faces of Mrs. Muller and Mrs. Morgan? Fear of what the neighborhood might think, what his parishioners might say?

Strange, he thought, to have your mind made up for you by a breeze from a cow barn. But who was to say that it *wasn't* an answer to prayer?

He turned quickly and went back into the house. In the bedroom, Anna gave him a wan smile. He saw her hand tighten on the patchwork quilt, grip it until the knuckles were white. She said, with a gasp, "I thought perhaps you had gone for the doctor."

He sat down on the edge of the bed. He said, "I've been thinking about it and praying about it. I'm going to be your doctor, if it's all right with you."

He saw the relief and the happiness come into her eyes. "Oh, Cliff," she said, "I was hoping you'd say that. He's our baby. Let's bring him into the world together!"

The child was born near daybreak. It was not an easy delivery for mother or baby, but the old God-given skill was still in his fingers, and he used it. When the child's head was finally born he saw that the umbilical cord was wrapped tightly around the baby's neck, shutting off the oxygen supply. The child's skin was blue, cyanosed. He completed the delivery, hardly aware in his haste that the baby was a boy. He freed the cord, tied it off, severed it, held the baby up by the heels, and slapped it smartly with the palm of his hand. . . .

Years later, describing the event to his eldest son, he would joke gently about it. "You took a deep breath, Norman," he would say, "and you began to squawk. What's more, you've been squawking ever since!"

CHAPTER II

"Be Somebody!"

❦

Clifford Peale was so proud of his baby that he found it hard to choose a name; none seemed good enough. He was inclined to call the baby Vincent, after Bishop Vincent, his friend and ecclesiastical superior. But he was still procrastinating when Anna's sister, Mae DeLaney, arrived for a visit. Mae was a brisk, decisive person. "Cliff," she said, "if you don't name this baby, I will!"

Actually, Mae did have a hand in the final decision. She had a fondness for poetry, especially Tennyson. One of her favorite quotations was from *Lady Clara Vere de Vere:*

> *Kind hearts are more than coronets,*
> *And simple faith than Norman blood.*

Norman, she said, was a strong, resonant name, and Norman Vincent had a fine, chivalric ring to it. Nobody could propose anything better, so Norman Vincent it was.

He was a bright-eyed baby, blond and round-faced like his mother, much petted and admired by the neighbors who soon forgot the unorthodox circumstances of his birth. ("If anything had gone wrong that night," Clifford Peale said wryly, "I think those women would have formed a posse to lynch me!") His mother, not very surprisingly, was delighted with him. "Look," she cried when he was photographed in his christening gown at the age of four months. "He looks like a bishop already!" And indeed there *was* something faintly pontifical in the benign yet penetrating baby stare and the oratorical gesture the upflung left hand was already making.

In those days it was the policy of the Methodist church not to allow its ministers to remain too long in one place. In 1900, therefore, when Norman was two years old, his father was called to Highland, a town not far from Bowersville and similar in most respects. Here a second child was born, another boy christened Robert Clifford and destined to become a doctor like his namesake, great-grandfather Robert Fulton.

Norman's reaction to the arrival of a new brother and possible rival for his parents' affection was in the classic two-year-old pattern. "Dead the baby, Mummy!" he said urgently, peering at the unwelcome stranger in the crib. "Dead the baby!"

But the baby was there to stay, and there was nothing Master Norman could do about it.

Two more years of rural service passed quickly for the Peales. Religion was a dominant force in Ohio; there were few towns, however small, where revivals were not held regularly and with enthusiasm. Evangelists moved from place to place, their coming eagerly awaited. Successors to Dwight L. Moody, forerunners of Billy Graham, they were judged by the force and fire of their preaching and the number of their conversions. Sometimes the meetings went on for days.

The emotional impact of these gatherings on small-town life was enormous. Not only was religious fervor "revived," but human lives and personalities were dramatically changed. One of young Norman's earliest recollections was of a service at which his father issued the familiar invitation to "come forward and surrender yourself to Jesus Christ." Down the aisle, his footsteps loud in the sudden silence, came a huge, white-haired man who was one of the town's flintiest characters—profane, hard-drinking, irascible, tough. He knelt at the altar while the congregation, hushed and awe-stricken, tried to help him with their prayers, tried to "pray him through," as the saying went.

He knelt there, not ten feet from the wide-eyed child in the Peale family pew. He knelt there, his face transfigured with a blinding inner happiness. And it was no mere momentary impulse: afterwards the man was different. He stopped drinking; he stopped swearing; his anger left him. He became calm and self-assured and kind. The whole town knew this, even the children knew it. Young as he was, Norman never forgot the radiance of the man's face or the feeling of power that came into the church, the mysterious power of religion to reach deep into the human heart and in an instant produce a miracle of personality regeneration.

Not all the moments spent in church were so solemn. One morning in the old Highland church, when Robert was still a baby in arms, he became so fretful that his cries began to distract his father in mid-sermon. "Norman," whispered Anna, "run home and get some crackers for Robert, quickly!"

Norman slid out of the pew and scampered over to the parsonage next door. In a few moments he reappeared with a huge bag of crackers—the way they were sold in those days. He couldn't lift it, but he dragged it the length of the aisle, to the delighted snickers of the congregation, and finally presented it to his mother.

Late in 1902, the family moved to Asbury Methodist Church on Vine Street in Cincinnati. The church authorities had become increasingly impressed with Clifford Peale's enthusiasm and spiritual effectiveness. Now they were willing to give his abilities broader scope. For the next seven years, first in

Asbury and later in Norwood, the Peale family were city-dwellers.

Looking across the broad Ohio, Cincinnati at the turn of the century was a lusty, vital town, "the most eastern of western cities, the most southern of northern cities." The Germanic influence was strong: the language was taught in the schools and heard on the streets. The wheels of industry hummed, trolley bells clanged, the first horseless carriages snorted alarmingly, saloons and beer gardens did a roaring trade despite the dire warnings from almost every pulpit in town on the horrors of drink.

From the start, the young minister and his wife felt happy and at home. Money—or rather, lack of it—remained a problem, more acute now that a friendly farming congregation could no longer be counted on to help fill the larder. But there was no real hardship; no one was ever ill-clothed, or hungry, or deprived of any necessity. Anna preached frugality constantly to her husband and—as they grew older—to her children. Perhaps she overdid this, but she had seen more than one underpaid minister yield to the temptation to borrow money, sink into debt, and destroy himself and his career. She was determined that no such fate should overtake her own family, and she counted the pennies grimly.

She also found, somewhat to her surprise, that she had a talent for organization and a flair for public speaking that made her an ideal committee woman. Soon she was as busy with church and civic affairs as her primary role of wife and mother would permit. Far from resenting this, her husband was delighted, urged her on, praised her lavishly, and rarely made a move of any kind without consulting her first.

As for Master Norman, his earliest recollection of Cincinnati was the ear-splitting screech of wheels as the trolley rounded a curve just outside the parsonage on Gilman Avenue. He was a bright child, with a quick mind and a retentive memory.

But he was sensitive—a sharp word could reduce him to gloom. And he was painfully shy.

His parents, extroverts by training if not by birth, felt that such diffidence was a handicap, something to be fought with and overcome. Now and then, acting on the old sink-or-swim theory, they would call upon their bashful boy to recite a poem to an admiring circle of friends or relatives. The chief result of this was that whenever he saw any visitors arriving, Norman would hide in the attic. His Uncle Will used to tell of being sent to find Norman and dragging him from his hiding place to the living room where, like an early Christian being thrown to the lions, he was ordered to speak his piece about the boy on the burning deck.

Brother Bob, two years younger, suffered from no such exposed nerve-ends. But, lacking Norman's flypaper memory for verse, he was spared such ordeals.

From the start, Bob was the more rugged, the more athletic of the two. He was tough and aggressive, ever self-assured, always ready for a fight. Norman, on the other hand, was thin for his age and soon became self-conscious about this. He had the competitive instinct and the desire to excel, but he lacked his brother's heft and physique, and this troubled him.

Like all small boys, Norman admired strength and leadership, and to him the embodiment of these manly qualities was his father. The fact that in church his father led the congregation and spoke with authority enhanced the aura. In one of Clifford Peale's early churches, the omnipresence of God was depicted by a great all-seeing, all-knowing eye painted above the altar. This eye made a deep impression on most young worshippers, and Norman was no exception. It was an awesome reminder that God was always there, watching every action, judging every thought. The eye looked out unblinkingly above the minister's head, and it seemed altogether appropriate to Norman that his father should be the spokesman for God.

Sometimes the minister would be asked to return to one of his former churches as guest preacher. He would board a train with his wife and two little boys, and often spend the whole weekend with old friends in the country. One of Norman's most vivid childhood recollections was of such a day: a country church by a dusty road somewhere, hot sunlight slanting through the open windows and glinting on the great green ocean of corn, "corn knee-high by the 4th of July," that lapped almost at the foot of the church steps. He could remember the lazy summer sounds, the creak of harness where the buggies were hitched outside, the smell of horse, the liquid mourning of doves, the clear sleepy whistle of quail. . . .

He could see it all with photographic clarity: his mother sitting in the pew between Bob and himself, nodding her head as she listened to the sermon and smiling now and then—she was never one to be solemn just because she was in church. And his father up in the pulpit behind the Book, gesturing with both hands, pointing to the flag sometimes, talking about the love of God and the greatness of America and the essential goodness of people in general and Ohio people in particular.

And the timeless old hymns, and the familiarity of the liturgy, and the security and the sense of belonging to an era and a culture that considered itself, without conscious arrogance, to be the apex of civilization. . . . All these things made their mark on his growing, impressionable mind, a mark so deep that in later life, when he encountered anything that seemed to be a threat or a challenge to such values, to such a way of life, he would oppose it fiercely and instinctively —and sometimes unreasonably.

In those days, before radio or television, movies or automobiles, the church was the social center, the intellectual forum, and the conscience of the community. Its only competition came from the saloons; "hell-holes," the clergy called them, and they were not far wrong. For many a family the critical problem to be faced each week was how to keep the wage earner from taking his pay check to the saloon where it was readily cashed and quickly spent, either at the bar or in an upstairs bedroom or both. Despite the thunders from the pulpit, alcoholism was rampant. It was a state of affairs that one day would lead to national prohibition.

As a practicing physician, Clifford Peale had seen more than his share of the consequences of drink. Sometimes, on visits to Lynchburg, he would take his two boys out to the cemetery—ostensibly to visit the graves of their ancestors—but actually to point a moral. With Norman and Bob walking beside him, he would go from grave to grave solemnly shaking his head.

"Here's old Jim Clements," he would say. "Died young. Took his own life—blew his head off with a shot-gun. But you know what really killed him?"

The children knew, all right, but they would shake their heads in horror and fascination.

"Whiskey!" their father would say heavily. "Now over here is Noah Worthington. Started off real well. But he died in the gutter, without a friend, without a cent. Know what did it?"

Again the mute and questioning glance.

"Whiskey! See that grave over there? That's where Maud Hancock is buried. She went from bad to worse. Got so no decent person would ever speak to her. They found her in a snowbank one day, frozen stiff. Know what did it? Whiskey!"

Once on the way home from one of these terrifying object lessons young Norman—always impressionable—found himself overcome with despair. It seemed to him highly probable that, despite their best efforts, he and Bob would come to some dreadful and rumsoaked end. "I don't want whiskey to get us," he cried. "What can we do? What can we do?"

His father smiled and ruffled his hair. "Life is full of temptations and problems, son. Whiskey is just one of 'em. Try to remember this: no man, however resourceful he may be, is a match for the difficulties he will encounter in life. His only hope is to attach himself to some force that is superior to and more powerful than the world of things." He hesitated. "It took me a long time to find that out, the simple fact that you can't get by without God's help. I hope you and Bob will be smarter than I was."

This sort of practical, everyday religion ran like a steady current through the family. There was always grace before meals. In the evening there were family prayers and Bible reading, then individual prayers at bedtime. Visiting churchmen frequently stopped in for a talk or a meal, and then the air was full of vigorous conversation and strong argument, often with everybody talking at once. As Anna Peale once said, "the whole world seemed to troop into our dining room."

The children lived on the fringes of theology, but this did not mean that life had to be somber or dull. Clifford and Anna Peale had too much humor and imagination for that. Anna could even make household chores seem gay. She invented games that dramatized bed making or dish washing. She recited poetry while she swept or dusted. She kept the house full of fun.

Clifford Peale's sense of humor included the capacity to laugh at himself. On the back of a rather glum photograph that showed him wearing a formidable plug hat he wrote, "Of course, if a man has a grouch like this, he ought not have his picture taken. If he *insists*, this is certainly what he deserves!" Another snapshot, partially light-struck, showed him with a sort of nimbus in the general area of his head. "Note the halo!" he wrote gleefully. "A trifle premature!"

Once in a while a practical joke would kick back on him. There was the time, for example, when he went to the dime store, bought a spectacular "diamond" ring, put it in an expensive jeweler's box, and presented it to his wife with great ceremony and affection.

Anna was thrilled to the core of her romantic soul, and wanted so badly to believe the unbelievable that her mind rejected completely the possibility that the ring was anything but genuine. When Clifford finally told her, she burst into tears and was inconsolable.

"But you must have known it wasn't real," her bewildered husband cried. "Where could I have found the money for a real ring that size? I'd have had to rob a bank!"

But Anna only wept the more. She forgave him, finally, but after that he was careful never to tamper with the unpredictable fabric of feminine dreams.

Young Norman inherited a good deal of his mother's strong sense of romance. At the susceptible age of five, or thereabouts, he fell in love with a dark-haired beauty named Marjorie. Years later he could still remember her vividly, and it is unlikely that she ever forgot him, either, since on one occasion he gave an impulsive shove to a lawn mower she was examining and almost severed two of her fingers.

This diminished his interest in the fair sex for several years, but later, when the family was living on Spencer Avenue in Norwood, he became enamoured of a blue-eyed, golden-haired little girl named Evelyn Flowers who lived, appropriately enough, on Floral Avenue, just a few streets away. He used to watch her yearningly as she sat in church, the sunlight bright on her shining hair. In his daydreams he was always rescuing her from a variety of cruel fates. But that was about as far as his passion ever got; he was too shy to mention it to Evelyn.

Evelyn's aunt was a teacher of music, and Norman's mother arranged for him to take piano lessons. She tried to fire his ambition by painting glowing pictures of him as a famous concert pianist. "Just imagine," she would say. "In about twenty years I'll come to New York, and I'll stand outside Carnegie Hall, and I'll look up at the lights. And you know what those lights will say? They'll say, 'Hear Peale Play!' and people will come from everywhere. . . ."

It was a brave attempt, but what Master Norman really wanted to play was shortstop for the Cincinnati Reds. His enthusiasm for piano practice was strictly limited. Finally the dream of Carnegie Hall was abandoned.

But Anna Peale remained ambitious for her sons. "You've got to love life," she would tell them again and again. "You've got to read everything, study everything, be interested in everything. You've got to be citizens of the world!"

Perhaps to some extent it was her own frustration speaking. She loved the church, she loved her husband, she would not willingly have changed anything about her life. And yet, restless within her, was a sense of unused energies, talents, capabilities. Years later, when her children were out of the nest, she was to find partial fulfillment in the role of world missionary leader. But now the ambitions smouldered, only half recognized, and it was inevitable that she should try to graft some of them onto her children. *"Be somebody, Abe,"* the dying mother of Lincoln had said at the end of her own unhappy life. In a thousand ways, consciously or unconsciously, Anna Peale said the same thing to her own sons.

She tried to kindle their imagination with fairy tales and poetry. She thrilled them with "Hans Brinker and the Silver Skates," and the immortal story of the lad who saved Holland by plugging with his finger the hole in the dyke. She told them the tales she had heard her Irish father tell of elves and leprechauns and the strange blue lights that flickered over the bogs of Killarney. She dramatized the great triumphant stories of the Bible: David slaying Goliath, Gideon and his gallant three hundred, Joshua causing the trumpets to blow that sent the walls of Jericho crashing down.

She told them of boys who rose from obscurity to become great men. Hans Christian Andersen, for example, who sat in his Copenhagen garret, poor and unknown, and looked out at the moonlight silvering the water and said to himself, "Some day, Hans Christian Andersen, you will be the most famous man in all of Denmark!"

To it all young Norman listened, wide-eyed, spellbound.

Inevitably, his ambition *was* stirred. He loved his mother, he wanted to please her, to win her approval with achievement. And there were times when he felt that, like Andersen, he would turn out to be a famous man, if not in Denmark, then at least in Ohio.

But along with these surges of confidence came flashes of fear that he might not be able to meet this challenge, that he might not achieve on such a glittering scale, that the powerful and malignant forces of life, the forces his father had mentioned in the cemetery, might prove too much for him.

In response to his mother's urging, the image of himself as a person of ultimate importance began to take shape in his mind. But one step behind it walked another image: the image of inadequacy, the image of self-doubt. As one concept grew, so did the other.

These shadowy Siamese twins were to be his constant companions until, years later, deepening spiritual experience made it possible for him to rise above his own doubts and help other people, by the millions, to do the same.

CHAPTER III

Preacher's Kid

❦

The years pass slowly, when you are young. The Peale boys went to school, played ball in vacant lots, went on picnics, yearned for the arrival of the circus. They were teased, occasionally, for being a minister's sons. Sometimes they were piously reminded by their teachers that ordinary standards of behavior did not apply to them. "My, my—and your father a preacher, too!" Nothing infuriated them more. Like preachers' kids from time immemorial they gritted their teeth and swore that *their* progeny would never suffer such humiliation.

Sometimes on a Saturday afternoon their parents would take them on the trolley car to the zoo at Eden Park. To Norman and Bob, scrubbed and sedate in their middy suits, there was no thrill quite like a ride in one of the fast, open-sided interurbans with the airwhistle blowing hoarsely and the conductor swinging along the running board, ringing up the nickels with death-defying nonchalance.

Out the trolleys would go through the golden afternoon, their varnished benches crowded with parents and their broods, girls in long skirts and starched shirtwaists, young men in high collars and derby hats. The wind would blow, the ladies would clutch their hats, wheels would screech as the trolley swayed alarmingly round the curves. Whenever the car stopped, the compressor would pant feverishly underfoot, and the acrid smell of hot electric motors would come wafting up through the floor boards.

When the new passengers had somehow wedged themselves aboard, the conductor would reach up, tug the signal rope twice—*ding ding.* The motorman would grandly swing his brass-knobbed controls, and they would be off again.

Going out was all anticipation. Coming back through the lilac-colored dusk was a pleasant weariness—a dream-state, almost—for a tired small boy half asleep in his mother's lap or his father's arms. Dimly he would hear the impromptu quartet on the rear platform singing the old barbershop songs. From under half-closed eyelids he would see the purple sputter of sparks whenever the trolley passed a junction point. And for the rest of his life, clear and timeless, the memory of those faraway afternoons would come back to him with a wistfulness, a nostalgia, a sense of peace and perfection beyond all describing and all recapture.

On other memorable occasions their father would take them up the river to Coney Island, an amusement park considerably less elaborate than its famous namesake, but exciting enough. Getting there was half the fun: you had to board the old side-wheeler "Island Queen" and churn your way up the muddy river with the calliope on the top deck blaring tunes that echoed back and forth between the Ohio and Kentucky hills.

To young Norman, one of the most fascinating things about Coney Island was the maze, a labyrinth of artfully arranged mirrors in which it was possible to get completely lost. Wherever you looked, whichever passage you tried, you ended by running into yourself. Here again Father Peale saw a chance to point a moral. "You see," he said to the boys, "the maze is exactly like life. No matter where you go, you can't get away from yourself. In yourself is hell and heaven, joy and sorrow, victory and defeat. You had better try to make yourself into a worthwhile person, because you'll never get away from that person, no matter what you do."

Almost half a century later his eldest son was to say the same thing, in almost exactly the same words, from the oldest Protestant pulpit in America.

Often during school holidays the boys were sent to visit their grandparents, Samuel and Laura Peale, in Lynchburg. The Peale Brothers' store had long since ceased to function; its demise hastened by the too liberal extension of credit on the one hand, and Uncle Wilson's fondness for checker playing on the other. In the old days, so the story went, Uncle Wilson used to take his checker board and a few worthy opponents into the back room of the store. "Hush," he'd say if a customer was heard banging on the counter. "Maybe if we keep real quiet he'll go away!" The result was that finally there were no customers, although Uncle Wilson's fame as a checker player spread far and wide.

The boys' grandfather, Samuel Peale, was a kind and gentle soul who clerked for a company that sold coal and grain and livestock. He was a man of great personal integrity, highly respected in the community. His life had had its moments of drama during the Civil War, and he relived these briefly each Memorial Day. Otherwise, he set no worlds afire. Grandma Peale, a strong and dynamic personality, was still the deeply devout, God-fearing woman who had helped her son Clifford make up his mind to abandon medicine for the ministry.

For Grandma Peale and those around her, preparations for Sunday began at sundown on Saturday. She took literally the commandment to keep the Sabbath holy. She would not cook on that day; for children in her house there were no games, no diversions. This strict observance left its mark. Years later, when Norman decided to while away a rainy Sunday afternoon in Switzerland by going to a movie, he found that a nagging sense of guilt robbed him of all enjoyment of it. It was the one and only time he ever did it.

The house was full of little framed exhortations and injunctions. "The Devil finds work for idle hands to do. . . ." "Remember now thy Creator in the days of thy youth. . . ." "Honesty is the best policy. . . ." Thought-conditioners, designed to sink into the subconscious mind and work in a subtle alchemy there.

The front parlor was a chill and awesome place, so cold that it was often used to store perishables. In the center of the room was a round, marble-topped table on which rested the family Bible. There was also a stereopticon, with slides of the destruction of Pompeii—and Niagara Falls—and a conch shell in the depths of which small landlocked boys could fancy they heard the roar of the unimaginable sea. Against one wall was an old-fashioned horsehair sofa, as rigid as sectarianism and as uncomfortable as sin. Projecting horsehairs had a lamentable tendency to puncture small bare legs. Kneeling by the sofa during the interminable Sunday prayers Norman and Bob used to pull out as many as they could find. But the next time there were always more.

On Saturday nights the washtub was placed by the kitchen stove, filled with steaming water, and the boys were scrubbed to a painful state of cleanliness. Then, when their grandmother had put them into the big old-fashioned bed that they shared, she would stand and pray over them for a while. "Lord," she would say, "look down on these little boys, bless them and keep them, let nothing harm them through the night. They are only little fellows, Lord, and they may be afraid of the dark. Put Your hand on their pillow, Lord, and take away their fears."

These prayers were designed to be reassuring, but they sometimes left the children wondering if perhaps there might not be more to be afraid of than they knew. Truth was, despite her strong and genuine faith, Grandma Peale had some irrational fears herself. Every night, while her husband double-locked all the doors, she peered under all the beds, with what horrid expectations no one ever quite knew. Thunder-storms unnerved her and—fear being as contagious as it is—some of these phobias rubbed off on her children and grand-children. Clifford Peale was afraid of storms until he was a grown man, he struggled all his life with a strong fear of disease, and he never did shake off a morbid dread of being buried alive.

One night Grandma Peale's fear of storms took possession of Norman. He lay in bed, panic-stricken, as thunder crashed and branches of the great sycamore tree outside slashed against the window. In his terror he imagined the house struck by lightning, blown flat, carried away by a flash flood, crushed under a falling tree. In the morning, surprised to find himself still alive, he rushed outside to look at the devastation. There was none. The sun rode placidly in the burnished sky, the town looked clean and new-washed, the great tree still stood unchanged. He never forgot this. Years later he was to preach more than one sermon on the tyranny of imaginary fears, and to use this episode as an illustration. He could always preach with eloquence and sincerity on the subject of fear, and for a very good reason. He was always preaching at him-self.

Before the Peale family left Cincinnati, sorrow came to the house on Spencer Avenue in the suburb of Norwood. In 1909 Anna Peale gave birth to twins, a boy and a girl. For a while there was much rejoicing and excitement: Norman and Bob grew quite rich charging their friends one cent apiece for a look at the twins. But the infants were never strong, and they grew weaker as time went on. Everything possible was done for them medically. At night, Norman could hear his mother weeping and begging the Lord to spare her babies. But first in one, then in the other, the spark of life flickered and went out. "The Lord giveth," said Anna Peale through her tears, "and the Lord taketh away. Blessed be the name of the Lord."

In 1910, shortly after Halley's comet had flashed in the sky (causing Norman to wonder if he could see it on its return in 1986), Clifford Peale was called to Greenville, Ohio. He regretted leaving Cincinnati, but he could look back on a job well done: a congregation enlarged and strengthened and solidly established in a fine new church whose cornerstone contained, among other items of note, a photograph of Master Norman Vincent Peale at the interesting age of twelve.

At the age of twelve, the human animal accepts transplantation readily enough. Greenville was no Cincinnati, no metropolis, but it was much larger than Highland or Bowersville. After a brief period of strangeness, Norman settled down to life in the new town.

By now his awareness of things was expanding; he was beginning to judge, to question, to wonder. He admired his father as much as ever, but he was not at all sure that he wanted to follow him in his choice of a career. For one thing, the tenure of a Methodist minister was extremely uncertain. It depended, to a large degree, on the attitude of the more influential members of the congregation. Inevitably, Norman and Bob were cautioned endlessly to mind their manners, to watch their behavior, to be particularly sure never to antagonize Mr. This or Mrs. That. They would have had to be superhuman not to resent this. They did resent it.

Early in September the Superintendent of the District would visit the town, confer with the church leaders, and decide whether the minister was to stay or whether he was to go—and where. A man could be up-graded to a larger church, or downgraded to a smaller one, with a smaller salary. Thus the pressure to conform, to toe the line, to ingratiate was enormous. Always sensitive to moods and atmospheres, Norman became acutely aware of this—and he hated it. Clifford and Anna Peale were not the kind to be subservient to anyone— and the boys weren't either. But the fact that some people seemed to expect it was galling.

Another thing that galled Norman—not constantly, but on occasion—was the never-ending necessity for strict economy. The Peales seldom ate in a restaurant, but when they did the price of each item was a matter of grim importance. Once when Norman and Bob desperately coveted a pair of the rubber noseguards then in favor with young football players, their mother said flatly that they could not afford them. In the end their father bought them anyway, and this precipitated one of the few family quarrels that ever amounted to anything. Listening to it, Norman clenched his small fists and swore to himself that when he grew up he wouldn't be poor if he could help it. If this eliminated the ministry, he told himself, then so be it.

But there were also times when the ministry seemed to him a mighty and marvelous calling. When he heard his father preach and felt the words take hold of the minds of the congregation, this power to move people's emotions, alter their thoughts, change their lives, and lead them to Christ, seemed to him a thrilling thing. Once, on a rainy afternoon, coming into the deserted church Anna Peale was startled to find Norman in the pulpit, preaching with unabashed fervor to the rows of empty pews, faithfully copying his father's gestures and mannerisms. She went out quietly, too wise to interrupt.

And so the conflicting forces began to grow in him: admiration for some aspects of the ministry, resentment of other aspects of it. It was an ambivalence that was to plague him for the next ten years. ·

So far his religion was not a very intense or personal thing. It was there, it had always been there, a little dulled by repetition perhaps, a little blurred by complete familiarity. And yet, now and then, he would feel a flash of something vital and vivid and tremendous.

There was the time, for example, when his Sunday School teacher was describing Christ's decision to go to Jerusalem, knowing well that His journey could only result in His death. She was reading the story to them from the Bible and she came to the phrase: *He set His face to go to Jerusalem.* . . . She looked up and repeated it: *He set His face to go to Jerusalem.* Then she closed the Book and said to them, "There was a man!"

And suddenly the listening boy had an awareness (there was no other word for it), an awareness brief but blindingly clear of a tall, bronzed Figure striding south along a dusty road, heedless of His own safety, deaf to the pleas and warnings of His disciples. *He set His face to go to Jerusalem.* . . . All at once that face was no longer dim with the passage of time. The dust of two thousand years seemed to blow away, and for the suddenly electrified boy in the Sunday School class Jesus of Nazareth was *alive,* a living Presence. For the first time he felt the full impact of a personality stronger than death. All the latent hero-worship in him seemed suddenly to focus itself on this personality with a mighty surge of love and admiration, and he wanted nothing more than to give himself, to follow, to obey. . . .

Then the intensity of the moment passed. But he never quite forgot it. *He set His face to go to Jerusalem.* . . . There was a man!

The months sped by. At school, his grades were above average, although neither he nor Bob showed any sign of obeying their mother's constant exhortation to put scholarship ahead of everything. It was in this school that he faced the ordeal of his first public speech. He memorized it, word-perfect. He rehearsed endlessly in front of mirrors. And yet, when the time came, panic seized him. As he tottered to the front of the stage in the auditorium, his eye fell upon a little girl in the second row. She seemed to be regarding him with interest, and so in the awful hush that preceded his first words he looked directly at her in a mute and anguished appeal for sympathy.

Her response was instantaneous. "Gosh!" she said in a whisper audible for half a mile. "Look at his knees shake!"

In a way, the shaking knees were significant. They proved that their owner cared about the impression he was making. He cared so desperately that only two alternatives were possible. Either he would avoid public speaking entirely—like the little boy who once hid in the attic when he saw visitors coming. Or else he would conquer his fears and force himself to excel at it.

Actually, he had inherited a certain verbal fluency from both his parents. The basic problem was one of overcoming shyness. This was not easy, but the desire for distinction was also bred into him, and it was becoming stronger all the time. He could not satisfy this thirst for recognition on the playing field. He lacked the physical equipment to be a crack athlete, although eventually he did make the high school track team. As time went on he began to see, dimly, that if he was going to make a mark anywhere, if he was going to "be somebody" as his mother wanted and accomplish something worthwhile in life, he was going to have to do it with his head—and with his tongue.

As he entered his teens, this problem did not loom very large. For a bright and inquisitive mind, life was a succession of interesting discoveries. He got himself a paper route, delivering the *Cincinnati Post*. This endeavor came to an abrupt end one day when his mother happened to meet him coming out of a saloon. "Norman Peale," she said aghast, "what were you doing in that place?"

"Delivering the *Post*," he said happily. "The bartender says he can't get along without it."

"Well," she said, "from now on the *Post* will have to get along without you!"

On another occasion, determined to prove himself no sissy even if he was a preacher's kid, Norman went into a store, plunked down a nickel, and asked for a large black cigar. Assuming he wanted it for his father, the tobacconist sold it to him readily enough. Outside, Norman stripped off the band, lit up with a flourish, and went puffing down the street.

He was striding along, feeling sickish but hard-boiled, when around the corner half a block away came the familiar derby hat and compact figure of Clifford Peale. Norman snatched the cigar out of his mouth, hid it behind his back, and kept going with a glassy grin of unconcern. He hoped his father might be too busy to notice him. It was a vain hope. Clifford Peale stopped, blocking the sidewalk.

"Hello, Norman."

In a frantic attempt to avoid looking his father in the face, Norman glanced wildly around. On the fence near-by was a gaudy poster full of improbable-looking lions and tigers: the circus was coming to town. "Gosh, Dad," cried Norman, pointing with one hand and keeping the other riveted behind him, "I hope you'll take us to the circus this year! Will you, please? Will you?"

"Norman," said his father quietly, "never make a petition and at the same time hold a smoldering disobedience behind your back!" And walked on down the street.

Years later, when people would come to Norman and complain that their prayers seemed to go unheard, or unanswered, he would tell them the story—and suggest that they might do better if they would remove the 'smoldering disobediences' from their lives before asking for favors.

Anna Peale once more was expecting a baby. The pregnancy was not an easy one, and near the end uremic poisoning set in. They took her back to Cincinnati for the birth of the baby—a frail infant whose chances for survival were considered slim. A few days after the child was born, Norman and Bob were rushed to Cincinnati to see their baby brother before it was too late. But this time Anna's prayers were granted: little Leonard pulled through.

Two years went by. Young Norman decided that he didn't like his name, and began signing himself William Howard Peale, which had a fine presidential ring to it. A few old school books, saved from the past, still bear his adopted signature. He even went down to the Court House and asked an amused magistrate how he could make this legal. The judge, observing the boy chewing nervously on a toothpick, told him that he could consider his name legally changed, if he liked, but that he must never, *never* chew a toothpick in public. Norman retired, somewhat abashed.

He did achieve a presidency, though. He was active in the Boys' Congress of Ohio, an organization made up of youngsters with similar religious backgrounds and affiliations. Thanks largely to his speaking ability, Norman was elected president. One night shortly thereafter, Bob was awakened by a sepulchral voice intoning, "President Peale! President Peale!"

"What's the matter?" Bob demanded crossly. "Are you having a nightmare?"

"Of course not," said Norman happily. "I just like the sound of it, that's all. President Peale! President Peale!"

The Ohio Boys' Congress numbered several thousand members, and offered Norman one of his first opportunities to demonstrate his flair for leadership. He traveled about the State, speaking to conventions of the organization and presiding at business meetings.

One young lady in particular was impressed. A demure little brunette with the sultry first name of Zara fell into the habit of letting President Peale carry her schoolbooks home for her. This was a very sedate relationship until one fine day, with the trees showing feathers of green and the warm breath of spring blowing gently down his neck, Norman summoned up enough courage to ask for—and get—his first kiss.

Zara's reaction, unfortunately, has been lost to posterity. Norman was so flabbergasted by the results of his own daring and by the torrent of emotions roaring through him that he dropped his lady love as if she had been a hot brick and sprinted all the way home. As he arrived, breathless and shaken, a newsboy flung the evening paper onto the porch at his feet. He picked it up and stared at the black headlines: TITANIC STRIKES ICEBERG—HUNDREDS PERISH!

It was April 15, 1912. He lacked just six weeks of being fourteen years old.

The romance with Miss Zara got nowhere because soon the family moved again, this time to Bellefontaine—pronounced Bellfountain—in nearby Logan County. It was a larger town and a larger church—and for the Peale family it produced larger problems. The difficulty was almost as old as Christendom: friction between the pastor and certain members of his flock who seemed to consider themselves divinely appointed to tell the minister how the church should be run and how he should conduct his private affairs.

Clifford Peale was a man well schooled by this time in the frailties of human nature, and tolerant of them up to a point. But he could be pushed too far. Norman had one vivid recollection of parental anger for which he was directly responsible. As a small boy, sitting in church one morning, he was amusing himself by timing the sermon with his father's watch which he had "borrowed" for the occasion. At one point, unintentionally, he snapped shut the protective gold case that covered the crystal. The sound echoed all over the church, and Clifford Peale's face turned crimson. He leaned over the pulpit railing and glared at his congregation. "Listen," he said, "listen to me, whoever you are that snapped that watch! This is my pulpit, and this is my sermon, and I'll make it as long or as short as I please, is that clear? Nobody in this church is going to try to control the length of my sermons by snapping a watch on me!"

There was a ringing silence in which young Norman wished he could sink through the floor. He was terrified of telling his father the truth, but a guilty conscience finally drove him to it. His father was still angry enough to take him out to the woodshed and settle the matter with a razorstrop. But his anger stemmed more from years of lay interference than the transgression of one small boy.

In Bellefontaine the chief opposition to the new minister came from a pair of elderly brothers, who owned a prosperous grocery store and had firm opinions about almost everything. Perhaps political differences had something to do with it— Clifford Peale, a great admirer of Teddy Roosevelt, had been an ardent Bull Mooser in the election of 1912. The resulting split in the Republican party had allowed Woodrow Wilson to become the first Democratic president in 16 years, and rockribbed Ohio Republicans who had supported Taft considered Roosevelt and his Bull Moosers little better than traitors.

Another thing that irked the brothers almost beyond endurance was the fact that one day the Reverend Peale went out and bought himself a car. He bought the car—a Reo—because he had laboriously saved the money, and could afford it. But to the brothers, poverty was a sign of godliness—at least where clergymen were concerned. If the Reverend Peale bought a car, it simply meant that the $2500 salary the church was paying him was too much, that was all. In any case, why couldn't he walk, or drive a buggy, the way his predecessors had?

Clifford Peale heard the rumblings and decided to ignore them, although he could foresee trouble. What he almost certainly did not foresee was that more than forty years later his oldest son would have similar charges leveled at him by a professor of religion who argued that "ministers, like policemen, should be regarded with a certain dubiety if they become either rich or famous." He drove the Reo with pleasure, and even let his teen-agers drive it occasionally, to their delight, although he knew this might annoy his critics all the more.

Nothing flares up faster or burns hotter than a church fight. The brothers had their adherents, and they widened their area of disapproval. Clifford Peale did not insist on having his youngsters attend evening church. Sunday School and one church service in the morning, he felt, was enough—any more might lead to a distaste for religion that might be permanent. The brothers brought this up at a meeting of the official church board, and complained that the minister's sons were setting a bad example. Criticism of himself was one thing; an attack on his family was another. Mustache bristling, Clifford Peale roared that the behavior of his boys was his affair and nobody else's.

Actually, the conduct of Norman and Bob left something to be desired. They resented being resented, and showed it in a variety of ways. Bob, by now an ebullient thirteen and intoxicated by his recent discovery of the apparent relativity of morals, undertook to argue loudly in Sunday School that a hypothetical man might well be justified in breaking the Commandment against stealing if his hypothetical children were hungry. The elder of the brothers, who was Sunday school superintendent, promptly sent him home in disgrace—a gesture which ruffled the already disarranged feathers in the Peale household still more.

Norman took to racing the Reo up and down the main street of Bellefontaine. Whenever he passed the brothers' grocery store, he would open the cutout with a roar that rattled the windows, caused the canned goods to tremble on the shelves, and brought the owners close to apoplexy. They retaliated by hinting darkly that the activities of a high school fraternity, to which the boys belonged, were too nefarious even to mention, and campaigned to have the fraternity headquarters—a vacant room above a livery stable—closed and padlocked.

Matters came to a head when, during the minister's temporary absence, the anti-Peale faction held a meeting at the
church to discuss ways and means of having him transferred.
Young Norman happened to be observed passing the window
of the room in which the meeting was being held, and was
promptly branded a spy—an accusation which annoyed his
father intensely when he heard of it.

As it turned out, the meeting was a tactical blunder on the
part of the opposition. The more levelheaded members of the
congregation felt that the brothers and their supporters had
over-reached themselves. They made it clear that they wanted
their pastor to stay. Gradually the uproar subsided.

But it left its mark on Norman. A sensitive sixteen-year-old,
he resented fiercely the pressure that the 'leading members' of
a congregation could exert on the minister and his family.
The result was a tendency to regard all social bigwigs with a
certain amount of suspicion. It was to stay with him for the
rest of his life.

He was beginning to question other things, too. More and
more it was beginning to dawn on him that clergymen were
set apart, isolated by their calling from other men. This puzzled
and dismayed him, but it was an evident fact. People changed
when a minister came into the room. They became artificial,
self-conscious, almost wary. Even his father, warm and hu-
morous as he was, seemed to have this effect on people. Why
was it? What was it? He was too young to find an answer,
and his uneasiness only strengthened his conviction that, no
matter what his parents said or felt, the ministry was not for
him.

In this rebellion, Bob happily joined him. They had no
quarrel with parental authority; that was administered with
justice and tempered with love. It was the authority of the
church that they rebelled against without even knowing it:
the authority that could uproot the family at any time, could
reduce or increase the family income; the great, powerful, in-

visible force that controlled their lives and had decreed from the beginning—without consulting them—that they should be "P.K.'s," preacher's kids, with all the frustrations and exasperations that that entailed.

The forms that their rebellion took were mild enough: surreptitious cigarets behind the barn, painting the high-school sidewalk with class numerals in scarlet letters three feet tall (the principal made them spend one whole day scrubbing them off), racketing down Detroit Avenue in the Reo with the cutout open. And these harmless escapades siphoned off the surface tension. But deep down there remained—in Norman at least—a resentment of any authority that presented itself in institutional form. Some of this, too, was to cling to him through the years.

Most of the time he was unaware of such internal pressures. In high school he won some fame as a debater, while Bob's football ability began to be noticed. Bob's approach to things, unlike Norman's, tended to be simple and direct, as a letter he wrote to his father shows. It was written at Lakeside, Ohio, on July 14, 1914 when Master Robert was approaching his fourteenth birthday:

Dear Dad:
    Well, I will quit smoking provided you let me dance. Please hurry, for in the meantime I'm going to learn to dance.
                    Lovingly,
                        Bob.

Lakeside was the scene of many religious conferences that the Peales attended. For Anna Peale, particularly, these were exciting times. Famous missionaries described their work in strange, exotic lands. Great preachers were heard nightly. There were public speaking contests for laymen, and Anna won more than one of these. She began to interest herself in foreign missions, she made new friends, she felt her horizons and her personality expand.

But she kept a watchful eye on her three boys: Norman, the sensitive one, blue-eyed, blond, slender as a reed but endowed with much of his mother's driving energy; Bob, the rough-tough one, stocky and solid, like his father; Leonard, the baby of the family, still frail and somewhat isolated, separated from his nearest brother by a gap of ten years. Her interest in them was intense. It was also possessive. She was a woman who knew her own mind and made decisions quickly. Consequently it seemed altogether natural to her to make decisions for the children. They were almost always wise ones. But this did not increase the children's capacity to make decisions for themselves.

At one point, with his parents' blessing, Norman decided to go into business as a door-to-door salesman of pots and pans. Aluminum kitchen ware was something new; the brochure from the factory assured would-be salesmen that their fortune was practically made. So Norman ordered a complete line, practiced his sales talk until he could recite it in his sleep, and set out to convert the housewives of Ohio from their primitive reliance on iron and enamel to the new age of aluminum.

He didn't want any of his friends to see him peddling pots and pans, so he borrowed the family car and drove to the near-by town of Union City, Indiana. He picked a likely street, and then sat in the car for some time, feeling his enthusiasm dwindle rapidly. Just before it vanished entirely, he made himself walk up on a porch and knock at the door. It swung open, and he found himself confronting a formidable-looking housewife with broom in hand and dust-cloth round her head. "Well?" she demanded.

Norman opened his mouth, but no sound issued from it. He tried desperately to recall the beginning of his sales pitch, but his mind was a total blank.

"*Well?*" repeated the woman impatiently.

Norman backed away two paces. "You don't—," he said,

and gulped. "You don't want to buy any—any pots or pans, do you?"

He made it sound like a statement, and the woman nodded her head in total agreement. "I sure don't!" she said, and slammed the door.

The new salesman was so shattered by this rejection that he climbed into the car and drove all the way home. There, in an effort to salvage something from the disaster, he sold a half interest in his venture to a friend of his who was a breezy extrovert.

The friend talked Norman into making another attempt the next day. While Norman fidgeted in the car, the friend knocked on a door, disappeared into the house, and promptly came out with a sale.

"How'd you do it?" Norman asked, amazed.

"I just told her she needed 'em. Matter of fact, she does. If you believe in what you're selling, you can sell anything."

"Gosh," said Norman weakly. "The brochure didn't say that."

"Never mind the brochure," his friend said. "Just have faith in the product! And somewhere along the line, tell 'em something nice about themselves!"

By nightfall, all the pots and pans were gone.

By the autumn of 1916, Norman was ready for college. There was no question about where he was to go: for a Methodist minister's son, Ohio Wesleyan was the inevitable choice. Clifford Peale had always regretted his lack of a classical education and had more than once felt ill-at-ease and excluded in a group of Wesleyan graduates. He wanted this label for all his sons. It would be a strain, he knew, on the family budget. But with the ministerial discount that he could claim on tuition, he felt that he could just about manage it.

He and Anna accompanied Norman to the little college town of Delaware, Ohio and saw him safely installed in the

Phi Gamma Delta fraternity house. Then Clifford Peale took his son aside and offered a few ministerial words of caution. "You're on your own, now, Norman," he said, "for the first time in your life. Four years from now, if you behave yourself, you'll be an Ohio Wesleyan graduate—something I always wanted to be. Don't do anything to jeopardize that opportunity. Study hard, and stay away from liquor, and don't run around with women. . . ." He hesitated for a moment, then the doctor of medicine took over from the doctor of divinity. "But if you *do* get into any sort of trouble, don't lie about it or try to hide it. Just come and tell me, and I'll see what I can do about getting you through it!"

He clapped Norman roughly on the shoulder, and turned away. His mother kissed him, making no attempt to hide her tears. Norman stood on the steps of the Phi Gam house and watched them go down the path that led to the street. Then abruptly he turned and ran up to his room. He was a man of the world, now, a college undergraduate, a member of a great national fraternity.

He didn't want any of his brethren to see him cry.

CHAPTER IV

Bright College Years

". . . with pleasure rife,
The shortest, gladdest years of life . . ."

◆§§◆

The lives of freshmen are usually a happy blur; Norman's was no exception. Everything was new, challenging, a little frightening. The sudden withdrawal of parental guidance left him both exhilarated and bewildered. Said a classmate, years later: "Norman was so used to having his mind made up for him that he could hardly decide when to send out his laundry. The charm and energy and potential leadership were there. But he was very immature in many ways."

It never occurred to Norman that he was immature; he was too busy soaking up impressions. Everything was exciting: classes, co-eds, chapel, football games. Even the hazing. Overnight, lurid posters appeared with black death-heads printed on pink paper and dire warnings to freshmen of the Class of 1920. "Ye Skunks!" was the salutation in screaming headlines. "Your maggot-covered, stench-producing carcasses have become unbearable to the noble Class of 1919. Obey, therefore, the following mandates with diligence and trembling fear:

1. Keep off the streets after seven o'clock
2. Wear your freshman hats
3. Salute all sophomores
4. Don't disfigure the chapel steps with your presence
5. Wear black neckties and come-to-Jesus collars on the Sabbath
6. Steer clear of the fair sex at Monnett Hall
7. Wear no cuffs on your trousers
8. Don't go near the squirrels on the campus
9. Wear a pink ribbon around your right sleeve."

One of the rituals of fraternity initiations, unalterable as the law of Medes and Persians, was known as "running a summons." Freshmen were sent out in pairs at midnight with instructions to go to some remote place, find another set of instructions, and keep going from point to point until the "summons" was completed.

Ordinarily, this meant four or five hours of hard walking in the dark. Norman and his partner, however, decided it would be more practical and comfortable to hire a horse and buggy—which they did. They were back so early and looked so smug that the upperclassmen checked the livery stables, exposed the crime, and sent them on a new "summons" that set a record for distance and difficulty. The pair of culprits staggered home at ten in the morning, having covered thirty miles and come to the deep conviction that, even where sophomores were concerned, honesty was the best policy.

If Anna Peale expected glowing reports that year of her son's scholastic aptitude, she was in for a rude shock. His grades for the first semester did not show a single A, or for that matter a B. The trouble would not have been hard to find, had Anna known where to look. It had large appealing eyes, soft blonde hair, and was named Helen.

She was a demure little co-ed who found Norman just as fascinating (because he took some pains to be) as he found her. She lived in Monnett Hall where chaperonage was strict and dreadful penalties awaited the girl who was out after nine o'clock. But that left a good many hours in which a boy could see a girl—and still more in which he could think about her.

It all began innocently enough: they met, they talked, they decided that they liked each other. One night, greatly daring, Norman held her hand all through a Mary Pickford movie. On the way back to Monnett Hall, in the shadow of the great elms, she let him kiss her—once. Norman felt as if Halley's comet had struck him. Weak-kneed, he watched her go inside. Then he floated dizzily back to the Phi Gam house, a helpless chip on the raging torrents of love.

It was only puppy love, but it had a bark that sounded loud to inexperienced ears, and it lasted for quite a while. Long enough to sabotage Norman's scholastic efforts, anyway. The end came, finally, when Helen began to seem a little proprietary. From Monnett Hall, via the campus grapevine, came a horrid rumor that she was spending her spare time embroidering table-napkins and other household items with the initials N and H, lovingly entwined. These dreadful intimations of matrimony so alarmed Norman that he began backing away at full speed. By the end of the year he was pretty well disentangled. A wiser man, he decided to spend more time with his books and less with blondes. It was safer, he told his roommate, and probably more fun to be just one of the boys.

The fraternity had its share of campus leaders, and indeed of national celebrities. Christy Mathewson, the great baseball pitcher, had been a Phi Gam. So was a persimmony-looking fellow named Calvin Coolidge, of the Amherst chapter, who was said to be a pretty good governor back east in Massachusetts.

It was an era of wonderful campus nicknames. No one knew exactly where they came from, but they had an aptness, an originality, an imagery and a euphony that was a reflection of pure genius. "Scoop" Wilkinson, "Fizzer" Guy, "Pinhead"

Castle, "Punk" McCord, "Slick" Burgess, "Beanie" Trawl, "Mother" Hubbard, "Sport" Detrick . . . the list went on and on, monosyllables balancing polysyllables in a manner that did honor to the noble rhythms of the ancient Anglo-Saxon heritage.

The reason for such perfection, probably, was that if a nickname didn't fit like a glove, if it lacked the fundamental poetry and insight, it fell by the wayside. Norman was sometimes called 'Doc' because it was assumed he might follow his father into the ministry. He was also known, on occasion, as "Policy Peale," a reflection of his fondness for demanding eagerly at fraternity meetings, "What's our policy in a case like this?" But neither of these nicknames had the glue of absolute aptness that made them stick.

The liberal arts course at Ohio Wesleyan required no mathematics and little science. It stressed English, Oratory, a certain amount of History with emphasis on Bible study and the history of Christianity, and Economics. It also called for a nodding acquaintance with at least one ancient and one modern language. Norman already had some knowledge of German, and he did well with Spanish and French, when he got around to them. But his grades in Greek were almost as dismal as his record in required gym, where he earned straight F's. The one bright spot in his freshman record was the A he achieved in Oratory—for extemporaneous speaking.

Two months after Norman entered Ohio Wesleyan the Democrats won the presidential campaign of 1916, re-electing Woodrow Wilson largely on the claim that he had kept the country out of war. Many Midwesterners supported Wilson for precisely this reason. But the pressures toward involvement were too strong. Six months later the nation was in it.

The nation was in it, and Norman was eager to get into it too. Burning with patriotism, he actually withdrew himself from college and hurried back to Bellefontaine to enlist. But he ran into an unyielding wall of parental disapproval. He was too young to go, his mother said; the Army wasn't looking for teen-agers. His education came first, his father said, and that was all there was to it. For two weeks Norman begged and pleaded in vain. Then he sadly went back to Delaware, where the university tolerantly re-enrolled him.

Clifford Peale saw in the holocaust of war confirmation of his long-held belief that some sort of international peace organization was essential if mankind wanted to avoid ultimate self-destruction. He admired Wilson's idealism, believed the President when he said that the country had gone to war to make the world safe for democracy. He preached this conviction both in Bellefontaine and in Findlay, where the family moved the following year.

In Findlay, for the first time, the Peales were able to afford a home of their own. Anna was so delighted that the day they moved in she ran from room to room, crying rapturously, "Ours! Ours! No more parsonages! It's really ours!"

Home from the excitements of his freshman year, Norman listened soberly to his mother's insistence that his scholarship would have to improve if he wanted to get anywhere in life. Then he set about making a few dollars to help meet expenses during his sophomore year.

One infallible way, he knew, to come at least within shouting distance of money was to associate with his Uncle Will. William Peale, Clifford's younger brother, was not so very much older than Norman—thirteen years, to be exact. But he was already an energetic and successful businessman. His churchgoing left much to be desired—a state of affairs deplored by his minister-brother's family. But churchgoer or not, there was one thing that Uncle Will did know how to do, and that was make money.

At this point he was making it in Iowa real estate, buying large tracts of land cheap, dividing it into small lots, and selling the lots at a solid profit. He said he would be glad to have his young nephew as an assistant. The result was that Norman spent some instructive hours out in the broiling Iowa sun painting posts and staking out lots for Uncle Will.

One thing that he learned from Uncle Will—and never forgot—was the value of lively advertising. Ordinary methods were all right, Uncle Will conceded, but they were a bit slow. He preferred to walk through the streets of the town holding aloft a ten dollar gold piece and proclaiming his intention of giving away that self-same gold piece at the corner of Main and Maple at two o'clock.

When Uncle Will proclaimed anything, everybody knew it. He often asserted—and no one disputed it—that William Jennings Bryan himself had told him that he had the greatest voice in the United States, next to William Jennings Bryan. Now and then, to make sure he was in top form, he would have Norman walk away from him and hold up his hand when he could no longer hear him clearly. If the wind was right, Norman would often walk half a mile and still hear every word Uncle Will was saying.

With the glitter of the gold piece and the resonance of his voice, Uncle Will never failed to attract a large crowd at the appointed time and place. He would have every onlooker write his name on a piece of paper and put it in a hat, a stratagem that gave him a useful list of prospects. Next he would have a small girl draw a name from the hat. Then he would present the gold piece to the lucky winner, and launch into a sales talk that invariably left him considerably richer.

He was fond of Norman, and helped him later by lending him money to get through college. But he never let sentiment or family ties interfere with business. Norman had to pay back every nickel. On time, and with interest.

The fall of 1917 found the campus at Ohio Wesleyan somewhat subdued and the ranks of upperclassmen thinned by enlistments. A branch of the Students' Army Training Corps was established, and Norman was one of those in uniform. He liked the precision and discipline of close-order drill, and because he liked it he was good at it. His marks in military science were consistently high.

His other grades began to move up, too, and this was partly traceable to an incident that made a profound impression on him. Aside from a certain glibness in public speaking, he was still plagued from time to time by agonizing self-consciousness. This was particularly evident if he was suddenly called upon to recite in class. The thought that he might seem ignorant or foolish to a room full of people paralyzed him, and often made his performance far worse than it had to be.

On one of these occasions the professor asked him, a bit grimly, to remain after class. When the other students were gone, he looked at Norman with evident distaste. "Peale," he said, "why don't you stop thinking about yourself?"

Norman stared at him. "Myself?"

"Yourself," said the teacher. "Why do you think you freeze up the way you do when called on in class? Why do you get confused and tongue-tied and red in the face? Because you're stupid? No. Because you're lazy? No. It's because you're so full of you that there isn't room for anything else!"

Norman felt a white-hot spark of anger begin to glow somewhere inside him. He clenched his fists and said nothing.

"You call it shyness, don't you?" the professor went on inexorably. "You think it's hypersensitivity, and maybe secretly you're a little proud of it. Well, it's about time you learned that self-consciousness is mostly self-centeredness. You know what this so-called inferiority complex of yours is caused by? It's caused by your desire to be smarter and wiser and better than anybody else—and your fear that maybe you *won't* be! Isn't that true? Admit it!"

Still Norman said nothing, but he knew from the blast of fury that roared through him that this was the truth, that the professor was stripping away the camouflage from a self that he had never clearly seen—and that he didn't want to see.

"I think you've got good stuff in you," the teacher said more gently. "Otherwise I wouldn't bother to tell you this. But you'll never get anywhere until you face up to this thing, and lick it." He pulled his books and papers toward him, and stood up. "And I'll tell you one more thing, while I'm at it. You'll never lick it alone. We all have our share of self-love, self-centeredness, and yours is bigger than most. You're going to need help, a lot of it. You're a minister's son, aren't you?"

Norman nodded, speechless.

"All right, then," the professor said. "You ought to know where to find it."

He nodded pleasantly and walked out of the classroom.

Norman stood there, motionless, feeling the anger slowly drain out of him. For the first time in his life he had wanted to smash his fist into another man's face. Respect for authority —or perhaps simply fear of the consequences—had prevented that. Now the rage was gone, leaving an emptiness, a weakness that was almost worse.

He walked slowly out into the clear autumn weather, along the path where fallen leaves lay like a golden rug. He came to Gray chapel and sat down on the broad steps—as a lordly sophomore he had this privilege now. *It's not true*, a voice said frantically somewhere inside him, *you're not self-centered, you're just shy, you've always been shy, ever since they made you stand in the living room and recite those silly poems, you can't help it, it's the way you're made. . . .*

But he knew, in a sudden flash of deadly insight, that this was false, this was rationalization, this was self-justification. The professor was right: he was so full of self that there was no room for anything else.

Abruptly he crossed his forearms on his knees, bowed his head until his forehead rested on them. "Help me, Lord," he prayed. "Help me get over this thing, this selfishness, this desire to be better than anyone else. Show me what You want me to do with my life, and then help me do it. Please help me . . . I'm not strong enough to help myself. *Please* . . ."

It was not a long prayer, but it was the most profound, the most intense, the most sincere one he had ever uttered.

After a while, he looked up. Nothing had changed around him. The paths stretched away, bisecting the emerald lawns. Students sauntered past, calling greetings to one another. Squirrels scampered through the fallen leaves. Nothing had changed, and yet he had a feeling that everything had changed.

He glanced at his watch and stood up quickly, not wanting to be late for his next class. He moved down the chapel steps, a thin, serious-faced boy. He was not fully aware of it, but he had taken his first long step toward understanding human nature. He had begun to understand himself.

Not all of his sophomore year was so serious, by any means. Initiations came again, but this time Norman and his friends were the tormentors, not the tormented.

Perhaps the most fiendish skulduggery practiced on gullible freshmen was the ancient bit of black magic known as the empty house trick. This required the most elaborate preparation and build-up. First an unoccupied house had to be located, preferably in a somewhat isolated spot. Then the innocent victim had to be convinced, by gradual and masterly persuasion, that in this house lived a lady of generous and amorous nature, married to a railroad man who was mostly elsewhere. On a given night, the freshman was offered the opportunity of accompanying a sophomore allegedly invited to visit the lady—and the inference was clear that if the freshman didn't take advantage of this offer he was no man at all, but a lily-livered mouse.

Around midnight, out would go the pair of them, the sophomore debonair and care-free, the freshman considerably less so, but more afraid of seeming a coward than of anything else. They would come to the house where a single light burned in an upstairs window. The sophomore would caution his companion once more on the need for utter secrecy and

discretion. They would tip-toe up the porch steps. The sophomore would rap furtively on the door. It would swing open—
to reveal the gigantic figure of the fiercest-looking upperclassman available, complete with black mustache and railroader's
cap.

"So!" he would bellow. "You're the ones who're trying to
break up my home!"

"Run!" the sophomore would shriek wildly, tumbling backward off the porch. "He's got a gun! Run for your life!"

The freshman rarely needed any urging. Down the road he
would bolt, the "husband" in furious pursuit, while from behind fences and bushes other sophomores would join in the
chase like a pack of hounds in full cry—or roll on the ground
convulsed with laughter. When the trick really worked, the
wretched freshman might flee for miles. One was reported
to have run right out of the county, swimming several rivers
that got in his way, and another was said never to have been
seen again—tales that in time acquired an almost Biblical
authenticity.

Sometimes, when the football team was playing a rival elsewhere, a group of impoverished students—lacking the railroad fare—would go down and hop a freight. Trainmen were
usually lenient where students were concerned, but railroad
authorities grew increasingly unhappy. When they ordered the
practice stopped, one enterprising student looked up the regulations and found that livestock-attendants were authorized in
freight cars. The boys chipped in, bought a bewildered pig,
crated him up and shipped him by freight complete with
two dozen solicitous valets who hovered over him all the
way to the town where the game was to be played. Then they
escorted him home and sold him—at a profit.

Except for his old nemesis, Greek (and of course required
gym,) Norman's grades were respectable by the end of his
sophomore year. He suffered from a chronic shortage of cash,
but this was no great hardship because most of his friends

and fraternity brothers were in the same boat. To earn a little money, at one point, he got a part-time job with a clothing merchant in town. His first assignment was to drive a truck-load of outdated suits into the rural areas where nobody knew or cared anything about fashion, and dispose of them to the unsuspecting farmers. "When they try on a coat," his employer told Norman earnestly, "hold it for them and grip it good and tight in back—like this, see? That makes it look like a good fit from the front!" The ethics of this struck Norman as somewhat dubious, and he contented himself with simply showing the suits. Fortunately they were priced so low that the farmers bought them anyway.

At the beginning of Norman's junior year, Bob showed up as a freshman. He too pledged Phi Gamma Delta. By this time Norman was president of the fraternity, and quite a man of the world—too much so to suit young Robert, who came trailing clouds of straitlaced Methodist morality.

In a fraternity house, a pledge was supposed to be less than dirt under the feet of an upperclassman, and unworthy to speak to the president at all. Nevertheless, on one occasion when a mild party was in progress in the basement and Norman was watching it benevolently, he was startled to find Bob at his elbow, eyes blazing.

"Come upstairs," commanded the lowly pledge. "I want to talk to you!"

Somewhat startled, Norman obeyed. When they were alone, he faced his brother. "What is it, Bob? What's the matter?"

"Nothing's the matter with me!" roared Bob. "It's you and those friends of yours. Do you know what some of those men are drinking? Beer—that's what they're drinking. Beer! Never, never, *never* let me catch you in such a disgraceful situation again! Is that clear?"

All Norman could do was concede that it was crystal clear and hope that Bob's iron-bound standards would relax a trifle, once the solvent of college life got to work on them.

In November the war ended, to universal rejoicing and relief. The Students' Army Training Corps was disbanded, and
just before Christmas Clifford Peale got a flowery communication from Norman's commanding officer:

Dear Friend:
In a few days your soldier will receive his honorable dis-
charge and start for home.

He is bringing back many fine qualities of body and mind
which he has acquired or developed in the Military Service.
The army has done everything it could to make him strong,
fine, self-reliant, yet self-controlled. It returns him to you a
better man. . . .

The qualities he brings back will help you now as your encouragement helped him, and in your hands and his rests the
future of our country.

As his commanding officer, I am proud of him. He has done
his duty well. I, and his comrades, will bid him good-bye with
deep regret, and wish him every success after he returns home
—the spot in every man's heart no other place can fill.

Sincerely yours,
W. P. Loman
Captain Inf. U.S.A.
Commanding Officer

This was high praise indeed. The only thing that dimmed
its lustre slightly was the fact that an identical letter went out
to the parents of every member of the late S.A.T.C.

The rest of Norman's junior year passed pleasantly and
quickly. His grades continued to improve. Now and then he
would take a girl to a movie: Lionel Barrymore in *The Copper-
head*, or Wallace Reid in *Valley of the Giants*. Sometimes a
few romantic souls would go over and serenade the co-eds
under the windows of Monnett Hall. In the spring, the smell
of lilac hung heavy on the soft night air, and sometimes a
girl failed to make it back to Monnett in time for the nine
o'clock curfew. When that happened, she had to be smuggled
up a ladder and into a window, amid much stifled giggling.

Sometimes the ladder slipped, the guilty ones fell with a crash into a lilac bush, and there were grim sessions with the Dean of Women the next day.

Now and then Norman would take a girl home, vaguely hoping for maternal approval. Anna Peale was always pleasant and polite. But she was careful not to fan any sparks into flame.

Norman's prestige on the campus was rising. That spring he was among those nominated for class president. He didn't win, but he ran fourth with sixty-three votes, a respectable showing.

He was beginning to take considerable interest in journalism. Professor "Rollie" Walker, who taught Bible, had said dryly to his class, "Gentlemen, if you're interested in reaching large numbers of people, you'll do much better from behind an editor's desk than you will from a pulpit." This remark stuck in Norman's mind. He knew he had a certain verbal fluency; perhaps he could write as well as speak. In an effort to find out, he became a staff member of the *Transcript*, the weekly student newspaper.

These veering ambitions did not mean that he had ruled out the ministry. On the contrary, when anyone pinned him down, he admitted that he would probably follow in his father's footsteps. His love of the church was genuine and deep; it varied in intensity from time to time, but it was always there. Sometimes, after being quiescent for a while, it would be revived with a tremendous surge of purpose and power and excitement.

There was, for example, the time in 1919 when he went to Columbus to attend the convention of an organization known as The Student Volunteers. In Memorial Hall a great banner, six feet high, was stretched across the vast auditorium: *The Evangelization of the World for Jesus Christ in This Generation.* "Look at that!" cried Norman, his eyes shining. "What an idea! What a challenge! We're going to win the world for Jesus Christ in our own lifetime!"

Those were days when great ideals were on the march. The

world had been made safe for democracy. The League of Nations was being formed, and men like Clifford Peale were all for heeding Wilson's call to join it. National prohibition was no longer just a dream. It was about to become the law of the land, and its supporters honestly believed that a new era of morality and sobriety was at hand. The pulpit seemed to have won its ancient battle with the saloon. Overseas, the tyrants had fallen. Throughout the world, war was to be forever outlawed. International justice and national temperance would henceforth reign. To men of good will everywhere, civilization seemed to be advancing with giant strides.

The days of disillusion were yet to come.

It was in this mood of buoyant optimism that the country moved toward the presidential election of 1920. In Ohio, Hiram Johnson, Warren Harding, and General Leonard Wood joined battle for the Republican nomination, and the excitement spread even to the cloistered halls of Ohio Wesleyan.

One reason it spread was that Norman was busy spreading it. The manager of Wood's campaign conceived the idea that straw ballots on various campuses might be influential and useful—provided his candidate won them. He let it be known that funds might be available to any trustworthy undergraduate who would organize a "Win with Wood" campaign under the elms and capture the college vote.

Down to Columbus went Norman with his friend and classmate "Joe" Joseph, both burning with newly acquired political fervor. They sought—and got—an interview with Wood's campaign manager. And they must have talked loud and long, because when they emerged from his office they were the official organizers of a "Win with Wood" campaign designed to sweep the campus back in Delaware. Even more astounding, they had been given the unheard-of sum of one hundred dollars with which to win friends and influence straw voters.

In a happy daze they went out and toured the grounds of the State capitol where statues of Ohio's famous sons—Mc-

Kinley, Sherman, Garfield—were enshrined. One niche was vacant—each graciously prophesied that some day the other would undoubtedly fill it. They went to the Neal House and for ten cents had themselves paged through the lobby, nudging each other ecstatically as the bellboy called hoarsely for Judge Joseph and Senator Peale. When darkness fell, their delirium mounted still higher. They repaired to the steps of the capitol where, having elected themselves Governor in a dizzy plunge into the future, they took turns making acceptance speeches to a vast imaginary audience. Each introduced the other. Norman offered a sonorous invocation in which he asked Divine guidance for his friend, the newly elected Governor of Ohio, John Jerome Joseph. Joseph's address was shorter. He merely told the invisible throng that since they had seen fit to elect Norman Peale as their Governor, he hoped the Lord would help *them.*

As the primaries approached, their political fever became even more acute. Having triumphantly carried the campus for Wood, they were invited to come back to Columbus and sit on the dais with other distinguished guests to hear the General address a great rally. On this occasion, Clifford Peale did offer the invocation, a long prayer that dwelt at some length on the greatness of the Grand Old Party. As one newspaper commented dryly the next day, the prayer was the best political speech of the rally.

Back in college, Norman began to wonder seriously if a newspaper job might not be the best stepping stone to a political career. By this time he was Associate Editor of the *Transcript.* His classmate, Gardner Townsley, was Editor-in-chief, and the pair of them sat up night after night dreaming great dreams of owning a small country newspaper, building it into a mighty political force, and eventually making Hearst and Pulitzer look like midgets.

On one occasion, driving through a town, they stopped the car, went into the local newspaper office, and asked to see the editor. "We're from Ohio Wesleyan," they announced grandly, "and we're interested in buying a newspaper."

The editor looked the future titans of journalism up and down. "With what?" he inquired.

The interview ended right there.

All the same, the *Transcript* was a recognized training ground for future journalists, and Norman felt sure he could land a job after graduation on the *Findlay Republican* if he wanted it. The question was, did he want it enough to disappoint his parents' hopes that he would enter the ministry? More important, did he want it enough to ignore the emotional undertow that tugged so urgently at him from time to time, drawing him toward the church.

In the weeks that followed, Norman went through a dozen changes of heart and mind. At times he was sure that politics was his ultimate destiny, that a newspaper job would act as a springboard, and that once he took the plunge his gift for oratory would carry him far. He worked feverishly to improve this gift. He and another glib classmate, Oliver Jaynes, used to go out into a pasture at night, sit on the fence, and—fortified by a little elderberry wine—deliver impassioned orations, mostly on political themes. Then they would criticize each other's technique, pulling no punches. Ultimately Jaynes and Townsley did go into newspapering with notable success.

It was not just the glitter and power of politics that fascinated Norman. His parents had always tried to instill in their children the idea of service to mankind. From his father in particular Norman had inherited a high concept of the lawmaker and the statesman as guardians of the public good, righters of wrongs, leaders in the field of human welfare. One of his early heroes, William Howard Taft, had lamented the lack of social consciousness in the average man. "Too many people," he had said, "do not care what happens as long as it does not happen to them." The true function of the politician, as Norman saw it through the eager eyes of youth, was to teach people to care about one another, to pass laws that would raise moral standards as well as living standards, to be a selfless worker for social justice. If such a role led ultimately to the Governor's mansion or Capitol Hill in Washington, why, so much the better. The pomp and circumstance were not displeasing to him either.

And yet sometimes, if he passed an old church, or heard a choir sing, or came upon some magnificent phrase from the New or the Old Testament, he would feel a strange yearning, almost like homesickness. And he would have to make a conscious effort to push this nostalgia away from him, bury it deep, out of sight, in the lower levels of his mind.

Some aspects of the ministry appealed to him greatly; the opportunity and obligation to tell people the *good news,* the gospel of Jesus Christ, the chance to preach to them, stir them, give them help and encouragement and a sense of wonder and gratitude for the gift of life which, unasking, they had received. . . .

But the relative poverty, the relative obscurity, the pressures from church authorities on the one hand and opinionated laymen on the other, the necessity for self-discipline, self-abasement almost—how could these things compare with the excitement and freedom of newspaper work, the sense of influencing great numbers of people with the spoken or written word, the chance to rub elbows with celebrities, the glow of self-importance that would come from knowing the inside story or being behind the scenes? How could they compare with the bright kaleidoscope of politics, with the possibility of becoming a famous orator, rich, renowned, sought-after? The answer seemed all too plain: they couldn't.

Norman's parents were too wise to put any pressure on him. They knew that he was well aware of their desires, their wishes for him. If anything, his father leaned a little backward. "I didn't start out as a minister," he said. "But I've never regretted that. I think my medical training was of enormous value in my ministry. Perhaps it was part of God's plan, although I didn't know it at the time. Do what you think is right, Norman; that's the main thing."

"I think," the boy said, remembering the words of his old Bible professor, "that as a newspaperman I can reach more people, and perhaps help more, than any other way."

His father looked at him, knowing how tightly the strands of self-interest and altruism could be woven in the human heart. "It's your life, Norman," he said. "You're the one who has to live it."

So it was arranged that when college ended, Norman would go to work for the *Findlay Republican* as a cub reporter. Salary: fifteen dollars per week.

The last few weeks of college life fled by. Norman was not dismayed by the prospect of his final examinations: in six courses taken during his last semester (having learned to avoid subjects like Greek) he achieved four A's and two B's. The *Transcript* ran short profiles of a few prominent seniors, and Norman's somewhat tongue-in-cheek oratorical style was readily discernible when he wrote about his friends. Joe Joseph, his old political colleague, got the full treatment, starting with a resounding anti-climax: "Out of Egypt came the Wise Men, out of Rome came Caesar, out of the eternal hills of Southern Ohio came one John Jerome Joseph . . ." "Chid" Mills found himself glowingly described in iambic pentameter: "Tennyson, in his great poem, *The Princess,* must have had Charles B. Mills of Marysville, Ohio, in mind when he exclaims, 'Fineness often compensates for size . . .'"

But there was genuine affection and admiration under the purple prose.

June 16 was Graduation Day. Clifford and Anna Peale came from Findlay, bringing young Leonard with them and glowing with pride. The speeches were made, the diplomas were handed out, the farewells were said, the last songs were sung. The warm June air was full of the ancient blend of nostalgia and anticipation, wistfulness and eagerness, and the timeless sense of the past meeting the future.

All the Peales were affected by it, and when he said good-bye to his friends, Norman was quite carried away. "Oliver," he said to Jaynes, "Oliver, let's agree not to see each other again until we meet on the floor of the United States Senate!"

The bright college years were over. Now the dreams ended, and reality began.

CHAPTER V

The Greatest Literary

Device Known to Man

". . . is a period."

◄§◊►

The publisher of the *Findlay Morning Republican* was Lowell Heminger, the City Editor was Anson Hardman, and being wise old newspaper hands they started Norman off in the department where people were least likely to complain about treatment received at the hands of the press—obituaries. Norman's first beat, therefore, consisted of the town's funeral parlors, where he first ascertained who was dead, and then went back to the paper and wrote up the death notices.

The *Republican* was a morning paper, which meant that reporters came to work at four p.m. and stayed late. Following the grim reaper around in the dark was not the most cheerful occupation in the world, but there were lessons to be learned from it. Interviewing survivors of the deceased, Norman saw at first hand the impact of sorrow on a household. He saw, too, when his father accompanied him as he sometimes did, the strength and solace that religion had to offer at such times.

From obituaries he progressed to covering police and fire activities. Ordinarily this would have been a welcome promotion. Unfortunately the dispenser of news at police headquarters was a grim old sergeant who seemed to have been designed expressly for frightening the wits out of young reporters. His scowl was so fierce and his voice so gruff that Norman quaked in his shoes whenever he had to ask him for information. In vain he summoned up all his resolution. Every day, when he had to go into the sergeant's awful presence, his courage drained out of him like water. The collection and reporting of news, instead of being a highroad to romance, was rapidly becoming a nightmare.

In desperation he finally went to his father and told him of his inability to solve the problem. Clifford Peale stroked his mustache for a while. Then he said, "What does the sergeant like? He can't dislike everything. What's he interested in?"

"I don't know," Norman said fervently.

"Well, I do," his father said. "The sergeant happens to have a little granddaughter. He thinks the sun rises and sets on the child. Why don't you manage to get a look at her and then say something pleasant to the sergeant about her."

"About his granddaughter?" Norman sounded skeptical. "What good will that do?"

"Try it," said his father, "and see."

The results were as predicted. The dragon ceased breathing fire and started giving out news.

"Why, you know," Norman said, "he's really a nice old fellow after all!"

"Most people are," his father said dryly, "if you handle 'em right and genuinely love 'em."

There was much else to learn, and many people to learn from. One of Norman's fellow reporters in Findlay was an old-timer who greatly admired Clifford Peale. The affection was mutual, although the pastor had misgivings about his friend—the old-timer was a hard drinker. The copy he produced was often lush and grandiloquent. But he knew the value of emotion, and he tried to make Norman see the importance of adding color and warmth to a story—human interest, he called it. Sometimes he would be too befuddled to complete his story, and Norman would finish it for him, imitating the tear-jerker style as best he could. "My boy," the old fellow would say tearfully on these occasions, "watch out for tobacco and liquor. They did this to me. Don't let 'em do it to you!"

Now and then Norman would be sent to cover an out-of-town story. On one of these trips a manufacturer of paint took a fancy to him and offered him a job, selling paint, with the whole of West Virginia as his territory. "Why, you could make twice as much money," the manufacturer said. "And besides," he added, shrewdly sizing up his prospect as the idealistic type, "what could be more satisfying than the knowledge that you were personally responsible for brightening up the landscape and bringing beauty into people's lives? Just think, you could ride along a road and look at house after house that your product had changed from something faded and drab to something shining and splendid!"

"That would be fine," Norman said doubtfully. "But in five or six years wouldn't they all have to be painted again?"

"Sure they would," cried the paint tycoon. "That's the best part of it!"

Norman thanked him politely, but said that it was his ambition to improve things in a way that would be a little more permanent.

After a few months apprenticeship on the *Republican*, he was offered a job on the *Detroit Journal*. This was not so much the result of his inspired obituary-writing as his father's friendship with Grove Patterson, then managing editor of the *Journal*. Patterson interviewed Norman and asked a few probing questions. "If you were covering a political convention," he said, "how would you slant your copy—for a college professor or a ditchdigger?"

There was only one answer to this, and Norman gave it.

"That's right," Patterson said. "The main thing about writing is to keep it simple. Never be obscure. Never be involved. Never try to Write with a capital W. Use simple Anglo-Saxon words, and keep your sentences short. The greatest literary device known to man is a period. Remember that."

"Yes, sir," Norman said.

"There's almost no subject," Patterson went on, "however complex, that can't be made understandable if the writer will just think clearly and write simply. There are precious few writers who can do this. Maybe you're one of 'em. I don't know. Let's try it for a while and see."

So Norman moved to the big city. His salary was a little larger, but not much. He lived at the Y.M.C.A., ate in drugstores and cafeterias, reported sermons, religious conferences, trials, Rotary Club luncheons, and anything else that came along. He also lived in considerable dread of his City Editor, a man of vast and unpredictable rages and a command of profanity unlike anything Norman had ever heard back in Ohio. But he was a good newspaperman, and he hammered the disciplines of the craft into his reporters.

On one occasion Norman was sent to cover a trial across the river in Canada, and was told to check in by telephone before the proceedings started. The proceedings were delayed for an hour or so, and Norman took his time about calling in. When he did reach the City Desk he got a blast that almost jarred the receiver out of his hand.

"Where the unprintable unprintable have you been?" roared the editor. "What do you think I'm running here—an unprintable kindergarten?"

Norman tried to explain that the trial hadn't started and that technically he was following instructions.

"Don't give me any unprintable excuses," yelled the editor. "Am I a mind reader? Suppose I'd wanted you to cover something else! After this, if you're supposed to call in at a certain time, you call—to the unprintable minute, is that clear?"

"Yes, sir!" said the sweating cub. It only took two or three such incidents to give him a respect for deadlines and copy disciplines that was to last for the rest of his life.

The weeks went by, busy, exciting, and on the whole satisfying. And yet there were times when Norman wondered if he were cut out to be a newspaperman after all. Looking around him, he saw that the best reporters had a toughness, an aggressiveness, a ruthlessness almost, that he knew was lacking in himself.

One incident crystallized this for him. He was sent with another reporter—a girl, as it happened—to the home of a man who had been involved in some sort of scandal and therefore was newsworthy. Their assignment was to interview the man's wife, and as they waited for her in the livingroom, Norman was already feeling squeamish about this intrusion on privacy. Suddenly the girl noticed on a table a photograph of the husband. She nudged Norman and pointed. "Slip that under your coat," she said.

"What do you mean?" asked Norman, startled.

"I mean, steal it," she said. "It's a good picture. No other paper will have it."

When Norman still refused, she gave him a scornful look—and stole it herself.

This quality of moral callousness was something that Norman knew he simply did not have, and never would have. The basic training he had received at home was too strong. He began to see that this squeamishness—while it might not be a fatal handicap—certainly could not be considered an advantage when it came to rough-and-tumble newsgathering.

In a way, although he did not realize it, he was following the same pattern as his father. Thirty years before, in Milwaukee, young Dr. Peale had felt something in him shrink and wince whenever he brushed elbows with the sordidness and degradation that a public health officer had to encounter. This revulsion, on some deep moral level, was undoubtedly a factor in his ultimate decision to leave medicine for the ministry. Now the same sort of pressures were working on the same sensitivities in his son.

The crisis came in the fall of 1921. Norman had heard of a newspaper job back in Troy, Ohio, that seemed to offer a chance for more rapid advancement. He decided to look into it, and on the way to stop and visit his family. It happened that the Peales had gone from Findlay down to Bellefontaine to attend a Methodist conference. And so it was to this town of his boyhood that Norman went.

Nothing had changed. There was the church where he had heard his father preach so often, where he had overheard the Carter brothers agitating for his father's removal. There was the main street down which he and Bob had roared in the old Reo with the cutout wide-open. There was the sidewalk outside the high school where they had painted the class numerals. Everywhere he went, everywhere he looked, the past seemed to enfold him, familiar and reassuring and comforting.

It was in this mood of awareness and receptivity that he met his parents, felt their love and pride surround him, went with them to the church meetings. And listening to the old hymns, hearing the strong, simple words of the preachers, he felt once more the old, insistent tug at the roots of his being, the slow, majestic surge of something that lay deeper than thought, beyond all reason.

He knew what it was, and what it meant. He knew that his father had once felt it, and had resisted as long as he could, but in the end had had to yield. He remembered the story he had heard his father use so often as an illustration in his sermons: the story of the coal miner who only saw the world at night, but one unforgettable day came up into the full blaze of noon. He remembered, too, the older story of the tax collector who sat unmoved at his place of business until a Stranger came and looked once into his eyes and said, *"Follow me!" And he arose, and followed him.*

When the meeting ended, Norman did not go back with his parents to the house where they were staying. He walked the darkened streets through the calm September night, fighting a battle with himself. Some intuition, some sure instinct told him that this was the crossroads, that if he was to change the direction of his life it would have to be now or never. He had already invested a year of his life in newspaper work. If he climbed any farther up the ladder, he would never have the courage to climb back down. . . .

Lord, he prayed, *I'm willing to do whatever You want me to do. Help me to make the right decision. Send me a sign. . . .*

But there seemed to be no sign, no answer, just the sound of his footsteps echoing hollowly in the listening night.

He tried to weigh the alternatives dispassionately, balancing the pros and cons in his mind. What of his political dreams, he asked himself, his hopes of helping people through service in public life? If he turned to the ministry now, those dreams would have to be abandoned. What of his visions of himself as a great orator, another Wilson or a Bryan? A small-town preacher could hardly aspire to such heights. Even his own father, for all his talent and strength of character and medical background had achieved nothing more than a small amount of local prominence. Furthermore, if he changed now, might not the lingering fear always haunt him that he changed because he was *afraid*—afraid of not being a great success as a newspaperman?

He walked faster, past houses whose windows gleamed like sightless eyes in the light from the street lamps, out toward the deeper darkness that marked the edge of town. Suppose he did resign his newspaper job and go to divinity school—at Boston

University, probably; that was the accepted place for Ohio Methodists to go. It would take him three more years of study. How would he finance this? His savings were too small to carry him very far. Suppose he met a girl he wanted to marry? As a divinity student he wouldn't be able to afford a wife. Whereas in a year or so, if he kept moving up in the newspaper world, he probably could. And yet . . .

And yet, which was more important, to go on thinking about himself and his own advancement and his own convenience and his own welfare, or . . .

Or to tell people, confused, despairing, hopeless people, about the love and strength and compassion of a God who cared, a God who was not remote and vague and indifferent, but who had given Himself to his people in the person of Jesus Christ?

He stopped abruptly, and looked up at the glittering stars. Finding the right answer wasn't the difficulty. Finding the courage to face up to it—that was the real problem.

He walked on. The lights of the town receded. An old moon hung low in the west, and by its feeble light he could see the dim outlines of the rolling countryside, the stubbled fields, the dark trees massed behind. He came to a dirt road and turned into it, preferring the soft earth to the unyielding asphalt. The memory came to him of childhood Sundays, his father preaching in small churches along country roads like this one, his mother's face as she listened. . . .

He halted again. Was this what he wanted? No, was this what was wanted of him?

Abruptly he knew that, struggling with the problem alone, he would never come to a complete solution. Later, as he grew in spirit, he would conquer indecisiveness. Now all he could do was make one small move in the right direction. If he waited until he had the courage to take the whole plunge, he might wait forever. But if he just put one toe in . . .

He turned quickly, and started back to town. He would

write to Boston University. No, he would send a telegram. He would not ask for admission to the Divinity School; he would simply ask for permission to work toward a Master of Arts degree in their graduate school and possibly take some courses in theology on the side. That way, he wouldn't be committed. That way he would leave open a possible line of retreat. And besides, he thought, as he hurried along, there was every chance that the University would turn down such a belated request. It was already September; their vacancies probably had been filled long ago.

Back in town he hesitated, half persuaded that the gesture he was about to make was both foolish and hopeless. He knew that the main telegraph office was long since closed. The only way to send a telegram would be to walk down to the railroad tracks, climb the ladder to the dispatcher's shack high above the rails, and ask him to put a message on the wire.

He stood there, irresolute. Go on, he said to himself, you've spent half the night agonizing over this. Do one thing that's concrete and specific, anyway. *Do it!*

The station was dark and deserted. He saw the light in the dispatcher's shack a hundred yards down the track. He walked toward it, stumbling over crossties, wondering if the man would think he had taken leave of his senses. He came to the ladder that led up into darkness, set his foot on the first rung, and began to climb it. . . .

Five minutes later he came back down. The telegram was on its way, giving his qualifications, asking for admittance. For a moment he stood there, motionless. Ahead of him the railroad signals burned green and red and amber, the shining rails stretched away to infinity. *All right, Lord,* he said in his mind, *I've put one toe in. I'm sorry, but it was the best I could do. I guess the rest is up to You.*

He walked back to the house where he was staying, feeling no anxiety, no uncertainty. The tension was gone. That, he thought, was what prayer could do for you, even feeble, uncertain, fumbling prayer. He felt as if he had put the matter into hands far stronger and more competent than his own. However it turned out now, whatever the outcome, that would be all right with him.

He went to bed and slept soundly. The next day a telegram arrived from Boston University. His request had been received. His application for enrollment was granted.

CHAPTER VI

"Prepare Your Own

Sermons!"

◆§§◆

Norman's decision to go to Boston was received by his family with quiet rejoicing. "Don't worry about the year that's just behind you," his father said. "You'll find it wasn't wasted at all. On the contrary, what you've learned as a reporter will help you for the rest of your life. Might not be a bad idea if every young man took a job for a year before going into postgraduate work. It'd keep a lot of 'em from getting ivory-tower-itis."

His mother said little, but Norman knew how pleased she was. For her his decision was one more proof that prayers were always heard—and answered if the petition was a valid one.

Grove Patterson was sorry to see him leave the *Journal.* "If you find you're not cut out to be a minister," he told Norman, "your old job will always be waiting for you."

It was a promise that neither of them forgot. Years later,

looking down from the pulpit of the Marble Collegiate Church in New York, Norman saw his old boss in the congregation. Eager to impress, he preached with all the power and eloquence he could command. The sermon was well received, and after the service Norman waited with some complacence for a word of praise. But the kindly old editor saw right through him. "Well, Norman," he said with a twinkle as he came by in the long line of handshakers, "your old job is *still* waiting for you!"

In Boston Norman took up a residence in one of the oldest parts of the city, Louisburg Square. In terms of architecture and atmosphere he might almost have fancied himself in eighteenth century London: the high, narrow houses with their lovely doorways and fanlights, the tall iron railing around the green oasis of shrubs and trees, the marble statue of Demosthenes on which irreverent divinity students liked to place derby hats—or sometimes less dignified objects.

To supplement the money he had borrowed from various relatives, he got a job as dumb-waiter operator in the Y.W.C.A. cafeteria. For two dollars a day—and his meals—he would load dirty dishes into the dumb-waiter, give a heave on a hairy rope, and send the load plummeting to the basement. His partner at the bottom of the shaft was another divinity student, Webster D. Melcher, who liked to be called "Web" but was universally known as "Shorty." His function was to unload the dirty dishes and send up clean ones. Shouting up and down the echoing shaft, Norman and Shorty soon became as intimate as two galley slaves chained to the same oar.

Boston fascinated Norman: the sense of antiquity, of respect for and continuity with the past, the great religious tradition, the tacit assumption of cultural superiority—these aspects of Eastern living made an enormous impression on the boy from the Middle West. His four years at Ohio Wesleyan had taught him almost nothing about classical music, still less about art. He began to try to remedy these deficiencies by going to concerts and museums. He read everything he could set his hands on. He discovered William James, and promptly elevated the great psychologist to a pinnacle alongside Emerson in his pantheon of mighty American minds.

His studies went well. His grounding in orthodox Methodism was so firm that he had no doubts to resolve, no great intellectual battles to fight out within himself. As the weeks went by the conviction grew steadily within him that he had made the right decision—or perhaps had had it made for him —in leaving the newspaper world. He decided to work for two degrees: Bachelor of Sacred Theology and Master of Arts in Social Ethics.

The art that he wished above all to master was the art of leading a congregation to deep spiritual commitment. He knew that effective preaching was one of the chief means of accomplishing this, and he had considerable faith in his own developing talent. All the same, his first formal sermon was an ordeal.

In the spring of his first year at Boston word came that the Methodist church in the little town of Walpole, Massachusetts, needed some one to fill its pulpit on Sunday. Norman volunteered to go. For two full weeks he worked feverishly on his sermon, writing and re-writing it. For a text he chose his father's favorite: *"I am come that they might have life, and that they might have it more abundantly."*

He prepared the sermon in at least seven different versions. None of them seemed to him to have the slightest merit. Finally, on the Monday before the dreaded Sunday, he wrote in panic to his father. "I wish," he said, "that you would send me your notes, or any written copy you may have of the sermon I have heard you preach so often on this text. I want so much to do a worthwhile job at Walpole. Please send me anything you have *at once!*"

He did not have to wait long for a reply; it came by return mail in his father's familiar scrawl: "Prepare your own sermons. Just tell the people that Jesus Christ can change their lives. Love, Dad."

With this gentle kick still tingling in the seat of his spiritual pants, Norman went down to Walpole. It was a lovely blue-and-gold morning; the white spire of the church pointed serenely to heaven. In the tower was a little room with an old red couch and a table strewn with Sunday School lessons, hymn-books, church announcements. Here Norman was told to make himself comfortable and await the appointed hour.

He waited, all right, but he was anything but comfortable. He paced up and down, heart thudding like a triphammer, trying to fix his sermon in his mind. The palms of his hands, he noticed, were sweating and he found it difficult to breathe.

Looking out of the window, he saw with a heightened sense of terror that people were beginning to gather. They came up the walk, old and young, dressed in their Sunday finery. An elderly man approached, tall and stately, and the sight of him drained away Norman's last drop of assurance. *What do you have to say,* jeered the mocking voice within, *that could possibly mean anything to a man like that? Who are you to be telling him how he should conduct his life?*

His sense of inadequacy swept over him in a great wave. He fell on his knees by the old red couch and prayed with an urgency he had not known for years. *Help me, Lord, help me to say something that will help them. . . .*

How long he knelt there he did not know, but suddenly the panic was gone and he felt a great calmness in his mind and heart. The removal of the fear was so miraculous and so complete that for a moment he could not believe it. He stood up, hesitantly. It was true; the terror was gone, and in its place was a kind of exaltation that melted rapidly into a great longing to share this incredible source of strength, this healing power with people everywhere. In a surge of gratitude he cried out his desire henceforth to dedicate his whole life, his whole strength, and any talents he might have to persuading people to accept Christ and to live the Christian life. He said this aloud, standing alone in the little room, and he meant it with all his heart.

There was a knock on the door. It was the sexton, telling him that it was time for the service to begin.

He preached for only twelve minutes that day. He forgot all about his prepared speech. He simply tried to tell the congregation what Christ had done for him, and could do for them if they would let Him.

He tried to tell them about the hunger in every human heart for God. "It's the deepest of all our desires," he said to them. "We came from God. He is our home, and there is a deep homesickness for Him in all of us. He is in our bloodstream, in the meshes of our minds, in the intricacies of our souls. We are His and He is ours. We can't get away from God; even if we deny Him, He haunts us. In our conflicts, our misery, we must turn back to Him for peace. A carrier pigeon, released in the air, instinctively turns home. Birds in their migrations unerringly go back to the same bush from which they came. Every river feels the lure of the sea. Every human life feels the tug of God."

They listened to him. He could feel them listening, could see on their faces a rapt and wistful expression that moved him profoundly. And then, abruptly, he had nothing more to say. He bowed his head and offered a short prayer. His first sermon was over.

Afterwards a kindly old lady from the congregation took him home to Sunday dinner. "It looks to me, Mr. Peale," she said, "as if you don't get enough to eat half the time. Why, a good strong wind would blow you away!"

"I eat more than most people," Norman assured her, and this was the truth. "I even drink double milk shakes between meals. It just doesn't do any good."

"Well, you come back and preach here often," she told him. "I'll fatten you up in no time."

On the train back to Boston, his sense of excitement and elation vanished and a reaction set in. He had only preached twelve minutes; what kind of sermon was that? A thousand sermons lay ahead of him, two thousand, perhaps. What was he going to say in all those sermons? How could he possibly go on preaching for twenty or thirty years when he ran out of ideas after his first twelve minutes?

For a while he tormented himself with such thoughts. Then the memory of his prayer in the little tower room came back to him. With God's help, he had come through the first crisis, hadn't he? The rest would offer no problem equal to that. The thing to do, obviously, was not to think in terms of two thousand sermons, but to think about them one at a time. An old Ohio farm saying came back to him: "If you think about all the corn you have to hoe, your back is broken before you start!" Maybe, he thought, that was the way to handle any problem: take one step at a time.

He took out a stick of gum, unwrapped it, began to chew reflectively. Outside the train window the landscape rushed past, the trees blurred with green, their branches fuzzy with the promise of spring. He felt, suddenly, a glow of warmth and joy in his heart. He had preached his first sermon. He had rededicated his life to the Lord. He had had a fine dinner. . . .

It had been quite a day.

That summer he went back to Ohio full of enthusiasms for the ministry, for Boston, for the School of Theology, for the widening horizons that lay before him. He was full of a certain amount of self-importance, too, although he would have been the first to deny this.

By this time Clifford Peale was a Methodist district superintendent, with perhaps a hundred churches under his jurisdiction. He observed his son's ebullience with a tolerant eye, saying nothing. But when the minister of one of his country churches fell ill, he suggested mildly that Norman might like to take his place on the following Sunday. It would be good practice, he said. And of course, he added, it wasn't often that a country congregation had the chance to hear a preacher fresh out of one of the great divinity schools of the country.

Suitably flattered, Norman set to work to produce a sermon that would do credit to the erudition of his teachers and the cultural spirit of old Boston. For a subject he chose the atonement, a topic on which he had recently spent endless classroom hours. He gave it, he thought, the most profound and respectful treatment. Then he decided to try the finished result on his father.

He read it to Clifford Peale on Saturday afternoon as they sat on the porch of the house in Findlay. "There," he said, when he was through. "What do you think of that?"

His father put his feet up on the porch railing. "Do you really want to know?"

"Why, yes," said Norman a bit uneasily. "I do."

"My advice," said his father thoughtfully, "would be to take it out back and burn it."

Norman stared. "Burn it?"

"Well, put it away. In any case, don't try to take it into the pulpit with you."

"But why not?" cried Norman despairingly.

"In the first place," said his father, "I gather you intend to read it. In my opinion, sermons should be given without notes and without a written text. How can you look your audience in the eye, gauge their reactions and feelings, and watch a manuscript at the same time?

"In the second place, you have taken a big subject and made it sound terribly involved. The job of a preacher is to simplify, not to complicate. Remember what Grove Patterson told you on the newspaper. There's no subject on earth that can't be put simply, if you will just think clearly and logically about it, and use plain instead of fancy language." He looked at Norman quizzically. "In your desire to impress people with your own profundity, you seem to have forgotten that the way to the human heart is through simplicity."

Norman stared down at the floor boards of the porch. This was true. This was shatteringly true. He said at last, in a small voice, "What shall I do?"

"It's easy," his father told him. "Simply tell them—*simply* tell them—how Christ has helped you, and how He will help them if they will just give Him a chance. That's the greatest message in the world, and it's the only message you'll ever need. Just tell the people that, keep telling them that, and you'll never have to worry about the size of your congregations. They'll come from miles around, they'll break down the doors to get into your church."

"Why," said Norman, "that's exactly what I tried to do in my sermon at Walpole!"

"That's fine," his father said. "Try to do it again tomorrow morning. And keep on trying to do it for the rest of your life."

Years later, Norman told a New York congregation what happened the next morning at the little red brick church in the country.

"I can remember it all," he said, "as if it were yesterday. The church stood at the intersection of two roads that ran between the endless fields of corn and wheat. Back of the church, visible through the pulpit window, was a cool and inviting grove where the shade of the great trees was broken by long shafts of sunlight. The church was quiet and restful; some one had put a bunch of summer flowers on the communion table. Soon an organist arrived and began softly to play a medley of hymns while the people gathered. Most arrived in buggies, although there were a few Model T Fords and a Willys Knight or two that came chugging up to stop in the spacious yard.

"The peace and quiet, the radiantly fresh morning, the Sunday-go-to-meeting atmosphere moved me deeply. I felt a rush of gratitude at the thought that I was privileged to share my faith with these people—simple country people, and the salt of the earth. I studied their faces as we listened to the music of the choir. The men, bronzed and rugged, looked slightly uncomfortable in their Sunday clothes. The women, while not what you might call stylish, had that nice dressed-up look of old-fashioned mothers and aunts. The little girls were sweet in their flounces and ribbons. Families sat together; father on the end, the boys next to him with their feet barely touching the floor, then the girls, and finally mother. A parent at either end was accepted as the best policing method!

"When time came for the sermon, I heeded my father's advice and gave a simple sermon based entirely on my own spiritual experience. I tried to use plain, everyday language and homey illustrations to drive home what Jesus Christ could do for my hearers. I described some of my own conflicts, and made the sermon a personal testimony of what Christ had done for me.

"While I was preaching, I suddenly became aware of the stillness that sometimes comes over a congregation when something very near to the heart of life creates a unity of understanding between the preacher and the people. It was a depth of feeling that seemed to tremble in the still summer air. There was something in it that made me think of a phrase I had heard somewhere: 'An impingement like the hush of eternity.'

"I noticed then the strange look on people's faces that in the years that followed I was to see so often whenever that mystic hush comes as it does now and then. It is a kind of wonder, a look of blissful gratitude and goodness that appears when Jesus Christ is talked about and related to the simplicities of human lives.

"After church, I was touched by the friendliness of the people. They treated me as if I were a real preacher! A big, white-haired farmer and his wife invited me home for dinner. They lived in a large brick farm-house set back from the road in a grove of pine trees. Several families were having their Sunday dinner jointly. The women folk went inside, some to cook, some to set the dining room table. The men sat out on the veranda. Pretty soon the most tantalizing odors wafted out and whetted our appetites on the porch.

"My host, the big farmer, clapped a great hand down on my knee. 'That was a pretty good sermon, son,' he said, 'pretty good. Of course, you still have a lot to learn about preaching.'

" 'Yes, sir,' I said meekly, 'I know.'

" 'Well,' he said with a chuckle, 'practice makes perfect.' He rocked back and forth for a while in a creaky old rocking chair. Then he went on: 'But you're on the right track. Always keep the message simple, so that people can understand. And always talk about Christ the Savior. He's a wonderful Savior, my boy. . . .'

"His voice trailed off. I was listening, looking out across the fields, but no more words came. Glancing up at the old farmer, I saw that he was struggling with himself. There were tears in his eyes. He stood up, suddenly, and went into the house.

"For a moment there was silence. Then one of the other men said quietly, 'George had a lot of problems and a lot of struggles. He went pretty wild there for a while. But at a revival meeting down at the church he found the Lord, and the Lord saved him, and he has had a warm place in his heart for Jesus ever since!'

"I shall never forget the feeling that came over me at that moment, the feeling that it was Jesus who could win a human heart and change lives and give salvation to men. It was one of the great formative experiences of my early ministry, deeply impressive and never forgotten."

During his second year in Boston, Norman was ordained. He promised, as did all Methodist clergymen, to keep out of debt and avoid all use of tobacco. The former was easier than the latter. He had smoked to some extent while in Ohio Wesleyan, enough to wonder if the habit might be getting a grip on him. At one point he had confided this fear to Bob. "The craving for nicotine," said Norman gloomily, "can be a powerful thing."

"Craving, my foot!" said the forthright member of the Peale family. "It's a state of mind, that's all. If you believe you can quit, you can quit. Why don't you try it and see."

Norman tried it, and found to his astonishment that Bob was right. So he did quit, and took to chewing gum instead.

During this year at divinity school, Norman began to make a serious effort to analyze and understand the techniques and secrets of successful preaching. Outstandingly effective preachers, he knew, were few and far between; half-empty churches all over the land proved how rare the gift really was. Listening to his elders and betters, watching them conduct themselves in the pulpit or on the lecture platform, Norman began to ask himself seriously and earnestly what it was that made some good and some indifferent.

All, clearly, faced the same problem. They had to formulate a series of ideas inside their own heads, then project those ideas into space, using their lungs, vocal cords, facial expressions, and manual or bodily gestures. These ideas, so expressed, then had to be received by the eyes and ears of the target-audience, relayed along optic and auditory nerves to the appropriate centers of the brain, and there decoded—against varying degrees of inertia—into thought and meaning.

The physiological processes of all this were complicated enough, but they were simple compared to the hundreds of shades of meaning that words possess and the billions of possible combinations of such words. Add to this the inescapable fact that any large audience is bound to be made up of people of widely diversified tastes and backgrounds, all of whom had

to be made to feel momentarily the same emotions and reactions, and the problem became truly formidable.

Listening to other speakers, laymen as well as ministers,
judging their success or lack of it by his own reactions and the
reactions he could observe in their audiences, Norman began
to see dimly that the most effective ones had certain things in
common. They were *arresting:* they caught the audience's attention at the start with some striking statement or anecdote,
and then they held it. They were *logical:* their ideas were
presented in a sequence that led the listener eventually to the
point they were trying to make. They had *personality:* humor,
enthusiasm, dedication, sincerity, a quality of differentness. Almost always they were *simple,* clear, unpretentious—and brief.

And where the great preachers were concerned, there was
one more quality that was the most important of all: the
mysterious and incandescent impression that they projected
of *being used,* of being a transmission mechanism for a mighty
flow of truth and power that came from beyond them and
passed through them into the minds and hearts of men. To
Norman nothing was so impressive as these miraculous manifestations, and he wondered, humbly and hopefully, if some
day he too might be chosen to become such a channel. He
knew that this gift was totally beyond his power to command, and also that many saintly and godly men were never
granted it. All he could do was wait and hope and pray. But
while he waited he could at least practice and analyze and
try to avoid some of the more obvious sermonic pitfalls.

Poor preachers, he noticed, also seemed to have certain
things in common. They had little knowledge of what really
appealed to people—and consequently rarely made any appeal to people's interest in their own betterment. They were
unable to think clearly for any sustained length of time—and so
were unable to offer any logical progression of ideas. They distrusted simplicity for fear that they themselves would be

thought unlearned—and consequently added pedantry to obscurity. They almost never used the God-given faculty of humor—either because they had little to begin with or because they had somehow come to believe it was out of place in the pulpit.

They had a tendency to talk too long because, having no empathy with their audience, they were unaware of the degree of boredom they were generating. They had been taught to preach mainly about great social evils rather than the immediate problems of their parishioners, so they chose broad topics—and the broader the topic, the less the impact on the individual. Finally, a great many of them had adopted a hollowness of tone, a kind of empty ecclesiastical sonority that was both sanctimonious and soporific. They were dealing with the most thrilling, fascinating thing in the world, the Gospel of Jesus Christ, and they were making it sound dull.

"Why do they *do* it?" cried Norman to Bill Stewart, his close friend and roommate. "Why can't they talk like people instead of plaster saints?"

"They're preaching, not talking," Bill said. "There's a difference, you know."

"Why should there be a difference?" Norman demanded. "I'll bet Jesus never sounded like that. He was a story-teller, the greatest that ever lived. He kept things short and simple. He knew how to reach people. He drew crowds to Him. These men, good men though they are, actually drive people away from Him and from His church!"

"Well, it's your dragon," said Bill cheerfully. "Why don't you go out single-handed and slay it?"

Recognizing the dragon was one thing; exterminating it was another. Norman was ready and willing to try, but the first skirmishes were fought in arenas that were necessarily small.

That winter another church had him occasionally as guest preacher. This was the Congregational church in Hancock,

N. H., where it was so cold that the water in the wash-basin in Norman's old-fashioned hotel room used to freeze solid every night—and the church itself wasn't much warmer.

He enjoyed it, though. In the church tower hung a bell made by Paul Revere, and Norman's romantic soul liked to toy with the fancy that, even as Revere had roused the countryside to the defense of liberty, so he—Norman Peale— was sounding the call to Christianity and the deeper freedom to be found in God.

He preached with all the fervor he could muster. Even so, there was one granite character who always came in, sat in the pew nearest the stove, put back his head, and promptly went to sleep. This used to annoy Norman intensely. He found that he could rouse the sleeper momentarily by announcing hymns in a sudden bellow that rattled the windows and mystified the other parishioners. But the victory was only temporary. The sleeper would open one startled eye, look faintly displeased, then drift off to dreamland again.

Later, at the height of his preaching career, Norman was to have an even more disconcerting experience. In the Marble Collegiate Church on one occasion he preached so eloquently and persuasively on how to relax, abandon all cares, forget all tensions, that an elderly lady went sound asleep in the front pew. This in itself would not have been so bad, but she snored. She snored, moreover, right into the public address system amplifier, which wafted her blissful groans and whistles to the farthest corners of the church while the congregation sat entranced.

On one of Norman's visits to Hancock the old hotel porter asked him if he would be interested in hearing the champion "cusser" of New Hampshire. Norman was both intrigued and repelled by the notion of meeting a past master of profanity, but decided sternly that he had better listen to the champion cusser, and if he was really as bad as all that take some action that would lead him to see the error of his ways.

So while the cusser was holding forth in the lobby of the hotel, Norman listened to him from ambush—on the landing of the stairs. But aside from a prolific use of 'damns' and 'hells,' the cusser did not seem to be in the championship class—certainly not compared to Norman's old city editor back in Detroit. So he let him go, unreformed.

Walpole and Hancock were temporary assignments only. In the spring of his second year in Boston, Norman was given a chance to show what he could do on a more permanent basis.

The Bishop called him in and explained that there were two small churches in near-by communities that needed someone to come every week end to fill the pulpit on Sunday and minister to the spiritual needs of the people. One was in a picture postcard type of New England village, lovely and serene. The church was happy and well-organized, the Bishop said—Norman would have plenty of time for study and reflection. The other church was in a small Rhode Island mill town that was in the throes of a bitter strike. Moreover, the Bishop said, the Rhode Island church was split wide open by a furious intramural fight that had raged around the previous minister, evidently a divisive sort of person. If Norman chose the church at Berkeley he would probably have time for nothing but trouble.

"The choice is yours," the Bishop said, "and I don't want to influence you unduly. But if you want my judgment, I would suggest you take the Berkeley church. You'll learn more about people and more about yourself. What's more, if you can keep your balance and your temper, you'll learn the most important thing of all, which is how effective Christianity can be when its message—which is the power of love—is applied to a situation like that." He hesitated and looked searchingly at Norman. "Well, what do you say?"

Norman said the only thing there was to say. He chose the church at Berkeley.

The town lay in the rugged Blackstone Valley, halfway be-

tween Pawtucket and Woonsocket. It offered little in the way
of charm or natural beauty; just a handful of houses clinging
to the rocky hillsides and the grim brick rectangles that were
the mills. The church, a tiny frame structure, was perched
precariously just above the main road. It seemed to wear
a woebegone expression. Indeed, over the whole town brooded
a kind of malevolence, a spirit of strife and sullen discord.

The Methodist district superintendent had warned Norman
of this. "It's partly the bitterness in the town between the
workers and the mill-owners," he said. "But it's also in the
church itself. The people are good people, basically, but
they've forgotten that they're good. They're full of hate and
vindictiveness. It's reached a point where they actually sit
on opposite sides of the main aisle and make faces at one another."

Norman was well aware of his own inexperience. "How do
I handle a situation like that?"

"Don't take sides," the Superintendent told him. "Pray hard,
preach love, don't get discouraged, and love the people yourself, in Christ's name."

This was good advice—and like most good advice not easy
to follow. The congregation regarded its new minister with
coolness. They were textile workers, many of them from the
English Midlands, poor, proud, rigidly honest, clinging to their
native customs, reasonable and pliant up to a certain point,
and then as unyielding as flint.

They had reached this point both in the realm of the spirit
and in temporal things. They wanted certain concessions from
the mill owners, and when Norman saw the way they lived—
no inside plumbing, sometimes not even electricity—he felt
that their demands were justified. They were asking for better wages, better housing, shorter hours, compensation for in-
jury, better sick pay, and so on. But in 1923, with the Sacco-
Vanzetti case rocking the nation and wild talk of rampant
socialism everywhere, the owners were in no mood to be

conciliatory. The outcome had been a series of strikes for which the workers were not fully prepared or organized. The chief result had been increasing bitterness on both sides.

Inside the church, the warring factions took one look at the slender divinity student and came to the silent but almost unanimous conclusion that the Bishop had sent a boy to do a man's job. Old Mrs. Follett, a widow who lived next to the church and had a tendency to consider it her private property, was heard to remark that the new minister looked as if he didn't have sense enough to come in out of the rain. This was hardly an original phrase, but it had the effect of swinging to Norman's side several neutrals who were ready to disagree furiously with Mrs. Follett on almost anything. When the remark was repeated to Norman—as it was several times with relish—it stung him badly in the area where he was most vulnerable, his hypersensitivity. But he remembered the Bishop's advice about not losing his temper, smiled a bit wanly, and said nothing.

Praying one night as usual for patience, wisdom, and the chance to put love into practice with these people, he was rewarded by a sudden thought. Old Mrs. Follett, after all, was not so very different—in appearance or in temperament —from the fearsome police sergeant who had terrorized him back in his reporting days in Findlay. Why, he asked himself, could not the technique his father had taught him, or some variant of it, be applied to the present problem?

The next day he went to call on Mrs. Follett. She was busy in her kitchen, but received him grimly in her front parlor. After a few polite exchanges Norman leaned back guilelessly in his chair. "Mrs. Follett," he said, "you know, I heard Mrs. Lloyd say something very nice about you."

Mrs. Follett blinked. Mrs. Lloyd was one of the leaders of the other church faction. "Humph!" she said. "You must have been hearing things!"

"No," said Norman. "She said you were a very excellent

cook." (This was true: he *had* heard Mrs. Lloyd make some such grudging admission.) "I got the impression she considered you one of the best cooks in the town."

"Well," said Mrs. Follett, "I'm not too bad. And if it comes to that—" she tossed her head as if she could hardly believe what she heard herself saying—"Peggy Lloyd makes nice light pastry herself."

Norman smiled contentedly. "What's that I smell cooking now? Smells like cookies."

" 'Tis cookies," said Mrs. Follett.

"Well, I'd like one," Norman said boldly. "Two, in fact. They smell like the ones my grandmother used to make out in Ohio. And a glass of milk, too, please, Mrs. Follett. If you can spare one."

Twenty minutes later he came out of Mrs. Follett's house with an air of triumph and hurried down the road. Thirty minutes later he was seated in another front parlor, balancing a cup of black tea on his knee. "You know, Mrs. Lloyd," he said, "I heard Mrs. Follett say something very complimentary about you. . . ."

"Who?" cried Mrs. Lloyd incredulously.

"Mrs. Follett. She said you made the best light pastry she ever tasted. You don't happen to have a small piece of pie handy, do you? Or a glass of milk? I'm starving!"

And so it went, the spiritual therapy of injecting goodwill. There were no miracles, no dramatic changes overnight. But gradually the atmosphere began to clear. People who had ceased speaking began to talk to one another; neighbors who had come to despise one another began to be reconciled. And the reason, Norman knew, lay not in his little stratagems and flatteries, but in something much deeper and stronger. It lay in the gospel that he preached constantly from the pulpit: the Christian doctrine of love.

Week after week he preached on the futility of hate, the destructiveness of resentment, the healing power of love. "Listen to this wonderful text," he would say. "Listen carefully. 'A *new commandment I give unto you, that ye love one another as I have loved you.*' Those words were spoken almost two thousand years ago, but they are the most important ever uttered on this tired old earth. Why? Because they are the key to life, to happiness, to successful living."

He would look down from the pulpit at the strong faces in front of him, at the clean, shabby clothing, at the work-roughened hands. He would look down, knowing he had come to love these people truly. He would grip the railing in front of him in the intensity of his effort to make them understand.

"You want respect and affection, don't you?" he would cry. "Then you have to give it. In this life we only get back what we give. Give hate to the world and the people around you, and you'll receive hatred. Cultivate an attitude of superiority, and you'll be treated with the same sort of contempt. Practice feelings of ill will and prejudice and anger, and that's what you'll get back. The whole universe is an echo-cavern. What you send out reverberates back to you. In order to have the love, esteem, and affection of other people, you must give them affection and esteem and love. Please listen to me; I am telling you the truth—and in your hearts you know it!"

And they did listen to him; he could tell by the softening, the longing that came into their faces.

"Love," he would say. "It's the greatest power in the world. Nothing is equal to it. How did Christ heal the sick? Partly by loving them, I think, loving them so intensely that they were made whole. Perfect love casteth out fear. It casts out anger, too, and hatred, and malice. We must learn to utilize love the way we utilize heat and electricity and mechanical energy. And the way to do this is to express love more freely, and to think about it more. The more it exists in our thought, the more it will show in our actions."

Sunday after Sunday he hammered at them with the same theme. "Have you ever," he would say to them, "have you ever actually, wholeheartedly tried love instead of hate? When someone has annoyed or offended or injured you, have you ever tried loving him back into a good relationship instead of fighting him? Try it now; try it before sunset today! Pick out someone here in this church, and try it. There are people here in this town who have been made physically ill by hatred, by giving it as well as by receiving it. They must learn to love before they can be made whole."

He became utterly engrossed in the task he had set himself. Five days of each week he spent in Boston with his classrooms and his textbooks. But each Friday he would return eagerly to Berkeley and the people he had come to think of as his people.

He lived in an upstairs room of a house belonging to a family named Morris. They were sturdy English people with a sense of humor and much music in them. Arthur Morris played the organ at the church. His wife, Mary, tall and black-haired, fussed over Norman as if he had been an undernourished nephew.

Their thirst for music had impelled the Morrises somehow to acquire a radio, one of the early crystal sets. Norman's first experience with this newfangled gadget came one night when, with earphones clamped to his head, he heard the station at Providence come through loud and clear. "Gosh!" he cried enthusiastically. "Think of how many people could hear a sermon if the preacher could just talk to them through this!"

As it was, he was reaching as many people as his legs would permit. Arriving at Berkeley on Friday night, he would usually hold a prayer meeting at some parishioner's house. There would be prayers, hymns, Bible reading. It was all very relaxed and informal. Once the family cat jumped on Norman's shoulder while he was praying aloud and sat there comfortably until he finished.

On Saturday he usually made calls, drumming up new members for the church, cheering up shut-ins, listening to people's problems. His energy astonished and impressed the congregation. His predecessor had made no more than half a dozen calls a month, and these to a select few. Church records still in existence show that Norman averaged something like a hundred and fifty calls a month. The same records also show that at one meeting of the church board "it was decided to allow Mr. Peale to take over the janitor's duties," no doubt in an effort to increase his almost invisible salary.

In the controversy between the workers and mill-owners, Norman's sympathies lay with the workers. He lived with them, he ate with them, he listened to their troubles. Moreover, back in divinity school, much emphasis was being laid on the social responsibility of the church. Every young minister was taught that the establishment of justice and fair play between all groups of men was very much his concern, and he was also led to believe that in most cases involving industrial friction the employers were likely to be wrong and the workers right.

Actually, in the early 'Twenties this was often the case. Norman never forgot seeing a boatload of immigrant workers landed at the Providence docks, herded ashore like bewildered cattle, tags around their necks consigning them to this mill or that. There was a callousness about it, an indifference to human dignity that jarred the young minister and aroused his sympathy and indignation.

More than once he went with a grievance committee of workers to confer with representatives of the mill management. The owners listened to him courteously, and made a few minor concessions. But their attitude made clear their apprehension that if they gave the workers an inch, they would demand a mile—so why give an inch? It was an attitude that was to produce a social revolution one decade later.

This was the serious side of life in Berkeley, but there was another side, a side that became increasingly gay and light-hearted as the animosities inside the church began to disappear. Great, for example, was the excitement generated over the privy project. The church had no such convenience until Norman spotted an abandonned four-holer in back of an unused warehouse. When he asked about it, he was told he could have it—if he would move it away. It took the lifting power of most of the able-bodied men in the congregation, but they finally got it onto a truck, drove it triumphantly through the streets with the minister perched on top, and installed it with loud cheers on the hillside behind the church.

Sometimes members of Norman's family would visit him in Berkeley. By now Bob was enrolled in medical school at Harvard; he could get away occasionally for a week end. A member of the congregation, invited to have chicken dinner on Sunday at the Morris house, found Anna and Clifford Peale on the front porch happily analyzing the sermon their son had given that morning, and Bob in the kitchen, busily dissecting the heads of the chickens "to see if they have any brains." The verdict, which was received with interest: not many.

One of Norman's best friends in Berkeley was a craggy Yorkshireman named Robert Rowbottom. He had gone to work in textile mills at the age of twelve, but what he lacked in formal education he more than made up in strength of character and forthrightness. From the start he gave Norman all the support and encouragement that one man could give another. He defended him against his critics. He rallied him in moments of discouragement. He showed him how to hold the first baby brought to him for baptism. On one occasion, when Norman's only dark suit was at the cleaners, he lent him his own black suit so that he could officiate at the funeral of a Catholic who was thought to have committed suicide, and hence had been refused burial by his own faith.

Long after Norman had left the little church at Berkeley,

Rowbottom continued to take a fatherly interest in him. One day shortly after Norman had been called to the Marble Church on Fifth Avenue in New York, Rowbottom appeared and listened to the sermon. Afterwards he fixed a stern and penetrating eye on his former minister. "I wanted to make sure," he said, "that you're still preaching in accordance with your conscience, and not just to please people."

Norman gulped and said that he surely hoped so.

"I know you are," said Rowbottom. "But it's a good question for any minister to ask himself now and then!"

His pastorate at Berkeley was a great training ground for Norman. When a question or a problem was too much for him, he could always take it back to divinity school and discuss it with older and wiser men. And when at divinity school some theory or hypothesis was handed to him, he could go down to Berkeley and put it to pragmatic test in the laboratory of human experience.

He was lucky, in a way, that his first church was a divided one. It gave him insight both into the corrosive action of hate and the healing power of love. He was very young, very inexperienced, and there were many things he sensed rather than understood. But some of the truest friends of his life were made in the bleak little mill town, and some of the greatest moments of his ministry were experienced there.

One Sunday night, for example, preaching once more on the power of love to heal and reunite divided people, he found himself so moved by the ageless message that at the end of the sermon, for the first time in his life, he challenged any one in the congregation who sincerely wanted to be changed to leave his pew and come to the altar to make a decision for Christ.

To his astonishment, five people in the tiny church rose and came forward. And watching them come, hopeful and trusting, the young minister felt his enthusiasm melt away and consternation take its place. He did not know what to do with these people he had called. Who was he, a nobody still in divinity school, to be leading human souls to a rendezvous with their Creator? What could he say to them? What should he do?

They stood there, waiting, and the silence seemed to lengthen into light-years. Finally he did the only thing he could do. He asked for help. He knelt beside the five who had come forward. "Lord," he prayed silently, "I don't know what to do. These people are here, and I don't know what to say to them. Give me an answer—please."

When he opened his eyes he saw his answer, in the faces beside him. They were alight, they were shining, they were transfigured. They were radiant with the gladness he had glimpsed long ago on the face of the old ne'er-do-well in his father's church who had come forward to be touched by the same finger of light. Looking into the eyes of his five parishioners he knew that what he said or didn't say made little difference. He saw there the projected power of the Christian faith, the one element recognized through the centuries as unique and supreme, the power of God to change human lives in the twinkling of an eye.

Later, when they were all gone, he locked up the little church, then walked home slowly through the rocky Rhode Island hills. The moon was clear; the air was crisp with autumn. But it was not the spell of the moonlight or the frosty air that kept his pulses racing with an exhilaration unlike any he had ever known. It was the knowledge that, inexperienced and immature and groping as he was, one of his sermons had actually helped to bring five people to a public confession of faith. Somehow a sermon of his had had enough of the power of God in it to touch these people, to transform them, to give them re-birth. It was staggering. It was incredible.

He came at last to the parsonage. He stared at the weather-beaten shingles, silver in the moonlight, and he felt a sudden flood of love and gratitude for the little house, for the quiet, decent people he shared it with, for the Power that had brought him to this place and had, this night, given him a glimpse of the greatness of his calling, the power and the glory and the stupendous drama of human change. . . .

He knew he would never escape from this greatness.

He went inside, climbed the narrow stairs, said a prayer of thankfulness, and fell instantly asleep.

CHAPTER VII

"Anything Can Happen

in Brooklyn"

◆§◆

"This," said Norman, peering happily out of the train window, "is it!"

"What do you mean—it?" asked Johnny Bancroft.

They were on their way back to the Seminary from Christmas holidays—Johnny too was an Ohioan. As usual, the need for economy had forced them to share an upper berth, but since both were small this was no great hardship. The train was crossing the Jersey meadows. In the distance the skyline of Manhattan was sharp against the January sky.

"I mean this is the big town, the big league," Norman said. "This is where I'd like to have a church some day."

"New York," quoted Johnny gloomily, "the graveyard of ministers!"

"I know that's what they say," Norman admitted, "the cruel, indifferent, heartbreaking city. All the same, I'd like to take a shot at it." He sat up straighter, seized by a sudden thought. "We have some time to kill between trains. Why don't we go and see Bishop Wilson? I'll bet if we told him we wanted a New York church next spring, he'd assign us to one."

Johnny looked as if the idea of bearding a bishop in his lair held little appeal for him. "Why," he said, "I'll bet he wouldn't even see us!"

"We'll never know unless we try," Norman said. "We got in to see the President of the United States, didn't we?"

This was true enough. On a trip to Washington, Norman had prevailed on an Ohio congressman to arrange a visit to the White House. He and Johnny had shaken hands with the President, and Norman had given Mr. Coolidge the secret Phi Gamma Delta fraternity grip—whereat the wintry presidential countenance had cracked in a faint smile.

"I know the Bishop's address," Norman went on. "It's 150 Fifth Avenue. That can't be very far from the station. We'll walk down and see him."

The walk turned out to be a good deal longer than either of them expected, and Johnny's lack of enthusiasm became more apparent with every step. But Norman was in one of his moods of buoyancy and optimism. There was something about the atmosphere of New York that stimulated him, something electric, something challenging. "Look at those buildings," he said eagerly. "Think of the energy and the skill and the money it took to build them! Think of all the people around us—seven million within a rifle shot! Doesn't it excite you?"

"Nope," said Johnny, blowing on his cold fingers. "And furthermore, I've decided to let you talk to the Bishop alone. I'll just wait outside. I don't want a New York church. I'd rather start my ministry back home in Ohio."

They came at last to the building where Bishop Wilson had his offices, they went in, they were greeted by a receptionist. "We're from the Seminary at Boston University," Norman explained. "I want to ask the Bishop for an assignment here in New York."

"Well," the receptionist said doubtfully, "if you'll have a seat . . ."

They sat down to wait. The minutes ticked away. "This is crazy," Johnny whispered. "Maybe we ought to go."

"After walking this far?" Norman shook his head. "That *would* be crazy!"

He was ushered in at last, while Johnny waited in the reception room. The Bishop was a kindly looking man, silver-haired, with shrewd gray eyes. "Well, young man," he said, "what can I do for you?"

"Bishop Wilson," Norman said, "I'll be leaving the Seminary this spring, and I've decided I'd like to be assigned to a church in this area."

"Really?" said the Bishop with a smile. "Have you decided which one?"

"Any one at all," Norman assured him. "I'm not particular. I just want a place to serve where there are people—lots of people!"

The Bishop leaned back, considering. "After lunch," he said finally, "the District Superintendent from Brooklyn will be here. Why don't you come back then, and we'll see what vacancies, if any, he expects to have?"

"You see," cried Norman gleefully as he and Johnny left the Bishop's office, "he may have something for me. My father always said that the bigger a man was, the easier he was to talk to. Really important people are always approachable. Something will come of this; I have a hunch about it. You'll see."

Later, in the Bishop's office, they met District Superintendent Abram S. Kavanagh. He too seemed both amused and impressed by Norman's eagerness. After some discussion, Dr. Kavanagh said, "Well, young fellow, I like the cut of your jib. There's an area in Brooklyn that's growing very rapidly. In a few months the little Flatlands church out there will be too small. We've bought a lot, and some day we hope to build a new church on it. How would you like to go out this afternoon with me and look the place over?"

"Fine!" said Norman, "I'll take a later train up to Boston."

He drove with the Superintendent across the Williamsburg

Bridge, through the crowded streets of Brooklyn until they came to the Flatlands Church, a small, weatherbeaten structure with empty lots all around it. "This church," the Superintendent said, has been here for over seventy-five years. Right now the congregation is down to about forty people. But people are moving into the area rapidly. What this place needs is a minister who can preach a workable gospel with a light in his eyes! Come on; I'll show you the lot we've acquired for a new church."

The lot was on the corner of Kings Highway and East 37th Street. There was hardly a paved street in sight. The lot itself looked desolate enough, surrounded by muddy streets, overgrown with weeds, filled with rubbish and tin cans. "I know it doesn't look very inspiring," the Superintendent said. "You have to use some imagination." He glanced at Norman. "What do you see?"

"I can see a church here," Norman said enthusiastically. "A big one, filled with people!"

The Superintendent nodded approvingly. "A church should be more than money and bricks and mortar," he said. "A church ought to be a kind of spiritual dynamo giving off a constant flow of power. That's what I'd like to see here, some day. In any case—" he looked thoughtfully at the eager young man—"I'll keep you in mind."

He did. In May, 1924, armed with a master's degree in Social Ethics and a bachelor's degree in Sacred Theology, Norman was assigned to the little church in Brooklyn. Officially, he was made associate minister of St. Marks Methodist Church at Ocean Avenue and Beverly Road, an older and stronger congregation that generously sponsored the struggling little church. And some months later Bishop Wilson ordained Norman in a great service at St. Marks.

The fact that the religious life of the community was at low ebb did not discourage Norman. "I was always lucky," he said years later, "lucky enough to be assigned to churches that were down. In every case, when I came along, attendance was low and morale was lower. There was no place to go but up!"

This was certainly true of the Flatlands Church. On one occasion, soon after his arrival, he found the old sexton dragging one of the back pews out of the building.

"What on earth are you doing?" cried Norman.

"Well," the sexton said, "it's not in very good shape, and nobody sits in it anyway. I thought I'd just chop it up for firewood."

"Put it back," said Norman grimly. "Somebody *is* going to sit in it!"

He started ringing doorbells. One of his parishioners, he found, worked in the gas company. Every time a new family moved into the district, a gas meter was installed. From his friend's records, Norman acquired the names and addresses of such people. He would go to the house, ring the bell, address the householder cordially by name, and invite him or her to attend services at the church. The personal touch rarely failed to impress newcomers, lonely and rootless as they often were. Church membership began to grow.

The new minister was not content merely to call on prospective members. He kept reminding them of the existence of the church by mail. Every week postcards went out to an ever-expanding list, frankly designed to sell Christianity in general and Norman's church in particular.

Sometimes the cards would ask provocative questions. "Why have our congregations increased until the church is crowded to capacity? Why has Sunday school attendance increased 100% in six months? Why are unchurched people of every Protestant denomination coming to us in increasingly large numbers? Come around and your questions will be answered!"

Nobody was exactly offering to give away ten dollar gold pieces, but Uncle Will, back in Iowa, would have understood and approved.

Sometimes the postcards would reach unashamedly for an emotional effect. "Do you remember," they would ask nostalgically, "the hymns your mother used to sing? You can hear them again, you know!" Or, "Palm Sunday—what memories it brings! The warm sunshine of spring, robin redbreasts on the lawn, the unfolding flowers. Visions of Mother getting the family ready, then the crowded church, the stately old hymns, a great congregation lifting their voices in the triumphant chorus! You, too, can be a part of this! Come next Sunday!"

At the end of six months, crowds were so large that the little church had to be abandoned. Norman set up temporary quarters in a large tent on the lot where the new church was to be built. The atmosphere reminded him of the old-time revival meetings of his Ohio boyhood. He reveled in it.

By this time, the drive for the new church was well under way. All sorts of fund raising devices were employed. At night Norman would drive through the streets in an automobile camouflaged to look like a locomotive, bell ringing, railroad flares blazing. His assistants—Clarence Neese, Robert Brand, and Bob Mirrilees—would knock on every door and request householders to buy a piece of red cardboard representing a brick. Each brick cost a dollar, and the donor's name and address went straight onto Norman's mailing list.

It was not all easy sailing. When the contractors' bids came in, the whole project seemed suddenly impossible. Norman's flock soon learned that their leader could plunge abruptly from high optimism into gloom and despair. But these fits of depression did not last long; he believed too firmly in the goal he was pursuing. Cheaper bids were sought and obtained. On September 20, 1925, the new Kings Highway Church was dedicated by Bishop Wilson, who saw no reason whatever to regret the appointment he had given Norman—and who said so. Three services were held, one of which was conducted by Norman's father. Anna Peale sat in the congregation, watched her son and her husband, and felt as if the best of her dreams had come true.

The following year Anna Peale herself appeared in the pulpit of the Kings Highway Church. She gave a talk entitled "The Lifted Horizon" in which she told her son's congregation of the work being done by the Women's Foreign Missionary Society. She spoke easily and pleasantly, a stocky blue-eyed woman, hair now streaked with gray. "Let's be careful how we use the word *heathen*," she suggested. "The people we call heathens are degraded only in the sense that they do not have Jesus Christ to lift them out of their slavery. I have no doubt there are a great many places right here in Brooklyn where the people are just as heathen as the masses of India or China!"

She also had a few kind words to say about her own sex. "They tell us today," she said dryly, "that there are no really great women, that there is not a single field in which women excel, not even cooking! Well, I know of one area in which women do excel, and that is organization. Women are practical; therefore they can organize. Men are visionary. Men go around with their heads in the clouds. Women keep their feet on the ground."

Her talk was well received and reported at length in the newspapers. It was Norman's turn to be proud of his mother.

As church membership grew, Norman's self-confidence grew with it. But it was a fragile plant, easily frostbitten. One Memorial Day the American Legion held a mass meeting in Prospect Park. The guest of honor was Theodore Roosevelt, Junior. As Protestant Chaplain of the Legion in that area, Norman was invited to attend and offer a prayer.

The Catholic chaplain of the Legion was invited also, and Norman understood that his friend the padre was to make a speech. He got a shock, therefore, when he picked up the program and saw that the priest was offering a prayer. The address was to be given by the Reverend Norman Vincent Peale.

There were some twenty-five thousand people seated in the park, with hundreds standing in front of the speakers' platform, and Norman was understandably dismayed. He went to the chairman, explained that he hadn't expected to speak, and therefore had no prepared talk. The chairman, looking equally worried, replied that Norman was on the program for a speech, that they had to have a speech, and that he would just have to stand up and deliver one.

"I can't do it!" Norman declared. "Look at that huge crowd!"

T. R. Junior had been listening to this conversation. "Son," he said to Norman, "I'm sure you can do it. You couldn't be pastor of a church and not be able to make a talk on Memorial Day to fathers and mothers and sisters and sweethearts whose loved ones died for their country. Look out there—" and he pointed to a large section where Gold Star Mothers were seated as guests of honor. "Talk to those bereaved mothers. Tell them their sons died for freedom and for America. This crowd is just made up of the plain ordinary people you know so well. Stand up there and comfort them. Tell them to keep on loving their country and believing in it—and they'll love you for it. Besides," he added, "I'll be sitting right behind you, pulling for you!"

Thus encouraged, while the opening exercises were going on, Norman reshaped the Memorial Day sermon he had given in church that morning. He delivered it well, and it stirred the great crowd.

"Well, now," said Colonel Roosevelt when Norman returned to his seat, "that was fine. You've helped many people today, including yourself. Never let yourself get into a state of mind where you think you can't do something. The best way to avoid that state of mind is to think about other people, and what you can do for them. And remember this: if you *think* you can't do something, you can't. If you think you can, you can. Believe in yourself, my boy, and others will believe in you!"

It was advice, Norman knew, that would be hard to follow, but it sounded so good that he decided to work at it. In time it was to become one of the strongest motivating forces in his life.

In the summer of 1926, Norman had his first glimpse of Europe. To achieve this, he sold guided tours to nineteen girls and two men, and consequently was given his own passage free. Anna Peale was somewhat concerned about the proportion of girls to men, but Norman managed to avoid any serious emotional entanglements. He shepherded his flock through countless cathedrals and museums, and brought it home intact. His father, still an ardent internationalist, was particularly pleased with one incident. In Geneva, wanting desperately to see the League of Nations in session but having no visitor's ticket, Norman spotted a door marked *Foreign Ministers Only*. Before he had time to think twice, he presented himself at it. "I'm a minister from the United States!" he announced grandly and was promptly led to one of the best seats available.

Back in Brooklyn, he found the tide of religious enthusiasm still rising in the Kings Highway Church. By now the Sunday school was the largest in Brooklyn. Church membership was close to nine hundred. Even the new church was beginning to seem too small.

As Easter Sunday approached, Norman's chief usher Bob Merrilees came to him. "You know," he said, "we'll be turning away hundreds of people on Easter morning unless we do something drastic. There's a big theatre down the street—the Marine Theatre. What if we held our services in that?"

"How many people does it hold?" Norman asked.

"About thirty-three hundred."

Norman felt the familiar hollowness in the pit of his stomach. "Do you remember how many people we had two Easters ago? One hundred. Now you're talking about filling a theatre with thirty-three hundred!"

"Look, Norman," the usher said, "anything can happen in Brooklyn. Besides, you've been telling us to think big and act big, haven't you? You've been preaching to us that we can do anything through the power of Christ and with God's help. Let's take that theatre, let's advertise it all over this area, let's assemble a fine choir, let's say we're going to have the greatest Easter service ever held in this community!"

Norman stared at him, feeling the contagion of his enthusiasm. "All right," he cried. "We'll do it!"

On Easter morning it was pouring rain. Norman took one look out of the window and felt his enthusiasm shrivel down to a cold, wet cinder. He tried, without much success, to pray some courage into himself. Then he telephoned his head usher. "This is awful!" he moaned. "Terrible! Nobody will come. We'll have an empty house!"

"Norman," said the usher, "people are more interested in immortality than they are in a little rain. Christ rose from the dead on Easter, didn't He? You just come to the theatre prepared to tell the people about it. That's all you should be thinking about!"

"I guess you're right," said Norman, buttressing his faith. When he walked out on the platform of the theatre at 10:45 that rainy morning, he saw the visible results of faith:—the 3300 seats were filled, and people were standing, and some were turned away.

It was a fitting climax to a brilliantly successful ministry. One month later Norman was called to another church.

The call came from the University Methodist Church in Syracuse, N. Y. Norman had been recommended by Bishop Leonard, his father's old friend, and had preached one sermon there—well aware that he was being "looked over." The church was a handsome structure, with magnificent stained glass windows, and some prominent members of the University of Syracuse faculty were in the congregation. But it was never full, and its presence there seemed to mean little or nothing to the great majority of the six thousand students. This was a state of affairs, Norman knew, that he was expected to change.

When the time came, he said good-bye to his friends in Brooklyn, feeling more of a wrench than he cared to admit. In Syracuse, he knew, the opportunities for service and personal advancement would be greater. But Brooklyn had given him his first real opportunity to try his wings, unhampered by parental pressures or Seminary supervision. He left because, in a sense, the job was done, the challenge answered, the problem solved. But he knew that he was leaving three years of himself behind.

He drove up the Hudson Valley through the smiling May weather, his bachelor belongings piled carelessly in the back of the car. Perhaps, he thought, he might now be able to afford a new car—his salary was to be a princely $5,000 a year. Actually, the University Church had been paying its minister $6,000, and had offered Norman $4,000, which he would have been happy to accept. But Bishop Leonard had intervened. "Let's not have any bargain-basement arrangements," he said sharply, and would have insisted on the full $6,000 if Norman hadn't begged him not to rock the boat.

It was a great opportunity, Norman knew, and a great honor for a young man still in his 28th year. Already he seemed to have come a long way from the little tower room in the Walpole church where his inadequacies had overwhelmed him and where he had learned that the only way to overcome them was to throw himself upon a Power greater than himself, trust in it implicitly, and surrender himself to it.

Lord, he prayed, gripping the wheel, *I'm trying to be Your servant. You've helped me so far. Keep on helping me, please. I'm going to need You more than ever!*

It was no idle prayer. In his mind's eye he could see the church filled with solemn academicians, doctors of philosophy, men of vast erudition who would listen to his sermons, compare them with Plato's dialogues, judge, and perhaps condemn. He was no intellectual; how could he reach these giant brains? How could he even communicate with them, much less influence them?

He shook his head blindly and pressed down on the accelerator, as if by driving faster he could escape from the demons of self-doubt that pursued him. In desperation he reached forward and switched on the car's radio. Anything to break this train of thought—music—anything . . .

A newscaster's voice came through, strong and clear, vibrant with excitement: ". . . reported off the coast of Ireland! He's already been in the air more than thirty hours. His single-engined Ryan monoplane must have consumed most of its gas by now. But he's still going, and if he can keep going just a little while longer, he'll make it to Paris, the first man in history to fly the Atlantic alone! Keep tuned to this station; we'll bring you bulletins as fast as we get them. And in the meantime, why not add your prayers to the millions being offered everywhere for this brave boy who . . ."

Norman sat there, electrified, his own fears forgotten. Lindbergh was going to make it! Against all the warnings, against all the dire predictions, trusting in himself and his judgment and a pair of fragile wings, he was going to make it! Faith, thought Norman—that's the answer. When you have that, when you really have it, nothing can stop you, nothing!

He felt tears sting his eyes. I will say a prayer for Lindbergh, he thought. I'll add my little coin to the great offering. But he's going to make it anyway, because he's clean and decent and alone and brave, and the God who made us all won't let him fail.

He said the prayer. Then he drove on, at peace with himself, through the fading afternoon.

CHAPTER VIII

Bachelor Minister in a

Co-ed Town

◅§▻

The man who welcomed Norman to Syracuse and introduced him to his new congregation was Hugh M. Tilroe,
Dean of the College of Public Speaking at the University. He
was a huge man, outwardly gruff, inwardly gentle and sensitive
and tender as a woman. He was aware instantly of Norman's
doubts about himself, and in a kindly way he tried to make
the congregation aware of them. "You have a very young man
here," he told them. "You can make a good preacher out of
him, and a good pastor, or you can turn him into a very
ordinary fellow. Whether he succeeds here in the name of
Christ, or whether he fails, is largely up to you. And now I
take great pleasure in introducing to you our new pastor, Norman Vincent Peale. . . ."

Wearing a swallow-tailed morning coat, as the custom was,
weighing all of 126 pounds, the new minister looked more like
an uneasy grasshopper than a conquering hero. He felt like
one, too. Standing on a huge, raised pulpit-platform, he faced

an imposing church and an impressive congregation. Graceful Gothic columns marched down the vaulted nave. Through enormous stained glass windows, multicolored shafts of light slanted across the crowd of worshippers. The effect was more like some great European cathedral than the little frame churches of Norman's boyhood.

It was an important pastorate for so young a man; some church leaders had been startled by Norman's appointment. They knew of his fine record in Brooklyn, but they had no proof, as yet, of his spiritual stature. The next five years in Syracuse were to be a period of testing, of growth, of the slow development of that stature. But on this bright and sunny 22nd day of May, 1927, the promise of the future was yet to be fulfilled.

Norman was still convinced that his sermons would be judged lacking in profundity. Consequently he made his first one sound like a baccalaureate address. He kept it up, too. He chose scholarly and abstract themes. He bombarded his listeners with allusions. He took to carrying the Oxford book of English verse in his car. He quoted Carlyle, Victor Hugo, Addison, Jung, Dostoievsky, Marcus Aurelius, Plato, and anyone else who came into his fevered brain. The congregation was amazed and somewhat appalled.

At last Dean Bray, one of the most learned members of the faculty, asked Norman to have lunch with him. As a young man the Dean had once gone to scoff at Billy Sunday. Instead he was converted, and had been a loyal church member ever since.

"Norman," he said, "everybody likes you, and we all want to help you in any way we can. You won't mind if I make a small suggestion, will you?"

Norman said that he wouldn't mind.

"Well," said the Dean, "I get the impression that you think you've got to preach intellectualized sermons just because you've got a lot of college professors sitting out in front of you every Sunday. Really, that's a mistake! We may be experts in our respective fields, one in biology, one in geology, one in history, and so on. But *you* are supposed to be an expert in the realm of the spirit. You must realize that when we listen to you on Sunday, we regard you as the teacher. You must tell us what you know personally about all this, not what somebody said about it in a book or a poem that you're going to quote."

Norman stared unhappily into his coffee cup and said nothing.

"Remember this," the Dean said. "We're all men and women who've come to church because we need God in our lives. We're just poor sinful people, and you mustn't be so awed by us that you can't tell us directly where we are wrong and need repentance. Preach to us just the same as you would to anyone else!"

In his blunt way, Tilroe said much the same thing. At one point Norman asked him if he wouldn't listen critically to his sermons and give him a few pointers on how to improve them. The big man laughed and shook his head. "Not on your life," he said. "If you want instruction in public speaking, register with the university, and pay your money, and attend my class. But Sunday is my day off. Besides, when I come to church on Sunday I'm not Hugh M. Tilroe, Dean of the College of Public Speaking. I'm Hugh M. Tilroe, a sinner saved by grace. I want the Gospel from you as you yourself preach it."

In one way the knowledge that such men wished to humble themselves before him reassured Norman. But in another way it worried him more than ever. In their gentle criticism he found proof that his ministry was off to a bad start. He had had little experience with failure, or the threat of failure; it acted on him like a subtle poison. He became tense and irritable. He lost weight, which he could ill afford to do, and slept badly.

"Relax!" Tilroe said to him. "You're going around with your fist clenched all the time. Did you realize that? It means you're clutching some problem so tight that you can't cope with it. Take it easy! We're all behind you. Relax!"

But Norman could not relax. It never occurred to him that his capacity for worry, his susceptibility to fears, might be part of some master plan specifically designed to teach him— the hard way—how to understand and help the fears of other people. He already knew, intuitively, that the road to deepest human sympathy often led through the dark valley of personal suffering. But he was still too young—and basically too humble —to apply this knowledge to himself.

The crisis came, strangely enough, on a train. He had gone home to Ohio for a visit. Now he was on his way back to Syracuse, back to the church where he was beginning to feel that he had bitten off more than he could chew, the church where he feared he would always be a little man in a big pulpit. For the journey from Toledo to Columbus he had bought a seat in a parlor car, hoping to do some work. No one else was so extravagant; he had the whole car to himself.

Years later, he told a congregation what happened. "For some time," he said, "I had been under a great strain that was drawing heavily on my nerve-strength. Worries and fears were haunting my days and disturbing my nights. To add further to my unhappiness, a profound sense of failure was casting a pall upon my spirit.

"On this train, traveling through central Ohio, I was working on a sermon for the following Sunday. The title I had chosen was "The Secret of Power." It suddenly occurred to me that the topic was ironical, for I certainly was not the possessor of power, or the secret of it.

"Years before I had experienced the power of religion by conversion, which was in every sense real and valid. But the force of that experience of God in my life seemed to have become—if not totally spent—at least greatly reduced. I was trying to get along under my own power. I was neglecting the vast force of God.

"Suddenly I ceased working on the sermon, and in desperation of spirit bowed my head in prayer. I had prayed since childhood, but in that prayer of agony on the train the wonder happened. In a moment of illumination, like a flash of lightning on a dark night that reveals a hitherto unknown landscape, I saw into the secret of spiritual power.

"But even more remarkable than that, I felt under me a sense of lifting and support like a great incoming tide that raises a stranded vessel from the shallows. It was overwhelming and awe-inspiring. A deep peace settled upon my heart; a sense of rest came to me; and overtopping all was a realization of the presence of God as the source of strength. There on that train, when least expected, came an experience which changed my life, a rediscovery of God.

"All the skepticism in the world could not shake the reality of that experience. Let others call it unscientific if they wish, or disparage it in any way they desire. I know beyond the shadow of a doubt that in that instant of time the wonder which is God impinged on my spirit and took away all my weakness, all my fears, all my sins, and gave me strength.

"The secret was this: my prayer was one of absolute and complete surrender. Weary and discouraged by living on my meager resources, I had thrown myself upon God, saying: 'Anything You want to do with me is all right. If You want me to fail, I will fail. I give my life to You, I put it in Your hands. Do with it what You will.'

"I had said that often before, and had meant it after a fashion. But this time the surrender was not partial; it was complete.

"Since then the high tide of that experience has ebbed and flowed, but the shallows have seldom reappeared. By a constant daily surrender to God I have discovered that Divine Power is available for my life. I would not exchange this secret for anything in the world."

Back in Syracuse, Norman resumed his duties with new vitality and enthusiasm. He called together his official board and told them that he was not used to churches that were only half full. What, he asked them, did they think might be done about it? They replied in pained surprise that the church always had been half full, that this seemed to be the case everywhere, and that they didn't know what could be done about it.

"You know something?" Norman told them. "In the balcony of our church there's a ladder, resting across the empty pews. I see it every Sunday, when I preach. I asked the sexton why it was there, and he told me that nobody ever sat there, so it was the most convenient place to keep the ladder. Well, I didn't come here to preach to ladders. Ladders aren't going to change the world; only people can do that. So, let's get the people in there! I've been too sedate, too cautious about all this. Jesus Christ wants everybody, young and old, students or faculty, college people or town people. Let's go after them. Let's *really* go after them!"

He began using some of his old Brooklyn techniques. He placed advertisements in the Syracuse *Post-Standard*. "*Why are young people flocking to the University Church? Why is it suddenly hard to get a seat?*" This was the way he visualized it, and so to him it was already a fact. He conceived the idea of having a section of the church reserved each Sunday for a certain fraternity, the pews decorated with the fraternity colors. He assembled the best singers he could find under the direction of Dr. Howard Lyman of the University's Music Department and called the result "the greatest choir in the Empire State!" He revived his postcard mailing list. On a hotel menu somewhere he spotted a motto that appealed to him: "Where you're a stranger but once . . ." He adopted this as a slogan for the church, and printed it on all church programs.

He had professionals from New York come up and give readings of plays or dramatizations of Bible stories. . . .

Before very long, the ladder had to be moved from the balcony.

It was showmanship, perhaps, that attracted the curious, but it was not showmanship that held them, that kept them coming back. It was the message, old to some, new to others, that Christianity *worked*, that it was not a pious enigma shrouded in an ecclesiastical fog, that it was a specific set of principles which, if mastered and applied, would give the individual enormous power over his problems and shortcomings and weaknesses.

Actually, there were times when Norman felt that his devices for attracting people to the church were pale and colorless compared to some. There was in Syracuse a minister of another denomination whose methods would have filled Uncle Will with abiding admiration. One Sunday he would arrange with a bank to have a million dollars in cash piled up in the pulpit under guard to illustrate the age-old struggle between God and Mammon. The next week he would have the pulpit filled with ice to emphasize the importance of keeping cool while under stress. To dramatize the need for optimism, he would march up and down the aisle with raised umbrella, while the organist played "Singing in the Rain." At night he would preach silhouetted against a purple backdrop by a spotlight that glinted hypnotically on his wavy blond hair.

Norman did not condone such activities, but there were times when he felt there ought to be a blending of such extremists and the good gray traditionalists who had let the power and the vitality drain out of the churches.

He also saw no reason why religion should not be fun. "Rejoice!" the Bible said. "And again I say unto you, rejoice!" Norman was young enough to know that young people wanted gaiety and laughter. He felt that, within reason, the church should provide this. He set out deliberately to attract and hold a lively group of younger people, some married, some not. His thesis was that it was perfectly possible to have a marvellous time within a framework of morality and decency. The spiritual life, he insisted, was the joyous life. If they would give him a chance, he told them, he would prove it to them.

They were skeptical at first, but they thawed rapidly. One thing about the new minister that appealed to them was that in some ways he didn't seem like a minister at all. He had no cavernously pious voice, no pulpit mannerisms. He liked a joke, even when it was on him. He seemed as much at home in old clothes as anyone. He didn't drink or smoke, but he did chew gum. He even played golf—or made a valiant effort to play it.

It was an episode on the golf course—a minor one, to be sure —that first endeared Norman to some of the Syracuse businessmen. He was in a foursome where one of the players, ordinarily a crack golfer, was far off his game. On one hole this unhappy fellow made a good drive and a fine approach, then took five miserable putts. "Look at that, dammit," he groaned. "Consistent as hell!"

Every eye rolled apprehensively toward the man of the cloth to judge the effect of such language. But Norman was studying his own score-card, and spoke from the heart. "Me too," he sadly said.

His bachelor status let him in for a good deal of teasing. If he was seen with a girl more than once, tongues began to wag happily, so he usually took refuge with young married couples: Geoffrey and Elsie Brown, Gordon and Dorothy Hoople, the Ponds, the Chappels, and the Rich Whitneys, a lively pair who responded to his exhortation to let religion be fun by putting a well-picked wishbone in the collection plate one Thanksgiving Day.

But there was another side to the good-humored young minister, a side that became increasingly apparent as he stood in the pulpit Sunday after Sunday. It was a growing aura of authority, the projection of a power that he certainly did not seem to have in his ordinary daily activities. When Norman stood up to preach, having prayed as he always did for help and guidance, he became *different;* there was no other word for it. His voice, his bearing, his whole personality seemed to undergo dramatic alteration.

Hearing him preach for the first time, people who had met him only socially were astounded by this change. And they were equally amazed, later on, to find him once more his natural, affable self. His friends sometimes discussed this phenomenon. Various theories were offered to account for it, but the majority held the simplest view and came to the simplest conclusion. When he preached, Norman was not up there in the pulpit alone. He was being guided. He was beginning to be used.

Although the country was riding a dizzy wave of prosperity, the finances of the University Church were not in very good shape. There was a church debt of $55,000 which had existed for some time. The attitude of the official board seemed to be that debt, like low attendance, was the natural state of affairs where churches were concerned. But Norman's mother had schooled him so intensely in the evils of indebtedness that he could not be casual about it. He decided at last to take some action—and as a result ran head-on into his first dramatic example of the power of thought to sway men's minds and actions.

There was in his congregation a colorful old gentleman named Harlowe B. Andrews, a wholesale grocer who had the deserved reputation of being the smartest businessman in Syracuse. Brother Andrews, as he was called, was also on very friendly and intimate terms with the Lord, Whom he consulted constantly and served with all his might. His old family Bible was read to tatters and covered with marginal notes.

"Ha, ha!" Brother Andrews would write alongside the text when some Biblical villain finally got his comeuppance, "the Lord sure saw through him!"

When the decision was reached to try to do something about the church debt, it was inevitable that Norman should avail himself of Brother Andrews and his Midas touch. In a speech made nineteen years later, in Detroit, he told the story in loving detail:

Many years ago in a church of which I was pastor, an old man taught me a lesson I have never forgotten. He was a wonderful person. He never went beyond the third grade in school, so he had insight which he might have lost if he had carried his education higher. He just had natural sagacity—the ability to penetrate things from outside in, from underneath up, and down from the top.

He lived up in the David Harum country in New York State. He was the personification of old David Harum himself. Wherever he put out his hand, money just sprang into it. He had a marvelous alchemy in his touch.

When I went to this church, I found that they had a $55,000 debt. They all told me there was no money with which to pay it off, although this was back in 1928. Listening to some of the negative thinkers, I got the impression that they loved this debt, that they wouldn't lose it for the world, that they would be homesick without it. But finally we had a meeting, and after much discussion the most amazing resolution was passed. It said, in effect, "We are sure we can't do this, but we ought to make some kind of gesture. Therefore be it resolved, knowing that we can't do it, that we will try to raise—not the whole amount—but $20,000."

"Now," they said to me, "you had better go out and talk to Brother Andrews."

I did, the next day. He lived out in the country in a little old-fashioned house on a hillside. I rapped on the door, and he opened it. He always wore his glasses far down on his nose. They were those half-moon kind that you seldom see any more.

I said, "How are you, Brother Andrews?"

He said, "Come in."

When we were in the old-fashioned parlor, I said to him, "We had a meeting of the Official Board last night."

"I heard you did."

"I thought I'd come out and have a talk with you."

"I thought you would," he said. "What's on your mind?"

I said, "Well, we're hoping to raise some money."

"How much are you going to raise?"

"Twenty thousand dollars."

"M'mm, is that so? Well, all right. Speak up. How much do you want?"

"I just wondered how much you are going to give."

"Oh, the answer to that is easy. Not a nickel. Not a cent. Now that that's settled, what else do you want to talk about?"

I said, "I guess there isn't anything else to talk about."

He looked at me for a minute. Then he said, "I won't give you any money, but I'll tell you what I will do. I'll pray with you."

That didn't fill me with any burning enthusiasm. It wasn't prayer I was after. It was cold, hard cash. Furthermore, I didn't think prayer would get me anywhere when it came to raising money. I had been taught not to pray for material things. But I agreed.

"Get down on your knees," said Brother Andrews.

His carpets were thin, too, I will tell you. But this old man evidently knew the Lord pretty well, because he talked to Him in a very free and easy manner.

This was his prayer: "Lord, here we are. We have to raise some money. This young minister is a nice fellow, but, Lord, he doesn't know much! He's the biggest willy-nilly I ever met in my life. Why, Lord, he doesn't know the first thing about business or how to do something big. He has little faith. He doesn't believe in himself, or in the ministry. Now, Lord, if he is only going to try to raise $20,000 I won't give him a nickel. But if he will believe he can raise the whole $55,000, I will give him $5,000. Amen."

We got off our knees, and I was pretty excited. I said to Brother Andrews, "Where are we going to get the rest of it?"

He said, "Where you just got the first $5,000. You prayed for it and you got it, didn't you? Now, do you want to know where to get the rest?"

"Yes," I said, in some bewilderment.

He said, "Get down on your knees again."

He got me down on my knees again. Then he put a plain white card on the table. "Lord," he said, "we want to know where to get the rest of the money. Give me a name, O Lord."

There was a silence. Then he said, "I have it!" I guess he had it all the time, but he was giving credit to the Lord, and actually it *was* the Lord, working through him.

He said, "I am going to write down the name of Dr. So-and-so. He will tell you he hasn't got any money, but I am on the Finance Committee at the bank, and I know exactly what he has. It says in the Bible that if you have faith even as a grain of mustard seed, nothing is impossible for you, and I have faith, and I'm going to write him down for $5,000. Amen."

He stood up and said to me, "Now go downtown and get it!"

I had little confidence in the whole thing, but I drove downtown. When I came to the building where the doctor had his offices, I drove around praying I wouldn't find a place to park. I found one at once.

"Well," I said to the doctor, "we are raising money."

"I heard you were. Now I suppose you want some from me."

"That's right."

"Well, suppose you tell me how much you think I ought to give."

I looked at him and said to myself, "I wonder if he's good for $500. Maybe I could ask him for a thousand." Then I remembered Brother Andrew's face with faith written all over it. I took a deep breath, and I said, "Dr. So-and-so, I am going to give you the privilege of giving us $5,000."

He said, "Five thousand dollars! That's a tremendous amount of money!"

I said, "It sure is."

Well, he mumbled in his beard for a minute. Then he said, "I think it's preposterous. But something comes over me as I'm standing here. I'll give you the $5,000."

I didn't even say good-bye to him. I jumped into my car, drove back to Brother Andrews' house, screeched up to the door. I burst in on him. "He did it! He did it!" I cried.

"Why, sure he did," said Brother Andrews.

I stared at him. "How did you know?"

He said, "Listen, son. I sat here all the time you were driving downtown, not believing he would do it, and I just sent a thought hovering over you all the way down there that he *would* do it, and my thought hit him right between the eyes."

I said, "You know, I saw it hit him!"

He said, "It penetrated his brain and it changed his thinking." Then he shoved me back against the wall and held me with a hand on either shoulder. "Listen, son," he said. "I don't care whether they raised that debt or not. A little old debt is good for a church. I'm investing that $5,000 in you, to try and make a man of faith out of you. A long while ago I discovered an antidote for failure, and it's this. You're never defeated by anything until in your mind you accept the thought that you are defeated. It may have cost me $5,000, but by George, if I've got that idea into your head, it's worth it!"

So the seed was planted that grew, twenty-four years later, into a book that sold more than two million copies. But within a few weeks Norman had forgotten all about the relative merits of positive or negative thinking.

The reason was simple.

He met a girl.

CHAPTER IX

The Parson Takes a Wife

❧

Her name was Ruth Stafford, she was blonde and blue-eyed, and she had made up her mind long ago that whatever else she might do with her life, she would never marry a minister.

Her father was a clergyman. All through her childhood, back in Detroit, she had watched him struggle with financial worries, with unreasonable colleagues, with demanding parishioners. Being a singularly levelheaded girl, she had decided that, while the spiritual rewards might be high, one had to have patience and humility bordering on sainthood to be successful as a minister's wife—and she considered herself no saint.

She was a co-ed in the Roaring Twenties, but hardly the type currently being celebrated by F. Scott Fitzgerald or John Held, Jr. She was a serious-minded senior majoring in mathematics, which she planned to teach. Between her freshman and sophomore years she had taken herself out of college, had gone to work with the telephone company so that one of her brothers could have his chance at higher education. All three of the Stafford children had thus interrupted their education to help one another. Later Ruth was to see a certain significance in this. If she had not delayed her college career, she might never have met Norman. She would doubtless have been gone when he arrived.

Ruth was manager of her Alpha Phi sorority house, a job that provided her with free room and board. From the other girls she began hearing a good deal about the energetic young minister down at the University Church. Phyllis Leonard, Bishop Leonard's daughter, was Ruth's roommate. "You really should meet Norman Peale, Ruth," she said. "The young people's group are having a party at the church tonight. Why don't you go with me?"

"All right," said Ruth. "I'll take a look at this paragon. But no ministers for me, thanks very much!"

And so in the middle of a fairly hectic evening, Norman found himself introduced to a quiet girl with steady eyes that looked into him as well as at him and seemed interested in what they saw.

Norman was interested too. Behind Ruth's surface shyness he sensed a stability, a firmness of character and purpose that he found appealing precisely because it balanced his own volatility. He said, politely, "How do you do, Miss Stafford." And held her hand a tenth of a second longer than was strictly necessary.

Ruth knew that some sort of spark had jumped between them, and was both flattered and amused. But she had no intention of becoming involved. She belonged to another Methodist church; her religious convictions were solid and deep. She certainly was not going to join the group of admiring co-eds who appeared in Norman's church every Sunday and were more inclined to sigh romantically over his poetic flights of fancy than heed his exhortations to seek the spiritual life.

As for Norman, like most bachelors he valued his independence and freedom from responsibility. He lived at the Syracuse Hotel. He dined out often and well. At one point the *Post-Standard* had referred to him as the town's most eligible bachelor, a title which delighted him hugely, and which he had no desire to relinquish. But slowly, where Ruth was concerned, the mystical combination of biological attraction and psychological need known as romantic love crept closer and closer—until one day it reached out a lightning paw and caught him.

At first he pretended that it hadn't. He persuaded Ruth to attend his church regularly. She would meet more young people, he said. He assigned her to various committees with which he was in frequent consultation. They needed her, he insisted. He asked her to help him arrange the seating at some church dinner or other—and was apparently thunderstruck when he discovered that there were only two places left, one for each of them, next to each other.

He told himself that what he really liked about her was her mind: clear, incisive, practical. He decided that she could be very useful to him as a sounding board for some of his speeches or sermons. And so one Sunday in March, when he was supposed to give a commencement address at a small college not far from Syracuse, he asked Ruth to drive over with him. She said she would.

They stopped for lunch at the old Linklaen House in Cazenovia. Before the food had a chance to appear on the table, Norman produced his notes and started discussing the high points of his speech. It was to be called "Imprisoned Splendor," he said, and was designed to show how anyone could unlock this inner radiance with the key of faith.

This went on all through the meal. At the commencement exercises, Norman poured forth his message as if it were for Ruth's ears alone. On the way back to Syracuse, he asked if she would mind driving. Somewhat puzzled, she took the wheel. Then, while she battled the Sunday traffic, he told her all about "Imprisoned Splendor" for the third time.

This was hardly the sort of attention a pretty girl might have expected from the most eligible bachelor in Syracuse, but Ruth was not bored. She sensed in this young man who spoke so fluently to large audiences a deep need for a more intimate kind of communication. Lying awake that night, pondering the paradox of his surface assurance and basic insecurity, she wondered if a feminine listener might not be what he needed, a person to whom he could confide his innermost thoughts and feelings without fear of rejection or criticism.

She also wondered if, despite all her resolutions, life might be offering her the assignment.

Ruth and her mother were very close; there were no secrets between them. Next day she wrote home about her Sunday with Norman.

> I had a grand time yesterday with Mr. Peale. He gave the Baccalaureate sermon at the small agricultural college in Morrisville, N. Y. The farmers have to go out for spring plowing, hence the graduating exercises at this time of the year.
>
> We left Syracuse right after church, had dinner in Cazenovia, and arrived in Morrisville at just 3 o'clock. He hadn't much time to go over his speech, so I drove part of the way. We got back about 6:15.
>
> Now all this is just between you and me! He doesn't understand his sudden interest in the opposite sex, but while it lasts he is willing to take the consequences if I am! He is so frank that it is very amusing and refreshing. Thus I have a dinner engagement for Thursday. I am prepared to remain interested as long as he does. Now, I hope you smile over all this as I have smiled in writing it. I am not being kidded very much! And I'm thankful for the training my brothers gave me. The girls want to know when I shall begin calling him Norman! ! ! ! ! ! ! !

Clearly Norman had made some impression, but he had plenty of competition. In particular, a cheerful Psi U named Bill Salter was being attentive to Ruth. She did not go home for the spring vacation; she could not afford the fare from

Syracuse to Detroit. But things were far from dull. On April 6, 1928, she wrote to her parents again.

Dearest Mother and Father,

We have been having the most wonderful weather for vacation. It seems more like the middle of summer than the first of April.

I am thoroughly enjoying my first vacation in Syracuse. Bill and I have been together quite a bit, although we both decided that we would accept as many invitations for meals as we received regardless of each other. Thus the first meal I had to buy was this noon. Now I want to tell how good people have been to me.

Wednesday Don took me to Krebs for dinner. That day I tried my old stunt, which you dislike so much, of making two dates in one evening. And boy, was it a close call—not more than five minutes apart! My evening date was for the Beta Theta Pi dance with a graduate of last June. He was at the Student Church service last Sunday, and I guess he liked the way I read the scripture. Anyway, that is the excuse he gave when he asked Phillis to introduce us. I am going out with him again tonight to see the great air picture, *Wings*. His name is Bub (Norman, I believe) Seiter, and everyone to whom I have mentioned his name has said, "How wonderful—he is a peach of a fellow!"

You see, I like to tell you things just as if I were at home. If you ever get tired of hearing me ramble, just say the word.

Now I must tell you what I did last night. I had an engagement with Mr. Peale for dinner. He called up in the morning, saying that we could not possibly waste the beautiful day, so we would go driving in the afternoon. We started at 3 o'clock and got in at 12!

We had dinner at the hotel, and then at 7:30 he spoke at a Lenten service in Cicero, N. Y. that lasted until 9:00, and then the minister and his wife insisted that we come to their home for a little while. All the talk sounded so familiar. I guess one will always find clicks in a small church. The minister is a fairly elderly man, hard worker, and has taken a peculiar fancy to Mr. Peale. Well, we got away about 10:30, so just got into the city in time.

But the prize plan for the vacation is as follows: Mr. Peale, never having seen the Adirondacks, is taking me on a trip right up into them on Monday. He was talking with me this afternoon and has learned from a man who goes up regularly that the drive is just 130 miles! We will leave early and get there by noon and stay until perhaps 4 o'clock. I have always longed to go up in the mountains, and I am actually excited about this trip.

After this I am afraid I shall need the rest of the vacation to rest!

Things move quickly when it is spring and you are beginning to fall in love. In a letter that Ruth wrote nine days later, Mr. Peale had vanished forever. Now it was Norman, and the tone was deeper and less restrained.

Yes, I took my fur coat on my trip Monday, but did not wear it until evening. We did not go to the Adirondacks because we got stuck in the mud about 50 miles from our destination. So we turned around, went to Albany, had lunch, drove to Cooperstown, a beautiful place on one of the finger lakes, and arrived back in Syracuse about midnight.

It was a long day—we drove about 335 miles—but I guess I enjoyed every minute of it.

On Thursday I went with Norman to Watertown, where he had to speak before the Northern New York Conference. It was the first time he had done anything like that, and he was a little nervous, so I was glad to be along to divert his mind and attention.

Today I believe he preached one of the best sermons I have heard him preach. At least, it affected me most, making me feel so little and unworthy, making me wish that my life might be as sincere and consecrated as his, so that I might deserve the inspiration that he gives me through his friendship. If the whole thing should end here, I would be better for having known him. . . .

But he is not willing just now that it should end, so I am going out for dinner with him on Thursday night.

Norman was anything but willing. On the Thursday night, timidly, they exchanged their first kiss. The next day Norman had to go out of town. On the morning of his return, Ruth got a telegram. "Meet me at the station," it said. Full of misgivings, she went to the station. By the time the train pulled in, she was convinced that Norman had had a change of heart and wanted to call the whole thing off. But he walked up to her on the platform and kissed her in front of everybody. She decided it was still on.

They tried to be as discreet as possible. Even so, word got around. Hugh Tilroe took to winking broadly at Norman and giving him bone-crushing nudges in the ribs. Brother Andrews was entranced and—subtle as a sledge hammer—found great delight in showing the two young people various manifestations of the nesting instinct in nature; a couple of birds in a tree, two peas in a pod, anything that came in pairs.

Not everyone was so enchanted. Two spinster ladies of the congregation invited Norman to tea and informed him that it was highly unsuitable for a man of his age and position to be seen in the company of an empty-headed college girl. Norman's reaction was to hurry over to Ruth and repeat what they had said—hoping no doubt that she would refute the charges for him. Ruth smiled bravely, bit her lip, and said nothing.

Another girl in town, the daughter of a banker, had been entertaining some hopes of her own where Norman was concerned. She said some things about Ruth that were so bitter and furious that finally her own conscience rebelled. She came to Ruth and confessed, with tears, that she had not been acting in a Christian manner toward her. Ruth could afford to be magnanimous, and forgave her.

As for Norman, for the first and only time in his life he was completely and overwhelmingly in love. Letters that had begun with the formal salutation "Dear Miss Stafford" rapidly became addressed to "Dearest Ruth." They were full of endearments that were touching in their sincerity. After twenty-eight years, Norman had found a girl to whom he could confide his innermost thoughts and feelings.

My dear little Sweetheart,

I have wanted to call you that for some time, but did not have the nerve. But a letter is a little easier, so here it is. It is now late Saturday afternoon, and I am just about to go to Cortland for a money raising meeting with some ministers. Want to mail this before I leave.

Your letter came a little while ago and I have read it many times already. The unbelievable thing is not that I care for you, but that you could care for me. I am not worthy of you at all.

I have discovered depths in my own heart that I did not know were there. Only you could bring them forth. As I preach tomorrow, you will be there just as really as anything can be. How wonderful it will be when I can look down every Sunday and see you there! Your last letter touched me deeply. The faith you express in me will always hold me true. I want to be a good man and a great preacher, and you will be and are a great help. I love and honor you with my whole being.

I never knew I could write so many letters, but honestly I would feel lost if I did not write.

I love you, my dear, with all my heart. . . .

It was time, clearly, for a formal engagement, but something in Norman wavered. Some of his hesitancy was caused by doubt as to his mother's reaction. But finally, like a man being dragged by wild horses, he went to a jeweler friend of his. "Bob," he groaned, "I've chased this girl until she's caught me!" He bought a ring, had it boxed, took it over to Ruth's sorority house. "Here," he said, tossing it to her with desperate levity. "I guess you've been waiting for this."

A less perceptive girl might have thrown it back to him. But Ruth was wise enough to recognize the last frantic strugglings of the trapped male. "Oh, Norman," she said serenely. "It's lovely!"

It was a long engagement. Ruth wanted to make some use of her hard-won degree. She got a job teaching high school mathematics at $1800 a year. As for Norman, he was busier than ever with his expanding church and outside speaking engagements which sometimes netted him as much as fifteen or twenty dollars. They agreed it was better not to rush things.

Norman's mother agreed, too. She was always polite to Ruth, always pleasant. But she did not hide her opinion that, after all, her son was already in *Who's Who*, while Ruth— well, she hadn't exactly proven herself yet, had she?

For her part, Ruth observed the Peale family with quiet amazement. Their closeness and affection for one another impressed her, although she knew that this made it all the more difficult for an outsider to be admitted to the magic circle. She found their mercurial changes of mood fascinating, but utterly foreign to her own steady temperament. She was astonished by their demonstrativeness; they could—and often did—weep on taking leave of one another or on any sentimental occasion. She was baffled by the Peale family conferences, grandly called to reach a decision, which invariably ended with no decision at all. A born manager herself, she was sometimes irritated by Peale inefficiency or helplessness in practical matters. But she kept most of her reactions to herself, set herself the task of making a good impression on Anna Peale, and gradually began to win her over.

As time went on, she began to understand Norman more fully, too. She was firmly convinced that he was destined to do great things in life, but gradually it dawned on her that the qualities that made him outstanding were qualities that also left him peculiarly vulnerable. The sensitivity that made him so attuned to human needs, the self-doubt that gave him so much insight into other people's fears, these were great assets, but they were also potential liabilities.

She began to see, further, that although Norman thought he wanted candid criticism where his work was concerned, what he needed most was reassurance. Once, before she knew him very well, she told him that while his sermons always started out well, in her opinion the endings were sometimes a bit weak. Instantly Norman was crushed. "You're right," he said somberly. "Absolutely right. And what you say convinces me that I should never have entered the ministry in the first place. I'm totally unfitted for it!"

His despair might have been laughable had it not been so real. Then and there Ruth learned a lesson that was to govern the rest of her life with Norman: always to avoid the introduction of negative considerations into a mind already open to fears of inadequacy.

In October, the Wall Street crash jarred the nation. Bob Pond, Norman's jeweler friend, made an ominous prediction. "This country," he said darkly, "will never be the same again."

"Oh, sure it will!" cried Norman, his Ohio faith in the continuity of progress unshaken. "The stock market will come back."

"I don't mean the market," Pond said. "I mean the underlying values and relationships. I mean the whole philosophy and fabric of the country. Just wait; you'll see."

The onset of the Great Depression had little effect at first on Norman. Each year the church raised his salary $500 without his requesting it. He added to this with his lecture fees. He had helped Bob with his expenses at medical school; now he was contributing generously to Leonard's education.

By this time he had a radio program, *The Angelus Hour,* on Saturday afternoon that brought him into contact with a greatly expanded audience. Shorty Melcher, who had been in theological seminary with Norman, came to the University Church as student pastor and was impressed all over again by Norman's driving energy. "Most ministers," he told a friend, "would be too busy preparing their sermons on Saturday nights to want to handle a radio program as well. But Norman seems to thrive on it. He has a kind of lust for work."

One reason Norman worked so hard was doubtless his subconscious realization that the farther he climbed the ladder of success, the farther there was to fall. But there were simpler reasons, too. He was happy. He was engaged to a fine girl.

He had a circle of devoted friends. His church was growing. And he felt that he was growing too, learning, expanding constantly.

The chief thing he was learning was that the realm of the spirit was even wider than he had thought. There seemed to be no aspect of living that was not deeply and intimately influenced by it. Listening to people's troubles, trying to help them, Norman became more aware of this all the time. Business, health, marriage, friendships, adjustment to life—he began to see that success or lack of it in all these areas depended largely on the condition of a man's mind or heart, and that this condition in turn depended largely on man's ability to live in accordance with certain spiritual principles. The moral insights and way-of-life precepts of the Bible might be obscured at times by archaic language or by deliberate symbolism. But they were still true, they were still valid, they were the only unchanging yardstick for successful living. When people got into trouble, it was usually because they had violated these principles, had *sinned*—to use the old-fashioned and unpopular term—and were being paid off in guilt feelings, fear complexes, compulsions and neuroses that made full-scale living impossible. The wages of sin, said the Bible were death. Norman began to see that by *death* the Bible did not mean total extinction, necessarily, but a reduction of the capacity to live and enjoy life fully.

There were endless examples of this. At one point Norman began to get anonymous telephone calls in which a voice obviously disguised, warned him about a certain woman—call her Miss Jones. In venom-laden tones the caller would list a few of Miss Jones' alleged deficiencies—mostly moral—and then hang up.

This happened several times. Then one night, when the call came again, Norman had one of his sudden flashes of insight. "Don't hang up, Miss Jones," he said with sudden authority. "I want to talk to you."

There was a click, then silence, but he knew his guess was right. He called Gordon Hoople, his medical friend. Together they drove to Miss Jones' house, found her crouched over the telephone in a state of semi-collapse. Slowly, working together in the weeks that followed, the doctor and minister won the tormented woman's confidence and were able eventually to relieve her of the festering guilt feelings that had led her thus to punish herself.

Sometimes other doctors called Norman. On one occasion, quite early in his Syracuse ministry, the phone rang late at night in Norman's hotel room. "Sorry to bother you at this hour," a doctor said, "but I need your help. I have a patient here who isn't responding to treatment. Will you come?"

"Of course," said Norman, thinking that he was being asked to console a dying person. "I'll be right there."

But when he reached the patient's home he found that the doctor wanted more than just prayers for the dying. "I want this woman to live," the doctor said. "I've done all I can, but it isn't enough. I treat my patients, but it's God who does the healing. You know that, and I know it. Let's try to fill that sickroom so full of the healing grace of Jesus Christ that the patient gets well. We're going to be partners in this thing. I think we can do it. Anyway, we can try."

They went into the room and sat down, one on either side of the bed. The patient tossed restlessly, only half consicous. First Norman prayed aloud. Then the physician prayed. Then they began to quote Scripture passages. It was a strange and moving experience. Norman felt that there were two contending forces at work in the room, one regenerative, the other destructive, and that by praying he and the physician were adding strength to the life force. He felt strangely exalted. He found that he could summon to mind almost any Bible passage that he wanted, could recite it verbatim although this was not usually the case—and later, when he tried to repeat some of them, he could not do it at all. Now and then he looked across at the physician's calm face, remembering how his Grandfather Fulton had used prayer as therapy long ago in Ohio. Living in the frantic 'Twenties, he had thought medicine had become purely materialistic, that all doctors regarded religion as something outside their province. Evidently not.

Time passed. All at once the patient's restlessness ceased. She opened her eyes, smiled at them faintly, then fell into a quiet sleep.

The doctor reached out and put his fingers on her wrist. Then he sat back in his chair and watched her with shadowed eyes. "I believe the crisis has passed," he said finally. "I think she'll get well."

Norman took a deep breath. "You—a doctor—think that prayer can succeed where medicine fails?"

"I think," said the doctor, "that religion and medicine ought to be used together far more often than they are. The early Christians were familiar with spiritual healing. They used it all the time. Why should that power have disappeared? Human beings haven't changed. The relationship between mind and body is just as close now as it was then. I think we've got a lot to learn in this whole area." He stood up wearily. "Come on; we'd better get some sleep."

But Norman was in no mood for sleep. He went outside and walked until the streets of the city were gray with dawn. Then he went back to his hotel room and picked up his New Testament. There were passages that he wanted to reread with this tremendous possibility throbbing inside him, the possibility that Christ might be not only the healer of souls, but of minds and bodies as well.

He turned to the passage about the sick man whose friends lowered him on a litter through the roof so that Jesus might heal him. He noted, with suddenly sharpened perceptions, how before healing the man, the Lord had said, "Son, thy sins be forgiven thee." Prayer, forgiveness, self-surrender— these all seemed to be part of the mysterious process.

Just how the power worked he did not know, but he had no doubt whatever that it existed. He had seen it with his own eyes, had felt it with his own intuitions. The doctor was right: it was still there, waiting to be rediscovered—and used. Religion and medicine, he thought. Some day . . . Some day . . .

The seed of an idea was planted. Later on it would take root, and grow.

The weeks fled past, busy, constructive, full of work and gaiety and a buoyant sense of progress. Norman never knew what sort of adventure the next day might bring. One afternoon a well-dressed woman appeared in his office and announced that she had in her handbag a pistol with which she intended to shoot her son's fiancée at the altar of the church—if Norman went through with his plan to marry the young couple the next day. He sized her up, decided it was all a bluff, and told her that she might as well go out and get some target practice, because the wedding would take place as scheduled. It did, with no interference from the enraged mama.

On another occasion a jilted gentleman called up and demanded furiously that Norman persuade the authorities to refund to him the money he had spent on a wedding license. It was all Norman's fault, he said, for recommending matrimony to him in the first place.

One dark night in the dead of winter, Norman got a phone call from a stranger. A woman was dying out in the country, the voice said. She had heard Norman on the radio and wanted him to pray with her. A car, therefore, would pick him up at his hotel in fifteen minutes.

It was a curiously peremptory request, but Norman did not feel that he could refuse it. Twenty minutes later he found himself in a big black limousine being driven through the night by three granite-faced characters who said not a word. On and on they went, refusing to answer any questions, twisting and turning until Norman lost all sense of direction. This was the heyday of the rum-runner, the gangster, the kid-napper, and Norman's imagination went feverishly to work. By the time they reached their destination, he was convinced that Syracuse was about to lose its most eligible bachelor. He began to pray with all his might—and not entirely for the dying woman, either.

But nothing happened. His silent escort herded him into a house where there *was* a woman who seemed quite ill. He prayed, without eliciting any particular response. Then his grim-faced guardians drove him back to his hotel, left him on the sidewalk, and roared away.

Hugh Tilroe was always vastly amused by such episodes. The big man had a cabin on a lake back in the woods where he loved to fish and hunt. The cabin had two bunks, and Norman was always welcome in the upper one. He spent many an evening there, staring into the fire, unburdening himself to the older man until the affection between them ran strong and deep.

Years later Norman was to hear of an experience that another man had in that same cabin. The man was a minister whose wife left him. She ran away with another man, leaving a note that said she was sorry, that she hated to hurt her husband, but that she wanted never to see him again.

Dazed and unbelieving, the minister called Tilroe and told him what had happened. "Stay right there," the big man said. "I'm coming over."

As quickly as possible, the professor was there. He said nothing about the runaway wife. He packed a bag for the suffering man, then drove him through the night to the cabin. There he made a fire, persuaded the minister to eat something, then tucked him into the top bunk as gently as a mother with a child. "Go to sleep, boy," he said, "go to sleep. I don't feel like sleeping. I'm going to sit up and keep the fire going."

All through the night the minister would wake and see

Tilroe sitting by the fire, gigantic, solid, immovable. "And you know," he said long afterwards to Norman, "into my tormented brain there came an answer to a question I had asked myself all my life: what was Jesus Christ really like? When I saw that man sitting there, sharing my sorrow with me, I knew the answer. Jesus Christ was like that."

In the morning they had breakfast. Then the professor offered a prayer. "Dear Lord," he said, "Who met with people long ago beside a lake, like this one, come into the heart and mind of my friend and give him peace. Take away the sting of the hurt he has suffered. Build him up again, Lord, so that he can go out into the world and tell people about You. Give him courage, Lord—and leave the rest to him. Amen."

In the end, his prayer was granted. The minister resumed his life as a strong and worthy man of God.

With the coming of spring, Ruth and Norman decided to set a date for their wedding. They had been engaged for almost two years now. Ruth would complete her second year of teaching in June. The opposition from Norman's mother had subsided. There seemed to be no point in waiting any longer.

Friday, June 20, was a perfect summer's day. Bishop Adna W. Leonard, Chancellor Charles W. Flint of the University, and Norman's father conducted the ceremony. The church was packed—mostly, it seemed to Ruth, with tearful females, several of whom reached out imploringly to touch Norman's hand as he escorted his bride down the aisle. The happy pair moved down the church steps together, into the waiting car. The bride looked expectantly at her new husband, waiting for his first endearment. . . .

"Boy!" cried Norman ecstatically. "What a crowd! If only we could have taken up a collection!"

Ruth stared at him for a moment. Then she burst out laughing. "Oh, Norman," she said, "you're so *romantic!*"

"Let's drive around the block," suggested the ex-most eligible bachelor in Syracuse. "Then we can get another look at all these people."

"Let's *not*," said the bride with sudden firmness. "You're on your honeymoon, now. What do you care about crowds?"

Actually, the honeymoon was a little crowded, too. Most of the Peale family went on it.

Ruth and Norman did have a few hours alone. They drove to the old Cooper Inn at Cooperstown, where they had often gone for dinner during their courtship. They walked hand in hand in the meadows, feeling the sense of completeness, of fulfillment grow in and around them.

But their solitude was brief. For one thing, Norman was scheduled to make a speech on Sunday—the baccalaureate at Cazenovia Seminary, where his brother Leonard was a member of the graduating class. Clifford and Anna Peale would be there. Why, Norman asked Ruth cheerily, should not his parents come along and share the cabin some one had offered him for a week in the Adirondacks? The cabin had several rooms. His parents could have a vacation while he and Ruth were having their honeymoon.

So strong was Ruth's determination to get along with her in-laws at all costs that she made no objection. And so strong— to put it charitably—were the family affections of the Peales that they were genuinely incapable of seeing anything odd in such an arrangement. On Monday, therefore, in two cars, the expedition set forth for the mountains.

Once the concept of a multiple honeymoon was accepted, everything went smoothly except for the fact that the cabin was more isolated than any of them had expected. It stood far back in a wilderness which the Peale imaginations, soaring off in all directions, immediately populated with wolves, bears, escaped lunatics, runaway criminals, and all sorts of dreadful menaces. One evening, as darkness was falling, an ominous scratching sound was heard on the porch. Norman snatched up a hatchet, gritted his teeth, and flung wide the door. There sat a little chipmunk, looking almost as frightened as the bridegroom. Later Norman was to use the episode in more than one sermon on the foolishness of unjustified fears. But Clifford Peale slept with the hatchet beside him every night.

They came out of the woods, finally, and reached the parting of the ways where one road led back to Syracuse and the other to Ohio. The honeymoon was over. They stood in the road and said fond farewells. Everyone shed tears—except the bride.

Back in Syracuse, Ruth and Norman took a tiny apartment and settled down to the life of newlyweds. It was decided that Ruth should go on teaching for a while. She wanted to keep busy. Besides, the extra money was useful. All around them the Great Depression was deepening. The church budget was being curtailed. By 1932 it would be down to less than half of the 1929 budget, and the church would be closed six nights of the week—to save fuel.

With such widening cracks appearing in the foundations of society, some of Norman's colleagues kept urging him to preach more sermons on sociological topics. Norman tried to oblige, but his heart wasn't in it. He could and did preach occasionally against dishonesty in business or corruption in politics. But he was happier when he was hammering away at specific human problems.

He still believed wholeheartedly in the perfectability of man. He continued to support Prohibition, although by this time it was apparent to most observers that the results of that noble experiment were anything but ennobling. He tried to discourage women from smoking.

"Gosh, Norman," Shorty Melcher said worriedly after this sermon, "you'll get in trouble if you keep trying to reform everybody. Don't be so harsh with 'em!"

But Norman's popularity didn't seem to diminish. His female listeners sighed, watched him with worshipful eyes—and went right on smoking.

At one point Norman and Shorty went out to attend a religious conference being held on the campus of Ohio Wesleyan. Leaders from every part of the country spoke on the problems facing the world and the church. On their way back to Syracuse, Norman said thoughtfully, "You know, Web, there were essentially two types of men at that conference— the intellectual type and the popular type. I don't think I could ever be the scholarly or intellectual type of minister. I think my talents lie in the literary or oratorical direction. It may sound silly to you, but I have a feeling that I was born to do some good with my life. Therefore I've got to concentrate on the talents I think I have, and develop them to the fullest. By George, I've got to work harder at it!"

"You work hard enough as it is," said Shorty. "You work harder than anybody I know."

"I've got to work harder still," Norman insisted. "I've got to learn to get past that first layer of fatigue."

"Past *what?*"

"The first layer of fatigue. That's what William James calls it; he says it exists in all of us. We drive ourselves and work hard until we come to this point. Then we decide we're so tired that we can't go any farther. All our activity is halted at this first fatigue barrier. But if we can get past it, James says, if we force ourselves through, we come into a new area of energy. We get a sort of second wind. James says that the people who do great things in the world are the ones who drive through that first layer of fatigue. And he's right; I've done it once or twice myself. From now on, I'm going to do it more often."

"Well," said Shorty resignedly, "good luck to you. But I think you'll find it rather lonely over there."

"Maybe so," said Norman. "But it'll be worth it."

He did drive himself. He worked all day and half the night polishing his sermons, trying to improve his speeches, preparing his radio talks, memorizing poetry, filing away apt quotations, as well as attending to the endless administrative details of the church.

A lecture bureau offered to take him under its wing. It was a well-feathered wing; and the percentage it demanded from its clients was absurdly high. But Norman didn't care. He was impressed by the brochure that introduced him—with more enthusiasm than knowledge of French—as "the Beaux Ideal of Youth." "Culture and elegance," cried the leaflet, "walk right into your community with Peale!" Then, under the heading "Peale's Appeal," it went on to give synopses of various orations. "Poetry, philosophy, literature and all the sciences, in an amazing roll call, are called upon to testify to the worth of personality." This referred to our old friend, "Imprisoned Splendor."

There were several such choices, but the response was not overwhelming. People were beginning to find it harder and harder to make ends meet. The problem of food and shelter was rapidly becoming more important in the average American home than the quest for culture and elegance.

It was at about this time that Norman had his first meeting with Franklin Roosevelt, then Governor of New York. A woman who listened to Norman's radio program had a son who was convicted of rape. She asked his help. There seemed to be some element of doubt as to the justice of the boy's conviction and so, with the approval of the sentencing judge, Norman went to Albany to see the Governor.

Roosevelt received him pleasantly, but refused his plea for clemency. "A rape case," he said, "is dynamite—politically. The boy was given a fair trial and convicted. I'm sorry, but there's nothing I can do."

Norman went away considerably impressed by the Governor's affability and charm. It was an impression destined not to last.

By now, Norman was being sought by other churches. In the summer of 1930, he received a call from Bishop Edgar Blake, offering him the pulpit of a leading Methodist church in Indianapolis. It was said to be the largest Methodist congregation in Indiana, with a fine new church building. "It's quite a temptation," he wrote to a friend back in Brooklyn, "and yet in my heart I don't want to leave Syracuse. Things have gone so well here, and still offer such a challenge, that it is difficult to think of accepting this call."

In the end, he did not accept the Indiana invitation. The following spring, grateful for his loyalty perhaps, Syracuse University conferred on him the honorary degree of Doctor of Divinity.

That summer he and Ruth made a tour of the western states. Norman preached in various churches, notably the huge First Methodist Episcopal Church of Los Angeles where, at the conclusion of his sermon, he was startled to hear the congregation break into loud applause—a Californian custom that would have shocked his Ohio ancestors. They visited the Grand Canyon, Yosemite, the Pacific Northwest, and came back to Syracuse full of the majesty and grandeur of the country west of the Mississippi.

They were glad to get back. The hectic gaiety of the 'Twenties had vanished now, and there was a chill of fear in the air. But Norman regarded this as Christianity's challenge—and perhaps its opportunity. The churches had been empty during prosperous times; perhaps people in trouble would be more likely to turn to God for help.

The help was there; he had proof of it in his own experience, in case after case that he had observed at first hand. Those who refused to avail themselves of it were as foolish, he often said, as a man who knew there was oil under his back yard but refused to sink a well and went on living from hand to mouth. In any mature religious experience, he knew, there had to be giving of self as well as receiving. There had to be awareness of the Giver as well as the gifts. But self-interest, he also knew, was one of the most powerful of all motivating forces. If this self-interest could bring a potential convert to the doors of the church, he felt that it was a step in the right direction, however selfish the initial impulse might be or might seem.

The days flashed by, full and varied. In later years, he and Ruth were to look back to their Syracuse period, as they called it, as almost the happiest years of their lives. "You know," Norman said to her once, "we don't realize how lucky we are in the friends we have. People like Brother Andrews and Hugh Tilroe, Dean Nye and Doc Hoople, and Bob Pond and Geoff Brown. Every time I'm with them, I learn something new."

"I imagine," said Ruth loyally, "that they also learn from you."

"Maybe," said Norman. "But I get a lot more than I give."

Driving Norman home from the church one evening, Gordon Hoople said, "The more I practice medicine, Norman, the more convinced I become that the great majority of people who come to me for help are more sick in their minds than in their bodies. Oh, their symptoms are real enough. But the trouble starts—" he tapped his forehead—"up here."

The minister nodded. "That's what my father says. And he's both a clergyman and a doctor."

"I had a rather striking example of it today," Hoople went on. "You know the lady, actually. She came into the office about a month ago. Same old set of troubles: chronic sinus condition, cancer-phobia, all sorts of fears and aches and pains, some real, some imaginary. Well, it happened to be her fiftieth birthday, and we got to talking about her troubles— how long they'd been going on, how persistent they were, and so on. And suddenly it occurred to me to ask her if there was anything on her mind, anything that had been bothering her for a long time. 'You know,' I told her, 'I've done about all I can for you, and you're not much better than you were in the first place. I wonder if perhaps there isn't something inside your mind that's *making* you sick.'"

The doctor swung the old Marmon up to the Peales' apartment and stopped. "Well, sir, she looked at me for a minute. Then she said, 'Doctor, I'm going to tell you something that I've never told anyone, something that happened forty-two years ago.' And then she told me how, when she was eight years old, her sister died. This sister was a favorite child, adored by her parents. When she died, her mother was so beside herself that she screamed at this other child, 'Why didn't you die? I wish to God it had been you!'"

Norman winced. He said nothing.

"For forty-two years," Hoople went on slowly, "that woman has hated her mother. And with some reason, you'll agree. She tried to hide that fury, disguise it, pretend it wasn't there. But she couldn't really banish it. It showed up—in the mucous membranes of her nose and sinuses! Well, as I say, that was a month ago. Today she came in again, and do you know something? She's greatly improved! For the first time in all the years I've been treating her, she's *better!* Because she got the cork out of the bottle, don't you see? She let the poison out by telling someone. Norman, I'm sure you know the person I'm talking about. I believe if you went around to see her now, you might get somewhere. You might even get yourself a new church member!"

The minister nodded and climbed out. "I'll do that. Thanks for the tip, Doc."

He watched the Marmon drive away, turned, went into the apartment. Ruth was back from her schoolteaching. Something smelled good in the kitchen. He kissed her thoughtfully, then went and sat down in his big chair.

"Hey," said Ruth, perching on the arm, "why so pensive?"

He reached up for her hand. "I was just thinking about something Hoople told me. You know, that fellow would have made a marvelous minister."

Ruth ruffled his hair. "Just the other day he told me you'd have made a marvelous doctor. Go and wash up, now. We've got spare ribs—and I've attempted another pie."

Most of their days were full of laughter and sunshine, but there was shadow, too. One night Hugh Tilroe had a stroke: sudden, unexpected, devastating. It left him broken, and some months later took his life. He lay in bed like a great tree blasted by lightning, his body paralyzed, his mind appallingly clear. Norman stood at his bedside, trying to offer words of comfort and hope, but finding it almost too much to bear. He loved this man as one of the dearest friends of his life. He felt his affliction as if it were his own.

"I suppose I shouldn't say this, Norman," the big man whispered, "but I can't help wishing the Lord had taken me altogether. This is no good, lying here helpless. No more fishing, no more hunting, no more trips to the cabin . . ."

Norman said, through the iron band that seemed to be encircling his throat, "Take it easy, old man. Everything will be all right. . . ."

He turned quickly, left the room, and went blindly down the stairs, out into the park in front of Tilroe's house. Abruptly, like a dark cloud, a terrible sense of man's helplessness in the face of affliction swept over him. It seemed to him suddenly that goodness was no defense against pain and suffering and death. Even the majestic words of the Bible seemed to hold little solace, little comfort. *Why*, he kept asking himself, *why?*

He listened, but he heard no answer. He sat down on a bench in the pallid starlight, and put his face in his hands, and sobbed bitterly.

CHAPTER X

New York—Graveyard

of Ministers

❧

In the spring of 1932, Norman received an invitation to fill the pulpit of the First Methodist Church in Los Angeles for a month as guest minister. The pastor, Dr. Elmer Ellsworth Helms, was to be away at General Conference. He accepted— the chance to preach regularly to the largest Methodist congregation in the world was too challenging to refuse. He and Ruth went to Los Angeles for the month of May.

In this sprawling city he spent much time with his old classmate Oliver Jaynes, who was moving up steadily in the newspaper world. Neither of them had forgotten the nights at Ohio Wesleyan when they would retire to a cow pasture, loosen their vocal cords with a little elderberry wine, and take turns delivering impassioned political orations. Now Oliver and another classmate, Fred Reid, sat in the First Methodist Church, listened to their fraternity brother's sermons, observed the reactions of the congregation, and gave Norman full and candid reports.

It was an exciting month. Just before leaving Syracuse Norman had been approached by a delegation from New York that had offered him the pulpit of the Marble Collegiate Church, founded in 1628 and said to be the oldest continuous Protestant pastorate in the country.

A month earlier, on Sunday, March 13, 1932, Norman had supplied the pulpit of this famous Fifth Avenue Church, scene of the notable ministries of Dr. David James Burrell for thirty years and Dr. Daniel A. Poling for a decade. At the time Norman had not realized that he was being considered for the pastoral vacancy, but two weeks later he noticed several officials of the Marble Church in his Syracuse congregation. After the service that Sunday they met with him in his study and intimated that an official call would come soon. Shortly thereafter, at a breakfast in the Hotel Onondaga, a large delegation of New Yorkers read him the call in the ancient and majestic language that had been used by the Collegiate Church for over three centuries.

Impressed and grateful, Norman had asked for time to consider his answer. Acceptance would mean the end of his Syracuse ministry. It would also mean changing denominations, from Methodist to the Reformed Church in America. The decision was too important to be made quickly. Besides, he had an idea that the invitation to preach in California was no casual one. Dr. Helms, he knew, was retiring. If his preaching was well received, there was a chance that a call to Los Angeles might be forthcoming.

Norman liked California. He liked the climate, the friendliness of the people, the absence of certain conventions and formalisms that irked him in the East. He liked bigness, too, and the size of the Los Angeles church impressed him. The choice, so far, was not clear-cut; the pulpit in California had not yet been offered to him. Even so, he and Jaynes spent hours discussing West Coast as opposed to East Coast living.

"You'd be freer out here, Norman," Oliver told him. "You

wouldn't be so tied down, you could be yourself. Californians are easy-going people; they're much more like Ohioans than New Yorkers are. How are you going to handle a sophisticated Fifth Avenue congregation? You're not so sophisticated yourself, you know. You're just a country boy, and always will be."

"I know," said Norman. "But maybe they're tired of sophistication on Fifth Avenue. Maybe New Yorkers are fed up with intellectualized sermons. Maybe the reason so many of those churches are half empty is that nobody is telling the Gospel story in language that people can understand."

"Maybe," said Oliver doubtfully. "But if you go down there you'll be sticking your theological neck out. You can be sure of that."

At the end of a month, Norman returned to Syracuse. When he arrived, a telegram was waiting for him. It was a call to the church in Los Angeles.

Then came days of momentous indecision. All Norman's hesitancy and suggestibility arose to plague him. He sought advice from friends in the church and on the Syracuse faculty. One would urge him to go to New York, marshaling impressive arguments, and for a few minutes or hours Norman would be persuaded. Then he would ask for more advice, receive a contrary set of views, and find himself back in the valley of vacillation.

At last Ruth led him into their living room and closed the door. "Norman," she said, "you're driving yourself crazy and making life miserable for me and everybody else. This can't go on. We're not leaving this room until you've come to a decision. I don't care how long it takes you to reach one. We're not going to open that door until you do."

"But how can I?" cried her distracted husband. "Every time I make up my mind something happens to change it! How can we reach a decision?"

"By doing what we should have done much sooner," Ruth said. "By praying about it, and I mean *really* praying. We're going to ask God what He wants us to do. And He's going to tell us. And we're going to do what He wants, not what we want!"

Norman nodded slowly. "You're right."

They knelt beside the davenport and held hands and prayed. An hour passed, and another. Still they prayed, asking only for guidance. Then they were silent for a long time.

"Well," said Ruth finally, "do you have an answer?"

"I think so," Norman said soberly. "I think God wants us in New York."

"I think so too," Ruth said. She stood up and opened the door. "Come on; we'll call New York right now." She smiled suddenly. "You see, it's not so hard—when you stop trying to do it all alone!"

From that moment, Norman's doubts and hesitancies vanished. The phone call was made; a telegram was sent to Los Angeles. He felt a twinge of regret at leaving the Methodist denomination, church of his boyhood, of his family for generations. But it was more sentimental than theological. The Reformed Church in America was evangelical in spirit. It had a strong liturgical tradition. It was both progressive and conservative. Its clear-minded stability seemed to reflect its solid Dutch ancestry. It might be a different denomination, but it was still a Christ-centered, Biblical system of religious thought. Norman could see no need to change his thinking or his message in the slightest.

On July 26 he wrote to Oliver Jaynes, telling him of his decision:

Dear Oliver:

I have been intending to write you for some time, but I have been so busy that it has just been impossible. Needless to say, I have thought of you many times since leaving Los Angeles.

When I arrived in Syracuse, I received an official call to the pastorate of the First Church, Los Angeles. Then I was up against the proposition of deciding between that church and the one in New York. I talked to you a great deal about it, and I think you understand all angles of the question. After my return, I consulted with many church leaders here. The over-whelming majority seemed to feel that the New York church offered opportunities that were quite unique. Some even went so far as to say that it was the kind of opportunity that happens only once in a generation.

It was very difficult for me to decide in favor of New York, because I wanted to live in California. If I had followed my desires, they would have taken me to Los Angeles, but, after all, to decide a question of this kind on the basis of the pleasantest place to live would not be the highest motive. I envy you, for California is a garden spot. Moreover, it would have been a wonderful privilege to have been associated so closely with you. I thoroughly enjoyed the month we spent together.

You will recall that I told you that this New York position involves a three months' vacation every year, so I am sure the lure of California will draw me back out there. I found myself sweating blood in deciding where to go, but now that the decision is made, I feel better. I begin my work in New York on October 2nd, the day I was to have begun in Los Angeles. Think of me that day. I certainly hope that you will write me once in a while.

Ruth joins me in best regards.

As ever, fraternally yours,

Norman

Leaving Syracuse saddened the Peales. It was incredible how closely woven, in five short years, the network of associations and affections had become. There were farewell dinners with old friends like the Ponds, the Chappels, the Hooples, the Whitneys, the Browns. Norman had persuaded Geoffrey Brown, jobless, to try the insurance business—and Geoff had promptly sold his first policy to the minister. "You should feel awfully proud, Norman," Elsie Brown said. "I'll bet you'll be the youngest pastor on Fifth Avenue!"

"Maybe so," said Norman, "but if I ever start getting a swelled head, come down to New York and knock it off, will you?"

"You'd better hurry up and take the job," Geoff Brown said dryly. "At the rate people are jumping out of windows in New York, there won't be anyone left to hear you preach!"

The joke was based on grim reality. In less than three years, the suicide rate for male Americans had risen thirty per cent. It was a bleak city and a bleak church that the Peales found waiting for them. Men were selling apples on street corners. Women were wearing out shoe leather looking for jobs that didn't exist. Heart attacks and nervous breakdowns were daily occurrences. Fear and anxiety were everywhere.

The Marble Collegiate was the oldest and most famous sanctuary of an ancient religious organization known as The Collegiate Reformed Protestant Dutch Church of the City of New York. The word "Collegiate" stood for the ministry of Colleagues in Marble, Middle, West End, Fort Washington, and St. Nicholas Congregations. These congregations together comprised the Collegiate Church, which, in turn, was part of the Reformed Church in America, popularly known as the Dutch Reformed Church.

Its history dated from 1628 when the Dutch established it in Nieuw Amsterdam. The church had served under three flags, Dutch, British and American, and was the oldest institution of any kind in New York. The first colonial governor, Peter Stuyvesant, was a member, as was Peter Minuit, who purchased the island of Manhattan from the Indians for twenty-four dollars.

Norman's predecessor at the Marble Church had been Dr. Daniel A. Poling, an able and devoted clergyman who was destined to become one of Norman's closest friends. But after a notable ministry, Dr. Poling had left the Marble Church and had been gone for almost three years. In the meantime, under a succession of temporary pastors, the congregation had dwindled. No more than two hundred souls were attending services in the great nave capable of seating eight times that many.

Over the rows of empty pews seemed to hang a spirit of discouragement and defeat that matched the sombre mood of the city.

Norman sensed this atmosphere instantly. He sensed it and knew that while his basic message might remain the same, he was going to have to change his emphasis. The graceful, poetic type of sermon that had delighted the co-eds at Syracuse would have to be abandoned. These New York people were in no mood for literary allusions or verbal elegance. They were frightened, they were defeated, some of them were desperate. Many had lost faith in themselves—and in the process had lost faith in God. They were baffled and beaten. They needed practical, specific help, not pious hopes or empty platitudes. They wanted to be assured—reassured—that God was, and that He cared, and that He would help those who turned to Him with faith and trust.

Norman understood all this. He understood it because the fears swirling around him were magnifications of fears and insecurities that he had known in himself. He had found his own solution in surrender to a Power infinitely stronger than himself. Time and again that Power had come to his rescue, had sustained and supported him through the years. But this did not mean that the fears had been completely eliminated. He knew that mortal man must conquer his insecurities over and over again.

Because he understood the anatomy of fear, because it was never far from him, because he literally needed the power of God in his own life to control it, Norman knew that he could talk to these people in language that they would understand. Preaching to them would not be difficult, he would really be preaching to himself. The problem was to draw them back into the church and to get them to listen.

He decided to start slowly, feel his way, and let the healing power of his message do the work. He hesitated to use the promotional ideas and advertising techniques that he had employed in Brooklyn and later in Syracuse. A part of his mind told him confidently that human beings were the same everywhere, that for all of them the Gospel of Christ was equally valid. But another part remembered uneasily what Oliver Jaynes had said: that New Yorkers were different, that they were sophisticated, impatient, demanding, critical. . . .

New York, he thought apprehensively, gazing up at the soaring spire of his new church, *no wonder they call it the graveyard of ministers.* . . .

The first thing he wished to do, the first point he wanted to get across to his uneasy flock, was that despite the economic chaos of the nation, despite the breadlines, despite the unemployment, God was still in His heaven, and man was still created in His image, and that therefore there was no reason to feel defeated or to lose heart. He did not wish to minimize the difficulties; no one in his right mind in the autumn of 1932 was inclined to do that. But he believed with all his unshakeable Ohio optimism that the country was basically sound, that the qualities that had made it great still existed under the paralysis of panic, and that if the people could just regain their faith in God and in themselves the downward trend would be reversed.

He set out deliberately to restore that faith. Once more he preached his first sermon on his father's favorite text: *I am come that they might have life, and that they might have it more abundantly.* Abundance . . . the word sounded strange in such times, but there was hope and promise in it.

Throughout the sermon he tried to rekindle in his sparse congregation a spark of pride in themselves as individuals. "Almighty God meant us to walk the earth as men," he told them. "He meant us to be strong. He intended for us to stand up to our problems and solve them, to confront our difficulties with power in His name. I tell you, if you fill your life with an awareness of the presence of God, all fear and shrinking and sense of failure will be cast out of you!"

They listened to him dubiously, as if convinced that the message was too good to be true. He could feel their skepticism, but it did not dismay him. He had expected it.

"These are difficult days," he told them. "We all know that. But perhaps we dwell too much on how difficult they are. Perhaps we think so much in terms of failure that we have forgotten how to think in terms of success. Perhaps we have fallen into the habit of minimizing our powers and belittling ourselves. This is a dangerous thing, almost as dangerous as falling into the opposite sin of pride or arrogance. It is dangerous because self-doubt becomes a poison, if carried too far. Believe me, I know!

"The other day I heard some one say, 'What a mess man has made of things!' Well, yes, he has made a mess of things at times. But he has done better than any other creature that I ever heard of. He has discovered God. He has reached out for ideals. He has learned the really subtle truth that love is stronger than hate. He has delved into the earth and brought forth riches. His great ships sail over the waters and under the waters and through the air. He fabricates everything he needs from the forests and the fields and the hills. And he has courage, too. Here he stands in this vast universe, with silence behind him and mystery before him. He doesn't know where he came from, and he can't prove where he's going. Yet he whistles a cheerful tune and he sings songs of faith.

"Who says man is not wonderful? You ought to be proud of being a member of the human race!"

They listened to him; he knew that much. Whether they really responded, whether their spirits were truly lifted, he could not immediately tell. All he knew was that he found himself loving these people, loving them and believing in them.

Afterwards, at the door of the church, many told him that his sermon had helped them. Only one reaction was distinctly negative, but it came from an important source. One of the elders of the church was a man in his late fifties, austere, stern, rather forbidding. He enjoyed the authority that went with the role of leading elder. He made it clear that, in his opinion, this authority included the right to give the new minister the benefit of his advice whenever he felt so inclined.

"That was an interesting sermon, Doctor," he said when he had Norman alone. "Very interesting. I'm sure a lot of the congregation went away feeling quite pleased with themselves. But tell me—is that really the function of the pulpit, to remind people of how good they are? I should have thought it was just the reverse, to remind them of their shortcomings, the need for change, the necessity for improvement."

Norman felt something tighten inside him. Here it was, the old, unyielding authoritarianism that he had rebelled against even as a child. Here it was, the dusty voice out of the past saying, "It must be thus and so because it has always been thus and so."

He said evenly, "There's evil in all of us as well as good. I know that, and from time to time I will say so. But I think God wants His children to live fully and gladly. People can't be effective if they're frightened and discouraged."

"They won't be better people if they lose their humility," the Leading Elder said. "In effect, this morning, you were counseling those people to lift themselves by their own bootstraps. It can't be done. Wishing won't get an unemployed man a job."

Norman felt his face grow red. "No," he said. "Wishing won't. But confidence often will. Unless a man believes in himself, nobody else is going to believe in him. If a man has lost his faith in himself, it won't help him much if I stand up in the pulpit and tell him that he's a miserable worm, will it?"

"Perhaps not a worm," said the Leading Elder with a wintry smile. "But he is a miserable sinner who is helpless without the grace of God. Don't forget that—and don't let them forget it. Good day, Doctor."

The conversation left Norman discouraged and depressed. He told Ruth about it that night as she sat making curtains for their apartment. "I know that people need God's help," he said. "I made that point over and over again this morning. But that's not enough for some of these fellows. They seem to think that man ought to spend his life apologizing to God for being the creature that God made him. This pessimism runs all through Protestantism nowadays. I don't share it myself—and that makes me different. And anyone whose ideas are different is going to have trouble."

He began to pace up and down, shoving his glasses up onto his forehead in the familiar mannerism inherited from his mother. "I've about decided that you can't think independently or be yourself in a Protestant church. You have to be what the fundamentalists want you to be—or the narrow-minded liberals. Protestantism was founded on the right of every man to think for himself. But now it's in a strait jacket!"

"You're making a mountain out of a molehill," Ruth said reassuringly. "There are always a few domineering people in any church who like to tell other people what to do. That old boy was just seeing how far he could go with you. Once he knows you won't back down, you won't have any more trouble with him."

But Norman shook his head glumly. "We'll be hearing more from him," he said, "and from people like him."

In November, the voters of the nation overwhelmingly elected Franklin D. Roosevelt to the highest office in the land. Norman did not share the feelings of the majority; he resented the Democrats' intention of ending Prohibition, of "bringing back the saloon" as the drys put it. But he was impressed by the new President's inaugural address and the ringing declaration that the only thing to fear was fear itself. "By George," Norman said to Ruth admiringly, "Roosevelt's given the whole country a tremendous lift by saying that. And he's right. He's absolutely right!"

But Norman was not so receptive to the flood of political innovations that followed. He recognized the need for leadership, the imperative necessity for relieving human suffering. But this seemed to call for governmental action, and the individualism that had been bred into him resented instinctively the intrusion of centralized authority into private affairs. The National Recovery Act, he felt, might have a laudable purpose, namely, the restoration of the nation's economic health. But he also felt that it was unconstitutional—as the Supreme Court later declared it to be—in that it sacrificed the rights of individuals to the welfare of people as a whole.

The call for a "planned economy," the tendency to put expediency ahead of law in the guise of humanitarianism, the redistribution of wealth through taxation, the whole "leveling down" process—in all these ideas and trends he thought he saw the seeds of Socialism, and he did not approve. Many others felt as he did. But in 1933, driven by inexorable economic pressures, the political pendulum was swinging far to the left. The prediction of the jeweler in Syracuse was coming true: for better or worse, a social revolution was in the making.

The essence of revolution is change. Norman did not consider himself opposed to change as such. In his own calling, inside the church, he was a liberal—often in opposition to various aspects of the status quo. But in the policy makers of New Deal he saw—or thought he saw—a delight in change for its own sake, a determination to alter things whether they needed alteration or not, a kind of blind iconoclasm that delighted in destroying the beliefs and traditions of the past. For most of these traditions and beliefs his Ohio boyhood had given him a deep and sentimental affection. He believed that the greatness of the country was based on them. Anyone who attacked them, therefore, was suspect—and dangerous.

He did not always fully reason these things out. He was a firm believer in the validity of intuition—the surest road to truth, Bergson had called it. His intuition told him that while the pump-priming and other forms of social legislation might have a short-term remedial effect, the underlying philosophy of the New Deal was implacably anti-individualistic. And a glance at the map of Europe told him that when a regime became anti-individualistic, there was every chance that it would also become anti-religious.

The reason for this was clear enough. Individualism itself was a religious concept. The doctrine of the infinite dignity and value of the individual with equal rights for all was based squarely on the assumption of the brotherhood of man under the fatherhood of God. Any attack on individualism, therefore, logically involved an ultimate assault on religion. The disciples of Marx and Lenin had always known this. There were those who felt that such a chain of events was unthinkable in America. But it had happened in Russia, it was happening in Germany, and in 1933 with the Blue Eagle of the NRA wildly flapping its pinions it was by no means certain that it couldn't happen right in the U.S.A.

So Norman found himself pushed, intellectually, into the ranks of the conservatives. It was not, at the time, an entirely comfortable place to be. To the non-conservative, it looked too much like a do-nothing, let-'em-eat cake attitude. Moreover, the thinking on which it was based was too abstract to impress people who wanted and needed a job—and would vote for the Party that gave them one. But Norman felt that it was the only position from which to defend his church and his country, and consequently the only possible position for him.

During his first months at the Marble Church, he did not voice his political views from the pulpit. He was too busy trying to allay people's fears and restore their confidence. But later on he would do so—and make the inevitable enemies.

It was during this first winter in New York that Norman encountered his first serious health problem. His teeth began to trouble him. He mentioned this casually once or twice, but did nothing about it. By the time he got around to consulting a dentist, he had such an advanced case of pyorrhea that for a while it looked as if he might lose every tooth in his head. He was badly worried; such a disaster might have put an end to his preaching altogether. In the end, Dr. Arthur H. Merritt was able to arrest the infection and save his teeth. Indeed, the doctor improved Norman's mind as well as his teeth. He was an enthusiastic student of literature, and sessions in the dental chair took on a marked literary flavor. "Believe me," Norman said fervently to Ruth, "finding Dr. Merritt was one of the greatest blessings of my life!"

Norman's difficulties awoke some vivid recollections in his father. "You're lucky to have found a man like Dr. Merritt," Clifford Peale said. "I'll never forget the time I had a tooth-ache as a small boy. Grandfather Fulton took a look at it and said he'd fix it so that the aching would stop. He took a piece of wire and heated it over a kerosene lamp until it was red hot. Then he thrust that wire down into the cavity, killing the nerve and just about killing one small boy in the process. Later on he extracted the tooth, using a claw-shaped instrument like a miniature baling hook. You were lucky in those days if a piece of your jawbone didn't come out with the tooth!"

"Don't!" groaned Norman, rocking to and fro in vicarious agony. "I can't stand it!"

"I couldn't either," his father said dryly. "But I had to!"

His mother's health was beginning to fail. Anna Peale was only in her late fifties, but the intensity with which she had always lived and felt things was beginning to take its toll. After feeling badly for some time, she came to New England for a vacation and consulted a well-known physician in Boston.

The doctor made the usual examinations, then looked at her thoughtfully. "Madam," he said, "are you a Christian?"

"Why, yes," said Anna Peale, surprised and somewhat resentful, "I consider myself a Christian."

She went on to tell him of the various ways in which she thought she was rendering a devoted Christian service. He listened and shook his head. "In spite of all that, Mrs. Peale," he said, "I doubt if you're a real Christian. I'm not sure that I'm one, either, but I understand that being a Christian means to have a childlike faith and trust, to be convinced that God loves you and exercises a watchful care over you, to believe that you can receive, by prayer and faith, sufficient strength to offset the drain of life. In this sort of Christianity, like most of us, you are deficient. You say you believe in these things, and no doubt you think you do, but you don't really practice them. Isn't that true?"

Anna Peale bit her lip and her eyes filled with tears. She said nothing.

"Well," said the doctor, "here's my prescription. Go off to some quiet place, and shake off the ambitions and frustrations you are carrying around with you, and think about God, and get His peace into your soul."

So Anna Peale went up to Cape Ann, a rugged promontory on the Massachusetts coast. There each day she sat by the sea, listening to the roar of the water as it surged against the cliffs. At first, she said later, her eyes rested wearily on the nearby rocks and waves, but gradually she lifted them to the far horizon until presently the vastness of the sea brought home to her a sense of the vastness that is God. And the doctor was right; after a while her body and spirit took on a new vitality that was almost a re-creation.

"You can learn something from this, Norman," she said to her son. "You're a lot like me, and every bit of this applies to you. I was letting tension take over. I was thinking about nothing but myself. I was losing my sense of dependence on God. Tension seems to be an enemy of God—probably because there's so much self in it. Remember that, whenever you find yourself getting tense. And tell your congregation about this healing power, too."

He did. All his observations as a minister, all his experience in counseling people in trouble seemed to bear out the truth of what his mother had said. With anxiety or frustration came tension, and with tension came—ultimately—physical illness. The antidote was calmness, imperturbability, the capacity to relax—and these were precisely the attributes that resulted from faith in a mighty Power that would sustain, and protect, and guide, faith in a loving and omnipotent God.

Faith was the answer, faith and self-surrender—it was so obvious that at times he simply could not see why people failed to understand. *Trust God and live one day at a time:* there it was in nine simple words—nine syllables—the whole secret of effective living. There it was, shining like a diamond in a dusty road—and yet people had to be cajoled and begged and exhorted and persuaded to pick it up.

It was strange and bewildering and sometimes a little disheartening.

That summer Norman took Ruth to Europe to attend the three hundredth anniversary of the great Passion Play at Oberammergau. He had a few qualms about going, because Ruth was expecting a baby. "Maybe we shouldn't go so far from home," he said worriedly. "Maybe the boat trip wouldn't be good for you. Maybe . . ."

"Nonsense," said Ruth. "You're acting as if I were made of glass. The baby isn't due until November. Of course we'll go!" They went, and had a marvelous time; staying as guests in the home of Anton Lang who played the part of the Christ in the great drama.

After Oberammergau they went to Ireland to meet Norman's parents. On the channel steamer, while Ruth was making sure their luggage was in the right cabin, Norman stood by the gangplank watching the passengers come aboard. One beautiful and solitary lady, seeing him standing there, gave him a dazzling smile. Thinking she must be somebody he knew, Norman beamed happily back at her. At which point he heard a wifely voice in his ear. "Who," demanded Ruth, "is *that?*"

"That?" echoed Norman. "Why, I don't know, really. It must be somebody we've met. . . ."

"You have never met her," stated Ruth firmly. "What's more, you never will! Not while I'm around, anyway!"

The "other woman" had come and gone in the Peale family life. It was probably the shortest triangle situation on record.

In Ireland, Anna Peale was anxious to find the birthplace of her father. Andrew DeLaney had always described his native village as "a small place called Ballinakill—not too long a walk from the sea." After much poring over maps, Norman located three separate Ballinakills none of which—judged by American walking standards—was anywhere near the sea. Even so, they decided to hire a car and visit all of them.

In the very first one a friendly priest took them to the church, produced the dusty baptismal records, and triumphantly pointed out the name of Andrew DeLaney. Anna Peale was so overcome by emotion that she burst into tears. The good father took them down a rustic lane and pointed out the thatch-roofed cottage where Andrew had lived as a boy. Then he invited them all back to his house, brought out a bottle of smoky Irish whiskey, and proposed a grand toast to all the DeLaneys, past and present, and their descendants on both sides of the ocean. He was somewhat depressed to discover that his newfound American friends had ideas about whiskey that differed radically from his own. But he solved the problem by hastily sending out for some non-alcoholic ginger beer—and the toast was drunk in that.

Back in New York to begin his second year at the Marble Church, Norman found his congregation a little stronger, but not much. Certainly the gains were far from being as spectacular as the ones he had recorded in Brooklyn or in Syracuse. A spiritual as well as financial depression seemed to hang over the land.

The birth of the baby was imminent, now, and on November 17, after a long and difficult labor, Margaret Ann Peale was born. Norman was both relieved and delighted. He told everyone proudly about his new daughter, but showed no great interest—then or later—in the mechanics of baby-tending: the diapering, bathing, feeding, burping, or midnight floor-walking departments.

The winter of 1934 seemed harsh and long. Progress at the church continued to be slow. This was not for lack of effort on Norman's part. He preached three different sermons each week. On Sundays he preached two—one in the morning, another at the evening service. On Wednesday night he delivered a third. Preparing for this triple effort, he sat up night after night, doggedly driving himself past not only the first, but the second and third layers of fatigue.

More and more he found himself engaged in personal counseling with people whose problems seemed as urgent as they were endless. He was constantly involved in church administrative details, which he disliked, and with committees, some of whose members were always prone to suffer from delusions of infallibility—or worse, perennially hurt feelings.

The Leading Elder continued to be a problem. For one thing, he had an obsession about time. He proclaimed his conviction that the new minister should be at his office in the church by eight-thirty every morning, not a moment later. He felt that sermons should be exactly twenty-five minutes long, no more and no less. One Sunday he came up to Norman with watch in hand. "You ran two minutes over," he said accusingly.

"Well," said Norman, trying to conceal his irritation with humor, "it's hard to put a time limit on the Holy Spirit."

On another occasion the Leading Elder complained to the church board about the National Council of Churches radio program that Norman was conducting. "We hired this man," he said. "He should be working for us, not for some radio network!"

When this was repeated to Norman, he exploded. "I'm not working for any of you," he roared. "Nobody hired me. I'm working for Jesus Christ, and I'm going to spread His message as far as I can, and by whatever means I can!"

Such episodes sapped his strength and vitality, but these were renewed in other ways. One stormy evening he stood with his mother outside the Fifth Avenue entrance to the church. Only a few people were on the rain-swept Avenue. Suddenly Anna Peale put her hand on one of the great blocks of marble at the base of the church edifice and began to weep.

"What's the matter?" Norman asked, startled. "Why are you crying?"

"Because I'm happy," his mother said. "This old church is so solid. No storm can move it. Nothing can shake it. Always keep it strong, Norman. Preach the gospel so as to reach people and help people. And never forget to give them the heart of the message—faith in Jesus Christ, Lord and Saviour!"

Norman was deeply moved. Often in years to come he would stand on the same spot, rest his hand where hers had rested, and repeat his vow—to keep the church strong.

In his effort to keep that promise he drove himself unmercifully. One Sunday a new-found medical friend, Dr. William S. Bainbridge, listened to the sermon, then after the service went back to Norman's office. He found the minister stretched out on a couch, looking pale and exhausted.

"Norman," the doctor said after they had talked for a while, "Sunday is hardly a day of rest for you. Which day in the week do you take off?"

"Which day?" Norman rubbed his forehead wearily. "Why, none, I guess. But I get a long vacation in the summer, and . . ."

"Listen, Norman," his friend said. "The wisest Man who ever walked the earth took one day off in seven. Do you think you're smarter than He was? You'd better slow down. I'm warning you—you're in for trouble if you don't."

"All right," said Norman meekly, "I'll try."

But it was difficult for him. He had never mastered the art of leisure. He had no hobbies outside his work. Sports meant little to him. He liked to watch a baseball game occasionally, or play nine holes of very amateurish golf. But the fact that he was not very good at games kept him from being fond of them. Also, when he thus indulged himself, he always had a guilty feeling that somehow he was wasting time, was neglecting problems or responsibilities that needed attention.

There were always plenty of these. The lists of people seeking appointments to discuss their problems grew steadily longer. Many involved marital difficulties. There were times when it seemed to Norman that the root of the trouble in every unhappy marriage was the blind desire on the part of one person to impose his or her will on the other, to twist and change their marriage partner into something closer to their own desires.

"You've got to stop trying to dominate each other," he would tell them. "You've got to stop acting as if your husband or your wife were your own personal possession. Every individual must be permitted to develop his mind and soul and spirit in his own way; this is the inalienable right of every human being. The test of a true marriage is whether each partner aids the other in becoming a greater soul. Stop trying to force each other into a mold! Get down on your knees together and ask God to help you appreciate each other, support each other, be kind to each other. Do this and, I promise you, your problems will begin to melt away."

Then there were the shy ones, the self-conscious ones, the ones who said they could not make friends, could not be at ease with people. "Look," he would say to them, "lots of people have this difficulty. I know something about it, because there's a lot of shyness in me. Oh, I'm all right up in the pulpit, because then I'm telling the people about the spiritual life—I'm armored with authority. And I'm all right, maybe, in an interview like this, because in a way I'm still in the driver's seat. But at a dinner party, where I'm expected to make small talk, I'm tongue-tied. I don't know any small talk! I'm likely to freeze up completely, the way you say you do.

"But we might as well face the truth about this. The reason for such embarrassment is self-centeredness. In your case, judging from what you tell me, everything that happens around you is immediately interpreted by your mind in terms of self-reference. You personalize everything; everything is made to revolve around you as a center. The result is, you have an ingrown life, abnormal, unnatural.

"Now, what can you do about this? The obvious thing to do is put something else in the center of your life, isn't it? Why don't you try putting Christ at the center and yourself at the circumference for a change? You'll be cured, if you do this,— if you really work at it steadily and sincerely. Ask the Lord to be the center of your life. All He wants is the invitation. Open the door of your heart and let Him in!"

Some of these people needed little more than a sympathetic listener and a few words of common sense. In others the difficulties were so old, so deeply ingrained, so much a part of the person that their removal seemed almost impossible. Indeed, as time went on, Norman became convinced that people often clung desperately to their troubles, even though they thought they wanted to be free of them.

"Wouldn't it be wonderful," he said one day in a sermon, "if, when the collection plate was passed, instead of dropping in money you could drop in your secret worry, or trouble, or fear, or whatever was bothering you most? Wouldn't it be marvelous if you could see it removed from you, carried down the aisle of the church, left at the altar? You could walk out of here a new person, liberated, free at last! And yet, you know what would happen? As soon as some people got outside they would hesitate, they would turn around, they would come back, furtively they would go up to the altar and start fishing around in those collection plates trying to find their lost trouble, their departed sin. They wouldn't be happy until they *had* found it, until they were united with it again!"

Some of the worst offenders in this regard were people harboring a sense of guilt. Time and again some one with a guilty conscience would come to Norman, would confess a sin, would ask God's forgiveness and receive assurance that if there was true repentance such forgiveness would readily be granted. Then, a week or a month later, the same person would reappear and go through the same process all over again.

There was one little white-haired lady who thought she had forfeited eternal life, not for an actual sin that she had committed, but because of thoughts she once had had. She had not committed the sin, but she had been tempted, she had read the passage in the New Testament that seems to equate evil thoughts with evil deeds, and for years she had been miserable.

Norman tried to make her see that actually she had won a victory over temptation. "None of us," he told her, "can fully control the thoughts that come into our minds. It's like the old Chinese proverb: 'A man can't prevent the birds from flying over his head, but he can keep them from building a nest in his hair.' This feeling of guilt that you have is out of all proportion. The Lord isn't angry with you; I'm sure of it. Put all this out of your mind. Forget it!"

But she could not. She remained abject, inconsolable.

Finally he took her into the church Sanctuary. No one else was there. The great building was hushed, quiet. He robed himself in his vestments, asked her to kneel at the altar. "Now," he said, standing beside her, "do you believe that as an ordained minister I am the representative of God in this church?"

"Yes," she said. "I do."

"Very well, then," he said. "We are going to pray once more for the Lord to look down on us, as He always does, with compassion and tenderness and love. Then I am going to put my hand on your head, and in that moment you will be fully and finally forgiven for any wrong thing you may have done. Mine is just an ordinary human hand. But the power of God will come through it and you will have your forgiveness. Do you believe that?"

"Yes," she said, "I believe it."

And so, with the aid of a little dramatization, the forces of faith were finally mobilized to the point where the mountain of imaginary guilt was set aside, and a human soul was lifted out of its self-inflicted misery.

But there were also cases that he did not fully understand, that he could not seem to help. It began to dawn on him that often the troubled person himself did not know what his basic problem was, although almost invariably he thought he did. As time went on, there seemed to be more and more of such cases. His own inability to help these people began to loom larger and larger in his own mind.

It was weighing on his mind when he and Ruth went back to England in the summer of 1934. His second year at the Marble Church had left Norman close to exhaustion. Despite his best efforts, membership had increased only slightly. After two years, he was still preaching to empty seats. The depression still hung heavy on the land, and the innovations of the New Deal seemed to Norman to be more divisive and destructive than helpful. The gaiety and buoyancy of the years at Syracuse seemed to be gone for good. It was to get her husband away from all these sources of discouragement that Ruth proposed a tour of the English Lake District. They could leave baby Margaret with her grandmother. Norman would love the country of Wordsworth and Coleridge. He would come back revitalized and refreshed, a new man.

So Ruth thought. It did not work out that way.

The Lakes were lovely, Wordsworth's cottage was still there, gray and weatherbeaten and timeless. But Norman's mood of discouragement did not lift. If anything, as the time drew near to go home, it became deeper. Ruth watched him, worried, saying little. Ordinarily she could divert him, could coax him out of despondency. Not this time.

The crisis came in the little town of Keswick, in the Cumbrian hills. They were staying at a hotel that had a lovely garden shaded by great elm and chestnut trees. Here every afternoon tea was served ceremoniously with hot scones and jam and bread-and-butter sliced paper thin and tiny water-cress sandwiches. It was a peaceful place, full of quietness and dignity and beauty. Something about it, perhaps the serenity contrasted with his own inner turmoil, broke down the last barriers of self-restraint in Norman. Sitting there with Ruth while the long twilight faded around them he began to talk about himself in relation to his work.

He had thought, he said, that coming to New York was the right, the selfless thing to do, but now he knew he had been mistaken. He had been successful in Brooklyn, and again in Syracuse, but New York was too much for him. It was cold and impersonal; it did not seem to need or want the warmth that he was trying to offer.

He had been preaching for two years, he went on, with little or no results. He knew the message he was trying to offer was sound. It always had been and it always would be. But it wasn't getting across; people weren't responding to it. That could only mean one thing; there was something wrong with him. There *must* be something wrong with him.

Now he was facing his third year in a pulpit that evidently was too large for him. Did it make sense, really, to try to go on with it? The church was not truly united behind him. Oh, most people had supported him loyally, but he knew others who did not. There were some who wanted more scholarly preaching, who would prefer a great theologian in the pulpit. He was no intellectual; he had never pretended to be one. After all, his doctorate was only an honorary one.

Even in counseling, personal counseling, he said, his limitations were becoming more apparent all the time. His training had been too academic and theoretical for him to cope with some of the problems that were presented to him. And if he couldn't cope, what was he doing there? Wasn't he being a hypocrite? Wouldn't it be better to step aside and let someone more qualified take his place? "It's bad enough to be a failure," he said, "but if you are one, it's better to face the fact, don't you think? Face it and stop trying to pretend you're something that you're not?"

Ruth did not answer for a while. Her thoughts ran back over the years she had sat in Norman's church, hearing the sermons he preached, accepting every word of them, herself gaining encouragement from the message he delivered to his congregation. Finally, she said, "You want me to contradict you, don't you? You want me to tell you that you're not a failure. Well, I can't do that because right now, at this moment, that's what you are."

She had never spoken to him like this before. The silence sang between them. The whole empty garden seemed to be listening. At last she went on: "You're a failure, but not in the way you think. You're a failure because you've let yourself be overwhelmed by the fear of failure. You're thinking entirely of yourself, and your success and popularity—or lack of it. You're not thinking about what God may have in mind for you. Maybe He wants you to know despair so that you can help despairing people. Maybe He even wants you to fail; maybe He feels it would be good for you. In any case, why don't you practice what you preach? Why don't you do what you're always telling other people to do: trust God, put your life in His hands, surrender yourself to Jesus Christ, and ask for His guidance?"

Norman was staring at the ground. "I don't know if I can," he said in a low voice. "I don't know if I can get rid of myself. There have been times, before, when I thought I did. But now . . ."

"You can't do it," Ruth said quietly, "by yourself. But if you ask for help to rededicate yourself, you'll get it. It's strange that I should have to say these things to you, because these are your own words, Norman. I've heard you say them to countless people. Ask the Lord to help you get back to Him. You've lost contact for a little while, that's all. Once you're back in touch, these difficulties that seem so large will iron themselves out. The church will grow. You'll solve the counseling problem. It will all happen, as soon as you let yourself become once more a channel for God's power and stop fretting about yourself."

He looked at her hopefully. "You really think so?"

"I know so," she said. "Go on. Right now. Right here and now."

"All right," he said, and reached for her hand. Then he bowed his head and closed his eyes and began to pray.

CHAPTER XI

"I Preach Out of My

Yesterdays. . . ."

◄§§►

Many times in the years that followed, Norman was to say that the moment of rededication in the garden at Keswick was one of the most profound and rewarding experiences of his life. Certainly soon afterward the gloom that had been oppressing him lifted and the difficulties that had seemed so overwhelming began to disappear.

The solution of the counseling problem was not instantaneous, but when it did come it was marvelously simple. "If you don't feel equipped to deal with some of those cases," Ruth said one day, "why don't you ask someone who is qualified to lend a hand? Doctors are always generous with the time and skill they give to charity. Why not find a good psychiatrist and ask him to help you? You made a pretty good team with doctors more than once back in Syracuse, and you got aid from Dr. Bainbridge here in New York, didn't you? Why not set up something like that?"

Norman stared at her. "Why, of course!" he said. "Why couldn't I think of that?"

"Men are visionary," Ruth said demurely. "Women are practical. Doesn't that sound familiar?"

"I know that's what my mother always says," Norman admitted. "But I never really believed it, until now!"

As a result of this conversation, Norman went to see his personal physician, Dr. Clarence W. Lieb, and outlined the problem. "We'll need a good man," he said. "One of the best. I'd want him to be a sound Christian as well as a sound psychiatrist. It would also help if he had a sense of humor. Believe me, you need one to keep your balance in that sort of work."

"I think it's a splendid idea," Lieb said. "It's always been obvious to me that religion can reach some people who can't be reached by psychiatry, and vice versa. The pastor and the psychiatrist traditionally have never had much use for each other. But they're certainly working toward the same goal. Why don't you talk to Iago Galdston up at the Academy of Medicine? He knows just about everyone in the medical profession."

Dr. Galdston, too, was sympathetic. He gave Norman the names of several qualified psychiatrists. One in particular he thought might be helpful. "He's a very good man," he said. "Got his training under Freud himself, in Vienna. He's a Southerner, a good thinker. Religious, too, an Episcopalian . . ."

"How's his sense of humor?" asked Norman.

"Well," said Galdston with a smile, "I'm told that when he's lecturing in the South and comes to a point where he has to call a spade a spade, he usually prefaces it by saying, 'Ladies and gentlemen, I am a native of Tennessee, I am a great admirer of Robert E. Lee, and for saying what I am about to say to you now I have been severely criticized in the North!'"

"He sounds fine to me," Norman said, and armed with an introduction from Dr. Galdston he went to see Smiley Blanton.

From the start the two men liked each other. Blanton listened to Norman's proposal, then leaned back in his chair. "Do you," he asked, "believe in the power of prayer?"

"Prayer?" echoed Norman, somewhat startled. "Of course I do! Why do you ask?"

"Because," said the psychiatrist, "I've been praying for years that some minister would see that psychiatry and religion not only might but should work together. And now here you are!"

After more discussion, the doctor agreed to review any case histories that Norman chose to send him, give the minister the benefit of his diagnostic experience, and make recommendations as to curative procedures. It was to be an elastic and informal relationship; they would just get together occasionally for lunch. Neither of them foresaw, even dimly, the great religio-psychiatric clinic that was to grow from the seeds they were planting.

Norman was deeply impressed by the way the psychiatrist, given the salient facts of a case, could often penetrate the carefully erected defenses of the patient, brush aside the camouflage, and reach the heart of the problem. "It's simply amazing," he said to Ruth, "to watch him analyze a situation, probe into a maladjusted personality, find the basic reason why a man can't get along with his wife, or keeps failing in his work, or suffers from hypertension. Once the psychiatrist points out the basic cause, then we ministers can begin to apply the great remedies of religion: prayer, faith, and love. But the two therapies go together, don't you see? They complement each other."

"You've always said," Ruth reminded him, "that the Bible is the greatest of all textbooks on the science of human behavior."

"That's exactly what it is," Norman said. "If a person will get rid of the load of guilt and fear he's carrying around with him as the result of wrongdoing, if he'll clean up his life, if he'll learn to stop hating and to love God and his fellow man, then he'll have mental health. That's what the psychiatrists are saying today. That's what the Bible has been saying all along. And it's true—pragmatically, verifiably true. Every day some one comes into my office who has made himself sick by draining back into his body the poisoned thoughts that are in his mind. You should see what happens to some of these people when they clean out their minds and hearts! Why, they're born again, just as the Bible says. They're made over, they're new!"

"I'm sure they are," Ruth said quietly. "But in the last analysis, they don't do it, and you don't do it, and Dr. Blanton doesn't do it. Christ does it."

The mood of confidence and optimism and deepened faith in which Norman had come back from England was reflected in his preaching. His sermons had more vitality, more insight, more assurance, more authority. People began to urge their friends to come with them to the Marble Church. The empty pews began to fill up. Church membership began to grow.

Norman had long been aware that an audience or a congregation had a kind of corporate personality of its own. It could be alive, intent, aware of everything. It could also be apathetic, lethargic, dull. But it could be influenced, it could be coaxed, it could be challenged—and it would almost always respond. Now and then, when he sensed this responsiveness, a kind of exultation would come over him and he would lose himself completely in the message he was trying to transmit. Then preaching became a joy and a privilege, not just because of the heady sense of leading people to God, but because of the humbling sense of helping them.

He never used notes, or tried to memorize his sermons. He would choose topics for several weeks ahead, assemble provocative titles to go with those topics, and then mark the titles on cardboard folders into which he would drop newspaper clippings, apt quotations, and memoranda to himself about stories or anecdotes that might serve as illustrations of the main point.

Two or three days before the sermon was to be delivered, he would take the folder, go through it carefully, and make a rough outline usually consisting of three main headings for the beginning, middle, and end, with a few subheadings. He would study this outline, fixing the sequence of ideas in his mind, "picturizing" himself actually in the pulpit delivering the sermon. He would do this over and over again until the framework was solidly constructed.

These were the mechanical preparations. But there had to be a spiritual mobilization, too. Norman never entered the pulpit—never spoke anywhere, for that matter—without praying for help and guidance. And Ruth, who watched him through the preparation and delivery of hundreds of sermons, was convinced that he was more fully guided than he knew. Too many times she had seen him, impelled by a strange uneasiness, return to a sermon already completed in his mind, ready for delivery, and make changes of emphasis for no apparent reason—changes that on Sunday morning seemed to reach out unerringly and meet some individual's deep and heartfelt need.

Sometimes these changes or additions would occur in midsermon, with no warning or conscious forethought at all—and afterward some member of the congregation would seek Ruth out and ask her to thank Norman for addressing himself, with such uncanny accuracy, to his hidden problem. "I felt," they often said, "as if he were talking just to me!" This happened too frequently to be explained in terms of intuition, or any law of averages. It was almost as if the wish Norman had expressed in his letter to Ruth during their courtship, his desire to be "a good man and a great preacher" in order to be worthy of her, had been a prayer selfless enough to be answered.

Preaching a minimum of two sermons each week for nine

months out of a year, he went through this creative process at least eighty times between October and June. He believed firmly that if he did his part of the work, God would help him and use him. But preaching never became easy. He always had a certain amount of stage fright. Once on his feet, assurance and authority came to him. But waiting for that moment could be misery.

His voice was not big, but it was clear and resonant, and he had learned from Hugh Tilroe to "aim it at the balcony." His gestures, which always grew more pronounced and compelling as he warmed to his subject, were completely instinctive. So was his sense of verbal timing. He knew, to the split second, when to change his inflection, when to pause for dramatic effect, when to relieve emotional tension with humor. None of this was studied or acquired; it was a gift.

The most valuable public-speaking advice he ever received, Norman often said, came from an old actor who urged him always to "practice loving your audience." In the course of a long career, the veteran told him, he had found that he gave his best performance when he stood in the wings before going on stage and "sent love thoughts across the footlights." It created an empathy, he insisted, between performer and audience, helped establish a firm and sympathetic contact between them. From then on, Norman never appeared before a congregation or an audience without trying to condition both himself and his hearers by sending out thoughts of love or good will toward them.

Most of his illustrations and anecdotes were drawn from his own experience. "I preach out of my yesterdays," he once said to a friend. People liked this; they recognized the ring of authenticity, and were reminded of similar experiences in their own lives.

They were attracted by Norman's sermons mainly because they sensed the spiritual power in them, but also because he was not afraid to leave the theological, occasionally, in favor of the mundane. He could describe the peace of soul that followed self-surrender, and document it from his own experience. But he could be just as eloquent on the subject of home cooking.

"Those Sunday midday dinners," he would say, "back in Ohio when I was a boy, believe me, those were dinners! Fried chicken—not just one lonely, pale faced, city kind of chicken, but a great heaping platter of crisp, brown country-fried chicken. And the mashed potatoes—not a little metropolitan side-dish of a shade resembling a deathmask, but great dishes of snow-white potatoes, not a lump in all of it, covered with meandering golden butter. Ah, and the gravy! Well, it was a masterpiece! These city-restaurant waiters never saw gravy like this. Little globules broken by the spoon that came up with shreds of chicken and the yolk of eggs—what a taste! It went well with the hot biscuits, too. . . ." And so forth and so on while the congregation, its spiritual hungers momentarily forgotten, sat spell-bound and drooling.

They liked his sermons, also, because he stayed within their frame of reference. If, for example, he was preaching on the ultimate consequences of evil-doing, he would choose a strong Biblical text: "*Keep thy heart with all diligence, for out of it are the issues of life.*" But then he would turn to modern idiom and practical everyday illustration.

"You have to analyze your life as it is today," he would tell them, "and try to correct any bad tendencies now. Why? Because if you don't, you will eventually become what you now have only a tendency to be."

He would look down at the men in the congregation. "I never played golf very much," he would say, "but I did learn this much: if you don't hit the ball right, it won't go right. If the head of the club meets the ball squarely and straight and follows through, the ball will go straight. But if the head of the club is at an angle, even a tiny one, the ball will not go straight. It may go 250 yards, but it will not go straight. It will follow the error in the angle of the clubhead. Its flight is determined by the tendency that started it."

He would shift his glance to the women in the audience. "Somebody gave my little Margaret a toy phonograph. It plays nursery rhymes set to music, and she played it all day yesterday—to the detriment of this sermon. But I was impressed by one of those nursery rhymes. Margaret gave me her permission to use it. It goes like this:

There was a crooked man, and he walked a crooked mile;
He found a crooked sixpence upon a crooked stile.
He bought a crooked cat, which caught a crooked mouse,
And they all lived together in a little crooked house.

"Now, nursery rhymes can be very profound. I take this not as meaning crooked in body; it means crooked in soul. There you have it. The man starts out crooked, and everything he finds or does is crooked, and he ends up crooked. Of course he does! That is philosophy; that is wisdom; that is truth. That is the projection of how your life will come out if you don't start it straight and keep it straight—it will turn out crooked!

"A young person today, if wise, will say to this soft and easy generation, 'Tendencies are important; wrong tendencies lead to wrong ends; therefore I will keep my tendencies straight.' As Emerson said, the soul contains the event that shall befall it. As the Bible says, 'Keep your heart with all diligence, for out of it are the issues of life.' "

Some of his best remembered sermons were preached on Easter, on the great themes of immortality and the deathlessness of the human spirit. "We do not try to prove immortality," he would say to his congregation, "so that we can believe it. We try to prove it because we can't help believing it. It is instinctive with us, and a true instinct. Every person here will pass through the act known as physical death. But God makes none of His natural processes terrible. He is a God of love, and everything He does is done with love.

"Before you came into the world, you were unborn babies, weren't you? We all were. And in going from this into another world we are still unborn babies so far as that next world is concerned. If a baby not yet born could think, he might say, 'This is a warm place. I'm taken care of, I'm secure here, I like it.' That baby would look upon the process of birth as if it were death, since it would be the end of the state he was in. And he would say, 'I don't want to die; I want to stay here. I like it, I am secure, I understand it here.' What to us is birth, to him is death, and he resists it. But the day comes when he does die to that life, and is born into our world.

"What happens to him? He is cradled in loving arms; soft hands hold him gently. A kind face looks down on him, and he loves that face. Every one who comes near admires him. He is king of the world he surveys. He begins to grow, and finds life good. Oh, he has some hardships, but that is to make a man of him. He has some struggles, which toughen his fiber. But he learns to love God, and people love him.

"Finally he is an old man, and he is told, 'You have to die.' He protests, 'I don't want to die. I love this world. I like to feel the sun on my face, and hear the whisper of the rain. I like our familiar human ways. I love the faces of my dear ones. I have lived here a long time. I don't want to die.'

"But he does die, and is born into the next world.

"Can you believe that, all of a sudden, the character of God and the constitution of the Universe are going to be changed so that a person will be born into a place of terror and gloom, or suffer complete extinction? Why, that's preposterous!

"That man will awaken to find himself young again. Loving faces will greet him; loving hands touch him. More beautiful sunlight will fall upon his face; sweeter music will sound in his ears. And he will say to himself, 'Why was I so afraid of this thing that we called death when, as I now know, it is life?'

"Isn't that logical? Isn't that the way God has made the world? Is He going to change and do it differently over there?

He doesn't change! That is why Socrates said, 'No evil can happen to a good man, either in life or after death.' That is why you read in the Book of Revelations these words spoken by a man who was terrified of death: 'And he laid his right hand upon me, saying unto me, Fear not.'

"Some people may say, 'You can't prove this.' Well, you can't prove it isn't so either, can you? On our side we have the weight of the deepest instincts of man and twenty centuries of the Gospel of the resurrection of Jesus Christ and all the logic and common sense in a world in which nothing, so the scientists tell us, is ever destroyed. Oh, yes, you can hold this faith. It isn't false. It is sound. Get it into your mind. Hold it and believe it, and you will find that it is true!"

When he preached such sermons to hushed congregations in the packed church, beautifully decorated at Easter with lilies flown from Bermuda, the atmosphere of reverence and spiritual unity was deeply impressive. An Elder of the church, Carl L. Cleaver, tried to put these intangibles into words.

"Sunday after Sunday," he wrote, "people gather in Marble Church. They are from everywhere and from every calling, those who have heard Dr. Peale for years and those who have never heard him. They are the fundamentalist and the liberal, the devout and the nonbeliever, the seeker after religion and the mocker, the curious and the indifferent. Why have they come? What do they learn?

"Long before the service begins, the church is filled. The congregation waits quietly, some with reverence, some with curiosity. A door opens to admit three ministers: Dr. Peale and two associates who take chairs on the raised pulpit-platform. Someone whispers to a stranger, 'The one in the middle is Dr. Peale.' The stillness becomes a quiet expectancy.

"A song is sung, the Bible read, then Dr. Peale rises to speak briefly before he begins his pastoral prayer. He talks about prayer and what it will do, about what should and should not be sought by prayer, about when and why and how to pray.

Then he prays. The prayer ends. Faces lift once more to the altar.

"Another hymn is sung. Now the sermon begins, and soon two thousand people are held in rapt attention, hearing a talk about everyday life and the part Jesus Christ has in it. The sermon will have humor to bring cheerfulness and laughter. It will have homely illustrations to show how people can learn to live the way Jesus taught.

"The sermon ends, and as the congregation leaves the church, fragments of conversation reveal the reasons why people fill to overflowing the Marble Church, and auditoriums where Dr. Peale speaks. A young girl whispers to a young man, 'Let's write and tell Mother we have found a church.' A middle-aged man says, to no one in particular, 'I should have heard him thirty years ago.' And a man who needs no identification: 'There's a preacher who's as big as Texas!' "

So the people came, and they listened, and the church grew.

The Peale family was growing, too. In 1936, John was born, a solemn-eyed baby who took his time about learning to talk. He maintained his sphinx-like silence for so long, in fact, that his worried parents finally consulted their old friend, Dr. Smiley Blanton. The verdict, which they awaited anxiously: John didn't talk because his sister did enough talking for two. "He's really being very sensible," Smiley assured them. "He figures he doesn't have to talk because Margaret says it all. Just separate them for a while, he'll talk soon enough." They did. It worked.

In the summers the Peales went to Long Island where Norman, never much of a swimmer, became such a formidable floater that he was occasionally mistaken for a buoy in Peconic Bay. In the winter they continued to live in their apartment near the church on lower Fifth Avenue.

As a rule they were too busy to have much time for strictly social affairs. But now and then they dined out with friends. On one such occasion where there were three or four couples, the cook became ill, so their hosts took them downtown and into what seemed to be a small, dimly lighted restaurant with subdued music and expensive decoration. "Well," cried Norman with his usual exuberance as they all sat down, "this is very nice! Ruth, we're a couple of old stick-in-the-muds. We ought to come to places like this more often!"

But Ruth was more observant than her husband, or perhaps less naive. "Norman," she whispered, nudging him fiercely in the ribs, "this is a *night club!*"

"Gosh," said the President of the National Temperance Society, looking furtively around as if he expected to find a committee of bishops spying on him. "Do you think we ought to leave?"

"That would embarrass our hosts," Ruth said calmly. "But you don't have to be quite so enthusiastic!"

Actually, the food was good and the entertainer turned out to be the singer Edith Piaf, who gave her usual polished and refined performance. Nothing occurred that was in the least offensive. Norman enjoyed the singing, and later on told the story in one of his sermons as a joke on himself, even citing Miss Piaf as an example of a person who accomplished much by using the full force of her personality in her job.

It was at about this time that his views on drinking brought him into controversy with Mrs. Roosevelt. The First Lady was quoted as saying that intelligent young ladies ought to find out what their capacity for drinking was, and then stay within it. Norman was shocked that a person in her position would condone drinking at all, and said so vehemently from the pulpit. The New York newspapers played it up to such an extent that finally, at the suggestion of a mutual friend, Norman went to call on Mrs. Roosevelt to see if in some manner oil might be poured on the troubled waters.

The meeting was not a great success. Mrs. Roosevelt had prepared a written statement, clarifying her position, but it still was too tolerant to suit Norman. The episode did little to improve his opinion of the Roosevelts or the effect he judged them to be having on the country's manners and morals.

He was also somewhat concerned, in those days, by the popular success of the ministry of Emmet Fox, whose sermons were attracting thousands in the metropolitan area. It seemed to Norman that Fox's message was not sufficiently Christ-centered, that what he was preaching was more psychology than theology. At one point, with Dr. John S. Bonnell, pastor of the Fifth Avenue Presbyterian Church, Norman actually hired a ballroom and tried to add "orthodoxy" to the Fox technique of reaching large numbers of people. It never occurred to him, at the time, that some fifteen years later he would be charged with identical sins of omission himself.

Congregations at the Marble Church continued to grow, but there were moments when all was not sweetness and light. A few of the old guard continued stubbornly to resist all innovations. Norman, for example, wanted to expand the choir from the quartet that had led the music for many years into a strong and dynamic choral group. He felt that quartets were out of date, and said so, forgetting that hell hath no fury like a soprano scorned. The resulting uproar would have been comic had there not been some people who took it with deadly seriousness. Poison pen letters flew around the congregation like swarms of angry bees. Norman learned, abruptly and to his sorrow, that small-town churches had no monopoly on spite and pettiness. Actually, only a few held with the soprano, but what they lacked in numbers they made up for in volume.

One night he got an urgent summons from the husband of the embattled soprano. Would he come right over, please? He did, and found the poor man pacing the floor in a state of distraction. "She's locked herself in there," he cried wildly, pointing at the bedroom door. "She won't come out! She says she'll never sing again!"

Repressing a strong desire to cheer, Norman knocked on the door, managed to calm the lady, persuaded her to retract her awful threat, and reunited her with her husband. As a result of this Christian conduct, naturally, the choir war went on more fiercely than ever.

Being anything, temperamentally, but a lion in the fray, Norman might have given up the struggle if it hadn't been for the support of various members of the congregation, notably Carl L. Cleaver and Milton Ketchum who, along with many others, were to give him loyal support through the years. He also had the backing of one Herbert B. Clarke, a small, imperturbable man who, as an adventurer and world traveler, had ridden camels across the Sahara and fought in two or three Latin American revolutions. "Don't let this get you down, Norman," Clarke said. "Matter of fact, this row is good for you. Healthiest thing in the world is a good fight—if you know you're on the right side. Stick with it, boy!"

Norman stuck, and eventually got his choir. He got an organist with a sense of humor, too. On one occasion, during a long and somewhat boring committee meeting in the nave of the church, Norman decided he would sneak out. He was tiptoeing quietly down the side aisle when the organ suddenly came to life. From his vantage point in the organ loft, where he could see everything, the organist was softly playing "Steal Away!"

The months went by, crowded and eventful. In 1936 Norman's old university, Ohio Wesleyan, conferred an honorary Doctorate of Divinity on him. In 1938 he received another from Duke University. In 1938 and 1939 he published his first two books: *The Art of Living* and *You Can Win*. They were slender little volumes, printed in rather small type, that met with only moderate success. The spiritual message was there, and the tone of optimism and buoyancy. But he had not mastered the use of the short, illustrative anecdote, his paragraphs tended to be long and sometimes diffuse, and he had not fully grasped the fact that a passage which sounded fine when spoken from a pulpit could sound sententious or even bombastic when fixed in cold type.

His feelings about New York continued to be curiously

mixed. A part of him was fascinated by it, responded eagerly to its competition and challenge. And another part—the rural Ohio part, no doubt—resented it, distrusted it, and at times did not hesitate to disparage it. This was the familiar Midwestern reaction. The belief of the true Ohioan in the superiority of his own culture was profound, but not so profound that it could not be shaken by the assurance and sophistication of the East. The result was a tendency to decry this sophistication.

Norman had his share of this defense mechanism. Basically, pretentious or socially conscious people rubbed him the wrong way. The origins of this feeling doubtless went back to the days in Bellefontaine when the eldest son of a rather impoverished minister had to mind his manners lest he offend the richer and more influential members of his father's congregation. Actually, it wasn't the people he disliked—it was the manner of life they represented.

Like every human being, he had other odd quirks, the origins of which were obscure. He had an almost compulsive passion for neatness. If a shirt had the smallest spot on it, he had to change it immediately. If a room was disorderly, he was unhappy. "Norman," said Ruth to a friend one day, "would really like to have a maid appear every time somebody stands up in our living room, and fluff up the cushions in the chair." He didn't like dim lighting arrangements, either, and unless sternly controlled would ruin Ruth's candlelight dinners by turning on a blaze of electricity. He became upset if he thought an insufficient quantity of food was being served. Once some unexpected guests dropped in and were invited to share a meal, the main course of which consisted of one undernourished duck. Watching Ruth divide the wretched bird into almost invisible portions, Norman died a thousand deaths. "Don't ever let that happen again," he moaned to Ruth when the guests were gone. "I like to have abundance around me. Abundance!"

The childhood survivals were very strong. Generous with

large sums of money, Norman could be niggardly with small ones. The analytical part of his mind recognized this. "I'm going to start giving bigger tips," he announced one day to a friend who was lunching in a restaurant with him. "This is a bad habit of mine and I'm going to change it. Besides, the more you give in this life, the more you get back. That's a spiritual law. We must share with others, and this is a good way to do so!"

No doubt he meant what he said. But when a spiritual law collides with a conditioned reflex, something has to give, and it is seldom the reflex. Anna Peale's lectures to her small boy on the need for constant economy had been more effective than she knew.

More and more Norman found himself leaving practical matters in Ruth's capable hands. The family finances, the church committees, the mechanics of moving his parents from Ohio to Clifford Peale's new church at Olean, New York—in such areas Ruth excelled. She was a capable home manager, too. Sometimes, perhaps, she overmanaged people a bit. On one occasion when the Peales were invited to an elaborate wedding reception, she made Bob and Norman dress up in cutaways despite their piteous protests. Then, in the taxicab, she coached them so diligently as to what to say and do that Norman finally exploded. "Stop this cab!" he cried, and leaping out, stalked along like an outraged floorwalker for several blocks before he could be persuaded to get back in. When they got to the reception, they found the father of the bride so wilted and harassed that it obviously made little difference how anybody looked or acted, and the whole thing turned into a family joke.

Actually, Ruth had just one purpose in life: to make it possible for Norman to reach as many people as possible with the message that Christ had come into the world to give them a more abundant life. Married to a man who had had to struggle to victory over worry, she had plenty of opportunity to observe the emotional waste and dissipation of energy that worry entailed. She knew that she could not banish all worry from her husband's mind. Indeed, she knew that he would no longer be himself if she did. But she saw no point in having him fret about the simple mechanics of living when clear-minded, practical, common sense efficiency could eliminate waste effort and save time for more productive activity. This ingredient, so conspicuously absent from the Peale make-up, she knew she could supply—and did.

One thing that troubled Norman during his early years at the Marble Church was the apathy toward religion displayed by men. In his own church, and in most congregations, women seemed to predominate. One night when he was scheduled to speak at a large gathering of young businessmen, a man was introduced to him. "Tell me, Dr. Peale," the man said, "exactly what is your formula for living?"

"My formula?" repeated Norman, somewhat startled. "Well, I suppose it's twofold: to find the secret of effective living for one's self, and then, having done so, to try to help others find their answer."

"And you have found that secret in religion, is that it?"

"Yes," said Norman. "That's exactly it. Christianity works— when it is worked. It has worked for me, and it will work for you—or for anyone who will let it."

"If that's true," said the man, "why aren't more of us businessmen aware of it and interested in it?" He hesitated, then answered his own question. "I'll tell you why. Because nobody tells us about it in language we can understand. We've quit going to church, most of us, because we've come to associate churches with boredom. And the church never comes to us. Why don't you fellows come down out of the pulpit once in a while and talk to us on our own level and in our own language at meetings like this one, or at business conventions? Outside the church, anyway! The message would be just as valid, wouldn't it? Why don't you go out and buttonhole us wherever we are? If what you have to offer is worth having, we'll listen. And maybe after a while we'll start going to church. But first you've got to play the game on our home grounds, not yours. If you want us in your churches, some of you have got to get out on the road and sell your product! You've got to be missionaries to businessmen!"

Sitting at the head table, Norman found he could not get this exhortation out of his mind. "It was amazing," he said to Ruth later. "It came over me with a tremendous sense of urgency and importance that this fellow was right, that we ought to come down out of the pulpit and go after this great reservoir of manpower waiting to be recruited for the church. While I sat there, waiting to be called on to speak, I found myself praying. I told the Lord that if He would guide me, I would do everything in my power to bring about a resurgence of dedication among the men of America to Christ and His church."

"How will you reach these businessmen?" Ruth asked doubtfully.

"I'll just go where they are," said Norman. "Somehow."

Shortly thereafter a lecture bureau wrote to him. They felt confident, they said, that they could obtain speaking engagements for him. They specialized, they added, in business and industrial conventions. Would he by any chance be available?

It was the beginning of an endless odyssey.

New fields of endeavor were opening up for Norman, but some old and cherished relationships were nearing an end. On a visit to Syracuse, he heard that Brother Andrews was far from well and probably would not live much longer. So he telephoned and asked permission to come and see him.

As darkness fell, he drove out into the country where the old man still lived all alone in his little white house. Nothing had changed since the memorable day when Brother Andrews had demonstrated so vividly to the hesitant young minister the power of thought to affect human actions. The road wound peacefully through the hills; the planks of the old covered bridge rattled like thunder as Norman drove across it. He came to the house and rapped on the door. Brother Andrews opened it, an old-fashioned kerosene lamp in his hand, his half-moon glasses still sliding down his nose, his craggy old face alight with pleasure. "Come in, come in, dear boy," he said, and kissed Norman on the cheek as if he had been a six-year-old coming home from school.

It was a visit that Norman never forgot. Later, he described it for his New York congregation. "We didn't talk about little things," he told them. "Brother Andrews was never one for small talk. We got the weather out of the way, and the next thing I knew he got out the old family Bible. Every line had something written beside it in his own handwriting. He read in a feeble voice, following the text carefully with his finger, and I don't know when I have heard such music and melody. When he had finished reading, he said, 'Let us pray.' I knelt down, as he did. He prayed for a long time, there on that thinly carpeted floor. I opened my eyes and looked at him. His face seemed transformed; a great light shone there.

"Then he began praying for me, and never was I lifted so tenderly to the throne of Divine Grace as in that prayer. It was no little prayer, such as people sometimes pray; it was the great prayer of a magnificent old Christian talking to his God in the midst of the eternal hills, in an old house with a kerosene lamp burning on the table! Then I said good-bye, and went back across the bridge, and as my car climbed the hill I could still see the little house and the dim light and my friend standing there. It was the last time I saw him in this life. But we shall meet again. I know this. I am sure of it."

His other great loss was his mother. She was not well in the summer of 1939, but no one suspected that the end was so near. Anna and Clifford were living in Canisteo, New York, and Ruth and Norman visited them often. On Friday, July 28, after an evening spent talking of happy memories, Norman took a train to the city, fully expecting to see his mother again. She died the next morning, at 8:30. Ruth and Clifford were with her. A Bible lay on the bed beside her, open to the 91st psalm: *He that dwelleth in the secret place of the most High shall abide under the shadow of the Almighty.*

When Ruth gave him the news by telephone, he went and sat alone in the pulpit of the Marble Church. He chose that place because his mother had often said to him, "Norman, every time you go into the pulpit, I will be with you." He knew how much she loved the old church. He thought he might be closest to her there.

He found it hard to grasp the fact that she was gone; she had always been so vital, so alive. A thousand memories came crowding in upon him. One in particular seemed to epitomize all the rest. It was just a small episode, of no great outward significance. His mother had been arriving for a visit; her train came in at Hoboken, on the Jersey side of the river. He had gone to meet her late on a dismal winter afternoon, foggy, cheerless, cold. Her health was not good even then, and he was afraid that the long journey would have left her exhausted. Not at all. She stepped off the train full of enthusiasm, delighted to see him, interested in everything. Not even the miserable weather could depress her. As the ferry groped its way across the fog-shrouded river, another boat passed them, lights gleaming dully. Its whistle bellowed hoarsely; then it was gone. And his mother said happily, "Oh, I wish I were a writer! I'd like to write a mystery novel that begins with two ferryboats passing each other in a fog!"

She kept it to the end, this sense of adventure, excitement, romance.

He left the pulpit finally and went into his office. There was a Bible on his desk. He put his hand on it, staring out of the window at the traffic on Fifth Avenue. As he did so, he had an experience so startling and inexplicable that nothing in his whole life matched it, before or afterwards. He felt, or seemed to feel, a pair of hands touch his head, gently, lovingly, unmistakably. The pressure lasted only for an instant; then it was gone.

Instantly, the rational part of his mind leaped up with a negation—it was an illusion, a hallucination caused by grief. But a deeper, instinctive part of him had no doubts at all: his mother had touched him, trying to comfort him, trying to let him know that all was well with her. Later, when he told the story in a magazine article, scores of people wrote to him describing similar experiences.

When he told Ruth of this, she did not seem surprised. "I know it's hard for you to believe this now," she said. "But as time goes on, you'll find that your mother is closer to you than ever."

He could not believe this, not at first; the sense of grief and loss was too strong. It persisted through the funeral service in Canisteo, and the long journey back to Lynchburg, Ohio. A year and a half later, still preaching out of his yesterdays, he told his congregation about it.

"The night before my mother's funeral," he said, "when all the others had retired, I felt I would like to be alone with her for a few moments. I went into the room where she lay, and gazed upon her face. Her hands were folded. My mother's hands were very beautiful, soft and graceful; I can feel their touch, and shall as long as life lasts.

"Very tenderly I put out my hand and touched hers. It was cold, like stone. I drew back and said, 'This is not my mother. What is this transformation? This is not my mother!' And there went through my heart a terror that struck to the center of my being, a terror and a horror of death.

"I went to my bedroom and walked to the window. Moonlight was bathing the hills in silvery radiance. I had always loved the moonlight, finding in it mystery and romance. But now it seemed cold and hateful, and the hills themselves seemed to mock, and the stars were sharp and bright, like points of hard steel. The whole universe seemed like a stone wall—cold, vast, utterly silent. It was death, death, everywhere the stark finality of death, and that night I slept a troubled sleep.

"The next morning, early, I went down into the garden. Dew was on the grass, birds were singing, the sky was blue, the world was bathed in sunshine. Life was speaking to me, and I found a measure of peace.

"But after a few weeks, as autumn came, I wanted to feel my mother's presence once again; I wanted to go where she sleeps in a little cemetery in southern Ohio. So I took the train, and as it rolled through the night I became impatient, as I used to be when I went home in happier times and eagerly awaited those breakfasts where we all laughed and talked at once in the spirit of family reunion.

"So I came back, and pushed open the gate of the old cemetery and stood by her grave. Then, all at once, I had one of those experiences that I shall treasure all my life, because suddenly, like a burst of light, it came to me; 'She isn't here. Why seek ye the living among the dead? She isn't here!' And I knew that she was not there in the grave, for I felt her with me, closer and dearer than ever. Something warm and peaceful, a deep joy, was in my heart.

"She is here with me this morning, in this church where her poor, imperfect son is preaching. Her simple faith is with me, and always will be, until that same transformation takes place in me, and then it will continue unimpaired in the land that is fairer than day. That is what the Bible tells us; it is what Christian experience teaches us; it is what our faith verifies.

" 'Because I live,' He said, 'ye shall live also.' Hold fast to that. Become as little children in your faith. Let your heart open to the Easter message! Why seek ye the living among the dead?"

CHAPTER XII

The Expanding Audience

❦

The year of Anna Peale's death saw the outbreak of war in Europe. Like most Americans, Norman felt nothing but contempt and loathing for Hitler; "this obscenity," he called the Nazi regime. As for Mussolini, he compared him to "an old buzzard sitting astride a fence, waiting to jump in on the winning side."

In the rise of Fascism, in the plunge of Europe into war, he saw the inevitable consequence of the spiritual anemia of the age. "The hatred in human society today," he said, "is a tragic commentary on our so-called Christian era. Never in my lifetime have I known the equal of this present situation of division and conflict. Two decades of spiritual indifference have brought us a kind of social sickness that no man seemingly is able to heal."

He was not referring only to the war in Europe; he also had in mind the unrest that gripped the United States. He had bitterly resented Roosevelt's plan to enlarge the Supreme Court. He was equally opposed to a third term for any Chief Executive, considering it a drastic and unnecessary change in the political traditions of the country. "If we don't settle this third-term issue now," he said prophetically, "in four years we'll be faced with the fourth-term issue. This may not be dictatorship, but why risk even an approach to it? No man is indispensable!"

When you command a large audience, you do not have to seek out people who share your views—they will come to you. And with them will come those whose views are more extreme than your own. Up in Rochester, New York, a newspaper publisher, Frank Gannett, had organized a group of citizens to fight the court-packing plan. The members of this Committee for Constitutional Government, as it was called, tended to be rich, influential, and violently anti-New Deal. When Norman's opposition to a third presidential term became known, he was offered the chairmanship of the Committee.

He accepted, partly because he had known Frank Gannett for years, partly because he was strongly anti-New Deal himself. In the depths of the Depression he had seen in it a deliberate and cynical attempt to exploit unemployment for political purposes. There were still men in the Administration, he felt, who would not hesitate to use the alleviation of human misery to buy votes. He was alarmed by the increase of what he called government-by-edict—rules and regulations issued from Washington without legislative sanction. Finally, he was convinced that, in its zeal to end the abuses of monopolistic capitalism, the country was running the risk of handing itself over to exploitation and domination by powerful and irresponsible labor unions, and he felt that the Administration was accelerating this trend by painting all conservatives—even the thoughtful ones—as fiends from Wall Street.

These were the sentiments of a good many people who never even heard of the Committee for Constitutional Government. Unfortunately for those on the Committee who might have been termed moderate conservatives, who wanted only a brake on what they considered runaway liberal policies, there were also members whose political views, judged by almost any standards, were several miles to the right of Louis XIV.

Against these ultra-conservatives, or reactionaries as they preferred to call them, the liberals and the New Dealers launched a furious attack. Just as the extremists in the Committee for Constitutional Government tended to regard all New Dealers as Socialists or Communists, so the more hot-headed liberals labeled all C.C.G. members Fascists. Tempers grew short and feelings ran high. There were threats of congressional investigations on the one hand and libel suits on the other. Controversy and discord seemed to be the mood of the nation as it moved steadily toward active participation in the war.

For a long time Norman stuck to his guns—and to the chairmanship of the C.C.G. "A minister," he said in 1940, "is a man before he is a minister, and a man or a minister who sees dangerous issues should raise his voice against them." This was a strong and perhaps courageous attitude for a man of the cloth. It was also a philosophy on which Norman was to reverse himself completely within a decade.

Eventually he did resign the chairmanship, but not before he had had the unpleasant experience of hearing the epithet "Fascist" applied to himself. It was a strange label for a man who had called Hitler a maniac, Mussolini a buzzard, and had supported the deal that sent fifty destroyers to Britain. But it hurt just the same. No doubt Norman might have avoided it if he had resigned sooner, but there was in him a stubborn Ohio streak that often made him not only disregard unsolicited advice, but do the exact opposite. "Who are these people," he roared in private to Ruth, "to tell me what organization I can join or not join? It's a free country, isn't it? I'm not going to let them scare me out of anything!"

To avoid being motivated by timidity he sometimes maintained positions from which his own common sense counseled him to withdraw.

In the summer of 1940 he had a pleasant interlude; he was

invited to Hollywood to act as technical adviser on a film called *One Foot in Heaven*, the story of a Protestant minister. He accepted with a few misgivings; he was not sure how a clergyman would fare in such surroundings. But he was pleasantly surprised. Vice was *not* rampant; sin was *not* supreme in the movie capital. "Why," he said in amazement, "you need a spyglass to see anyone in the streets after midnight!"

In a newspaper interview he listed the things about Hollywood that impressed him most. The intensity with which people worked from early morning until late at night. The friendliness of everyone. The fact that the "bad actors," the ones whose antics gained them national notoriety, were frowned on by the rest of the movie colony. The interest of the producers, not only in money making, but in promoting patriotism and strengthening the nation in any way they could. The ingenuity and resourcefulness of the technicians. And so on. He did complain that movies showed too many drinking scenes, and too many broken homes. But in general he felt that the industry was doing an excellent job of policing itself. Later, when a pair of right-wing Senators criticized Hollywood for being Jewish controlled, Norman rose up furiously to denounce their action as unfair and unchristian.

Back in his New York pulpit, he kept hammering away at social themes. By this time, some of his sermons were being taken down stenographically. On April 6, 1941, he stirred a congregation to the point of actual demonstration—most unusual in a staid Manhattan church.

"Take, for example," he said, "that which is uppermost in our minds today—the bitter conflict between Labor and Employer groups. There is a situation into which we have never taken religion, and it means our undoing, this division between those who own and manage, and those who labor. The record of owners and managers certainly is not clean. It has many dark spots. There was an epoch in this country when dividends were good and profits were good, but the position of labor was paltry, poor, and underprivileged. Labor toiled long hours under iniquitous working conditions. I have seen it. You know it.

"Then there began to be gains in the labor movement, and religion contributed to these gains because it was interested in justice to all men. There grew up a social awareness, and I believe that had it been let alone there would have developed an understanding cooperation on the part of both employer and worker, because in the last analysis they both grew out of the same background. They would have understood one another. But one of the most vicious things that ever happened in the life of the nation was when the Government of the United States itself drove a wedge between capital and labor, as if to say, all labor is good and all capital is bad. One they tried to show as white, and the other as black.

"Thus there grew up in our social life an intense hatred and prejudice. Suspicions and recriminations arose. Now, I have known laboring men all my life; not all of them are good. I have also known employers all my life; not all of them are devils. There are good men and bad men in both groups. In fact, most of the men in both groups are good men—decent, law-abiding, honest American citizens. But today there is hatred between them, and it is growing.

"Labor, which is coming into its own, in my opinion is being exploited, and this is highly dangerous. I realize there may be some people who feel that to discuss this is not the function of the pulpit. But what is the function of the pulpit? I believe this is a matter of deep spiritual concern, this hatred between men. We must say to labor, 'Be warned, lest you lose your gains by being exploited by subversive men whose concern is not labor's welfare, but whose aim is either communism or fascism.'

"How do they work? They despatch men into industry and foment trouble. They make trouble not for the interests of the workers, but in order that the social life of a great nation will be disrupted. There are boys from this very congregation who have gone into Army camps at $21 a month, leaving good jobs and good pay and future homes. They cannot strike. But workers in industries can strike. The right to strike is not to be abridged, but the wages of workers in defense industries must be adjusted by some kind of adjudication. It seems to me that if the United States Government can control one group of men at $21 a month, not allowing them to strike, it ought to exercise authority on the leaders of labor, saying to them, 'If your grievances are real, you will have every fair consideration, we will have them weighed by thoughtful, impartial Boards of Adjustment, but you must not strike, you cannot strike against the United States of America!"

The congregation burst into applause.

"Don't applaud," he said, almost sadly. "This is no place for it. But if ever there was a time when we needed the application of religion to public affairs, it is now. There used to be a time when we stood in the pulpit and said, 'Please be religious.' That is no more. We have *got* to be religious, or it is the end of our society."

The war came. For a while Norman wanted to join the armed forces as a chaplain. His friends and family talked him out of it. His object was to be with the men in uniform, wasn't it? To help them all he could? Well, his church was already flooded with men in uniform. He would have contact with far more of them if he stayed where he was than if he followed his personal desires. He could not refute the argument. It was true.

His attitude toward the war was formulated instantly, and did not change. "We can't have international barbarism in the world," he said, "and it is necessary that we strike it down. But after we have done so, and while we are doing so, we shall love these enemies of ours. We'll love them, finally, back into the family of nations for the redemption of the world."

He was so busy and so preoccupied in the first weeks of the war that he was baffled one day when a lady came up to him after the service and offered her congratulations.

"Thank you," said Norman. "But what for?"

"Why," said the lady, "your happy news!"

"Happy news?" echoed Norman, mystified. "What happy news?"

The woman turned and fled. Ruth finally had to enlighten her unobservant husband. She was almost five months pregnant.

The baby was born July 22nd in Olean, under the medical auspices of Brother Bob. Ruth took the whole thing very casually. On the final afternoon she had some ironing to do, and she did it—while Norman gnawed his fingers in the background. Then she decided she had better go to the hairdresser. At five-thirty, with hair resplendent, she finally went to the hospital, and at seven-thirty, with a minimum of fuss and bother, Miss Elizabeth Peale made her appearance. The Peale family circle was complete.

During the war Norman continued to preach sermons that would have surprised his critics of later years. There were times when he seemed to be against more things than he was for. He attacked obscenity in current best sellers and on the New York stage. Though he was an admirer of Wendell Willkie, he took him to task for publicly using the word "damn." He objected to the proposed $25,000 ceiling on income on the grounds that it was an invasion of individual rights. He opposed, vainly, the induction of women into the Armed Forces. "It's not going to serve this country well," he said, "to stimulate the process of masculinizing women. Today an astounding number of women can drink and swear with any man. To enroll them in the Army isn't going to make them sweet and demure by any means. If women want to volunteer for factory and office work and air raid duty, that is fine, but let's have no drafting of women. It smacks of European regimentation."

The Catholic Bishop of Army Chaplains agreed with him, but the country as a whole didn't. The WACs and WAVEs proceeded to prove, that women could wear uniforms and still remain reasonably feminine.

Dan Poling went overseas as an Army chaplain. When he returned, Norman asked him to preach in the Marble Church.

Poling shook his head. "I'd better not, Norman," he said. "I know how you feel about Roosevelt. I've objected to some of his domestic policies myself, but since I've been in North Africa I've changed. I think he's a great war leader, and if I get up in your pulpit I'm likely to say so."

"Go ahead," said Norman to his old friend. "There's been free speech in that pulpit for three hundred years. We're not going to change now. Get up there and say anything you like."

There was a deep affection between Norman and Dan Poling. Whenever Norman needed support or encouragement, Dan came to his defense like an older brother. Years later, when the overflow crowds forced Norman to preach twice on Sunday mornings, he persuaded Dan to return to his old pulpit as Sunday night preacher.

The Peales spent the summer of 1943 at Pawling, New York, on the estate owned by their friend Lowell Thomas. They liked the little town, near enough to New York to be accessible, far enough away to be real country. While vacationing there, they heard of a small farm for sale on Quaker Hill where Thomas had such neighbors as Governor Dewey and Edward R. Murrow. They decided to go and look at it.

In all their years together, Ruth and Norman had never had a home of their own, a place where the children could put down roots. Ruth was enchanted by the old eighteenth century farmhouse, the great maples, the view across the valley. Norman wasn't so sure. The house seemed enormous; they might rattle around like dice in a box, he said. The big barn on the next piece of property cut off some of the view. Besides, the place with its twenty acres cost $25,000, and they didn't have $25,000. They didn't even have $5,000.

"We could borrow it," Ruth suggested.

The aversion to debt his mother had taught her sons was manifest in Norman. "How would we ever pay it back?"

"You can go out and give lectures," Ruth said promptly, "until it's paid back."

"Well," said Norman, "you had better forget about it, because I'm all against it."

"Yes, dear," Ruth said docilely.

They bought it the following January—with a mortgage plus $10,000 borrowed from a friend.

From the start they were delighted with it. They named it Sugar Tree Farm in memory of Sugar Tree Ridge, the little Ohio village to which Clifford Peale had taken his bride, half a century before. Norman went around extolling the hidden virtues of the barn that he once had thought such a disaster. "Finest hand-hewn beams in the whole state," he would say proudly—a bit of information that had been artfully dropped into his ear, at Ruth's request, by Lowell Thomas. A local farmer named Rockwell applied for—and got—the job of looking after the place. He was a salty soul who did not hesitate to speak his mind. "You stick to the preaching, Doctor," he said to Norman. "I'll tend to the farming." Rockwell was with them for years as farmer and friend.

This arrangement suited the new squire fine. He enjoyed eating the turkeys that Rockwell raised, and the vegetables that Ruth put up in endless frozen packages. But he was happier with a pencil in his hand than a rake or a hoe.

He liked to walk around the place with Elizabeth riding on his shoulders. From the start he had felt an almost mystical attachment to the little golden-haired, blue-eyed child. Once, just for fun, he tossed her onto an enormous pile of fallen maple leaves raked together for burning. Elizabeth promptly disappeared altogether. "Ruth, Ruth!" yelled Norman in a panic, burrowing frantically after his vanished child. He found her at the bottom, convinced it was part of the game and not at all frightened. But Norman was a wreck. "What if she had smothered?" he groaned.

By this time Margaret and John were ten and eight respectively. They were lively youngsters who got into their share of mischief. Once they were haled before their mother in disgrace for dropping water bombs from the apartment windows on unsuspecting pedestrians. "How could you do such a thing?" Ruth demanded sternly. "Don't you realize your father is a minister?"

"No, no, no!" cried Norman, anguished memories of his own childhood flashing before his eyes. "Scold them all you like, punish them, anything! But don't ever, ever say that!"

He spent as much time with the children as he could, playing games, making up stories with imaginary characters. One favorite was a faintly sinister type known as Jake the Snake. There was also a magical trio named Larry, Harry and Parry who kept airplanes in their pockets. They blew them up like balloons whenever they wanted to go anywhere, and every night at supper Norman had to concoct another chapter in the endless journeyings of Larry, Harry and Parry.

But the pressure of work was relentless, and Ruth was becoming almost as busy as Norman. Within her own denomination she was President of the Women's Board of Domestic Missions. She was also President of the Home Missions Council of North America, the first woman to hold the post. She was Treasurer of the United Church Women. "Well," said ten-year-old Margaret resignedly at breakfast one morning, "which board is meeting today?" As for John, there was so much talk of boards around the house that he was convinced his mother worked in a lumber yard.

When the war finally ended, Norman was optimistic about the future. The suffering and sorrow and separation, he felt, had reawakened people's interest in religion. The apathy and indifference of the 'Twenties and the 'Thirties were gone, he was sure of it. "We're on the brink of something big," he told Ruth. "A real religious revival, perhaps. We've got to do everything we can do to help it along. We need new ideas—big ideas!"

One such idea grew out of conversations he had had with a friend, Raymond Thornburg. Thornburg was a Pawling businessman. In the business world there were many weekly or monthly newsletters purporting to give subscribers inside information on industrial trends or forthcoming legislation. Why not, they asked themselves, put out a sort of spiritual newsletter for businessmen or factory workers with simple, down-to-earth stories of religious faith in action?

Such a periodical, they felt, might accomplish several things. It might help to break down some of the barriers that still existed between the church and the business world. It could remind people that the United States was one of the first countries to begin its existence on a religious premise, and that everyone's personal freedom was based ultimately on the concept of God as the head of the State. Being nonsectarian, such a "newsletter" might also tend to harmonize religious diversities and reduce friction between Catholic, Protestant, and Jew. It could utilize the old proven testimonial technique, encouraging ordinary, everyday people who had found a firm faith to stand up and be counted. Well-known personalities might be persuaded to tell how, through the application of religion, they had learned to live victoriously. Finally, it would serve as a medium for bringing to people Norman's faith in Christianity as a practical method for solving life's problems.

When they tried out the idea on various friends, they got a mixed reaction. It was a worthy notion, everyone agreed. But wouldn't the material have a deadly monotony? Wouldn't the people be reluctant to discuss anything as personal as the part religion played in their lives? Besides, if there was to be no advertising, where would the operating expenses come from?

Nobody had any final answers, but the businessman and the minister decided to go ahead anyway. They asked for—and got—a few contributions, rented a room above the First National Grocery Store in Pawling, hired a two-man staff that consisted of a jobless ex-Air Force flier named Leonard Le-Sourd and Fred Decker, a young advertising man, and went blithely into the publishing business.

Few experiences ever got off to a worse start. Everyone was totally inexperienced. The first *Guideposts*, as they named the new venture, consisted of four four-page leaflets that weren't even stapled. They flew apart when opened, and the magazine's creators actually thought this was a good idea, because they figured its message would thus be disseminated farther. The writing was often primitive. Design and layout were poor. Mailing procedures were chaotic.

People tried to help. Lowell Thomas lent them an empty house to use as headquarters. Fulton Oursler, Senior Editor of *Reader's Digest*, gave advice and encouragement. Grace Oursler, Fulton's wife, agreed to serve in an editorial capacity. Le-Sourd began grimly teaching himself the rudiments of editing. But on a cold winter night in January, 1947, the ancient furnace in the borrowed house started a fire. By morning there was nothing but a pile of ashes. Everything, including the only list of subscribers and their addresses, was gone.

There was every reason to abandon the whole project, but in a curious way the crisis seemed to galvanize everyone. Norman felt strongly that a publication that preached faith and prayer and courage now had a chance to demonstrate all three. "Actually," LeSourd said later, "that fire was a godsend! It burned up most of our mistakes."

Lowell Thomas devoted part of his radio program to describing the disaster and asking old subscribers to send in their names and addresses. DeWitt Wallace, a firm friend of the fledgling publication, had his *Reader's Digest* carry the story, with a similar appeal. As a direct result of the fire, *Guideposts* received more and better publicity than it ever dreamed of. Instead of having no subscribers, it shortly had more than it had had before.

The financial problems, however, remained. By early spring, the situation was critical. The magazine was $32,000 in debt, and the printer was refusing—not unreasonably—to print the June issue. Norman had virtually exhausted the patience and generosity of his friends. In desperation, LeSourd went to see a lady whom he did not know but who, he heard, was sometimes willing to support worthy causes.

Teresa Durlach turned out to be white-haired, serene, and a firm believer in divine guidance. One could obtain this guidance, she said, by asking for it, then by taking paper and pencil and writing down whatever came into one's head. Interested in what LeSourd told her about *Guideposts*, she asked if she might be introduced to the key people in the enterprise. As a result, a meeting was arranged on the veranda of Sugar Tree Farm. Present were the Peales, the Thornburgs, Len LeSourd, Grace Oursler, one or two others—and Tessie Durlach.

"First," said Mrs. Durlach, looking around the circle of faces, "I'd like to know if there is peace and harmony in your organization."

Norman and LeSourd exchanged glances; they were all close friends, but Grace Oursler and Thornburg could and did on occasion needle each other a bit.

"Well," said Norman cautiously, "I think you could certainly say we're all working toward a common objective."

"All right," said Mrs. Durlach. "Now let's have guidance."

Her technique was explained. Pads and pencils were brought. Everybody wrote for some minutes in silence.

"Now," said Mrs. Durlach, "each of you read aloud what you've written down, just as it came into your heads."

What had come into the heads of almost everyone, it seemed, was a dismal list of problems. Lack of money. Lack of subscribers. Lack of skilled personnel. Need for this. Need for that.

When all had finished, Tessie looked around the circle again. "If your thinking is as negative as all that," she asked, "why should I invest any money in *Guideposts*? If you have so little faith in your own future, why should I have any?"

No one could think of anything to say.

"The trouble with you people," Tessie went on, "is that you're thinking *lack*. Your minds are saturated with negative thoughts. Therefore everything you do turns out negatively."

Norman sat up straight. "Brother Andrews!" he said.

"I beg your pardon?" asked Tessie politely.

"Nothing, nothing," said Norman hastily. "I mean, Mrs. Durlach, you're absolutely right! What we need to do is think in terms of solutions, not in terms of problems."

"Exactly," said Mrs. Durlach. "You say you want subscribers. How many do you want—100,000? All right, believe you are getting them! Give thanks for them! Visualize them! And you'll have them!"

"Of course!" cried Norman. "I can see 'em right now, over there!" He pointed out at the sunlit valley. "A hundred thousand! I can see 'em." He looked eagerly at Thornburg. "Can't you, Raymond?"

"Well," said Thornburg, feebly, "I . . ."

"Sure you can!" Norman went on, carried away by his own enthusiasm. "We all can. We need a new approach. We've got to stop begging for charity and handouts. We've got to get some business loans—put this whole thing on a sound financial basis. We ought to ask some big companies to take it for their employees. People need the message we're trying to give. They want it. They'll go for it if we give them half a chance!

Mrs. Durlach, whether you give us any money for *Guideposts* or not, we'll always be indebted to you. This is the turning point, right here and now!"

Strangely enough, it was. Mrs. Durlach did make a financial contribution, but that was not the important thing. The important thing was the changed attitude she left behind her. The little group reorganized their finances. They eliminated waste. They paid off debts. The 100,000 subscribers ceased being a dream and became a reality. Then another 100,000 were added, and another, and another. The magazine remained physically small; readers seemed to like it that way. But the subscription list kept growing. The calibre of the writing and the art-work steadily improved. Within a decade it was self-supporting with more than 800,000 subscribers. It was, and still is, a publishing phenomenon.

During this period, Norman had been working painfully and laboriously on a book. At the church, the religio-psychiatric clinic was expanding steadily. Hundreds of cases were being handled, and there were long waiting lists. Already Smiley Blanton had had to bring in several additional psychiatrists and psychologists in an effort to keep up with the demand.

From the start, results obtained from this combination of therapies had been spectacular, and in 1940 Norman and his psychiatrist friend had described some of the cases in a book called *Faith is the Answer*. But the book had not reached a very large audience, and Norman felt the need of a new effort that would summarize all he had learned about the interrelationship of fear, worry, guilt, tension, ill-health and the therapeutic effects of applied religion.

He wanted to set it down so clearly and simply that any reader could apply the basic principles to problems and difficulties in his own life. Ideally, he knew, people in emotional trouble needed the personal guidance and supervision of qualified experts, both medical and religious. But only a fraction of those who needed assistance could ever get it under such circumstances. For the vast majority, the power of religion was the most available remedy. Norman had seen that power in action. He believed that, with a little direction, great numbers of people could learn to avail themselves of it.

Norman's interest in methods of teaching people about the benefits of applied religion went back a long way. He had never forgotten an incident in Syracuse where one of his congregation had left the Methodist church and turned to Christian Science. He knew the man to be both sincere and intelligent, no emotional weathervane, and so he went to see him and asked him to explain his decision. "Something must have been lacking in my ministry," he said. "I'd consider it a great favor if you'd tell me frankly what it was."

And the man had told him. "It has nothing to do with you personally, Norman," he said. "It's just that religion as preached in most Protestant churches is too vague. There's nothing for a practical person to get hold of. I go to church, and I'm told to have faith, for instance. But nobody ever tells me *how* to have faith. I'm told to be good, and pray, and trust God. But nobody tells me *how* to go about these things. In Christian Science I get a blueprint that I can follow—simple, specific, practical. I like that. I'm going to stick with it."

"But our church is practical," Norman protested. "The blueprints are there!"

The man shook his head. "Maybe they are," he said, "but they've become obscure. You've been using the same words for so long that they've lost their meaning. They have no handles on them any more. Go and sit in a few pews in churches around this town and you'll see what I mean. All you'll hear is a kind of antiquated jargon delivered in a sanctimonious tone. I really think a lot of preachers are just trying to impress other preachers with their sermons. They certainly have little or no meaning for the people in the congregation. I'm sorry, Norman—but I'm not coming back."

The episode made a deep impression on Norman. "You

know," he said to Ruth, "I hate to admit it, but a lot of what that fellow said was justified. We've got to revise our approach, or we'll lose more members. We'll certainly never reach the vast, untouched public. The message we're trying to give is sound, it's valid, it's right. But we need to find new words, new techniques. It's not enough to exhort people to love their enemies, or to go to church. We need to tell them specifically how to overcome hatred, or how to get the most out of a church service. Simple steps. One-two-three. A-B-C."

"Can you," said Ruth, "really reduce Christianity to A-B-C?"

"Not all of it, certainly. But it's like learning to read. You have to master the alphabet first. That calls for simplification and repetition. Endless, endless repetition."

He found himself saying much the same thing in the introduction of the book he was trying to write. "The principles of happiness and success," he wrote, "to be presented in this book are not new. They were not created by the author, but are as old as the Bible. In fact, they are the simple principles taught in the Bible. If the present technique possesses any uniqueness, it lies in the effort to show *how* to use these principles in a practical and understanding manner suited to modern man.

"The book may seem repetitious at times. That is because it is the textbook of a formula. It hammers on one basic procedure, and repetition is the master of studies, as the classic saying goes. Reiteration is essential in persuading the reader to practice; to try and try again. . . ."

Writing a brief introduction was not difficult; organizing a thousand fragmentary ideas into a unified theme was something else again. Over the garage at Pawling there was a room with a ping-pong table. Len LeSourd found Norman there one day with his head in his hands and the manuscript scattered all over the big green table. "It's no use," the minister groaned. "I may be a preacher, but I'm no writer. Never again!"

"Who's going to publish it?" asked LeSourd cheerfully.

"I don't know," said Norman. "Nobody, probably. No publisher in his right mind would touch it."

At one point he grew so disgusted that he threw the whole manuscript in the wastebasket. Ruth rescued it and gave it to her father-in-law to read. By this time Clifford Peale had retired and was living at a club in New York. Kenneth Giniger, a fellow-member of the club who worked in a publishing house, agreed to read the manuscript. He carried it off to his office, and there it stayed. Weeks went by. No reaction came from the publisher at all.

"You see," said Norman to Ruth in gloomy triumph. "I told you it was no good!"

Ruth did not agree; her faith in Norman and his message remained unshaken. Recently the responsibility for having her husband's sermons printed and distributed had fallen to her. In 1945 the list had contained fewer than a thousand names. By 1946 the number had risen to some 2700. By 1948 it was over seventeen thousand, and shooting upward at a tremendous rate. The printing and mailing were financed by voluntary contributions from those who received the sermons; the average gift was two dollars a year, with perhaps one-half of the recipients making donations. The whole venture, known as Sermon Publications, was—like *Guideposts*—more often in the red than in the black. But from the mail that came in Ruth knew how loyal these people were to her husband and the message he was trying to give. "It's a good book, Norman," she kept saying. "Sooner or later, somebody is going to realize it."

She was right. Her dejected husband wrote and asked for the return of the manuscript. But by this time the publishers had made up their minds. Contracts and suggestions for revision were placed before the astonished Norman. Before he knew quite what had happened, the book was on the presses.

They called it *A Guide to Confident Living*. In the next four years it was to go through twenty-five printings.

It was a supremely readable book. It spoke out with all the crispness and authority that Norman had in the pulpit. The message was the same one that he had been preaching for years, but now the illustrations were sharper, the psychological insights were clearer, and the practical how-to-do-it aspects were plainer.

The message was simply that Christianity worked. That it wasn't vague or impractical. That it was a specific set of principles which, if mastered, would give the individual great power over his thoughts and emotions, and hence over his environment. Religion, the book told its readers, was a system of spiritual and mental discipline. If a person would avoid wrong-doing, if he would consciously exclude hatred, resentment, malice, fear, and worry from his mind, if he would believe in the reality and goodness of God, submit to His will, and surrender his life to Jesus Christ, then an inner peace would come to him that would greatly aid in the solution of all problems.

The appeal to self-interest was strong, and some of the promises made were large. But no larger, certainly, than some of the staggering statements in the four Gospels. "If ye have faith," the Master had said, "nothing shall be impossible unto you." Norman believed that He meant exactly what He said, literally, factually, and completely. "The basic secret of the Christian religion," he wrote, "is not effort, or will power. The secret of Christianity is faith."

Faith, the book said over and over, was the contact point between the finite individual and the infinite power of God. Weak people, with little faith in themselves, could become strong people if they would put their lives in God's hands. Norman could write about this with total sincerity; he had experienced it himself.

He was astonished and gratified when the book jumped onto

the best seller list. It meant that at last he was reaching great masses of people with the message of a dynamic and creative faith. This was thrilling to him; he considered it his mission in life. In addition, the success of the book meant that he and Ruth would be able to travel in the summers to places they had always wanted to visit, and that the children would be able to go to better schools.

It meant other things, too, which he did not foresee at the time. Perhaps this was just as well—fame brings mixed blessings. Ahead lay some complicated years.

CHAPTER XIII

"Trust in God —

and the Realizable Wish!"

❦

The success of the book increased the family income, but it also increased the family pressure and expense. The volume of Norman's mail—already large—jumped enormously. Requests poured in for magazine articles, for speeches, for additional radio broadcasts.

Strangers called him up on the telephone at any and all hours to drop their personal problems in his lap. He loved to tell—on himself—the story of the gruff old tycoon who called him long distance from Chicago. "Are we together?" demanded this character without preamble.

"Why, yes," Norman said. "At least, this phone is connecting us. Why do you ask?"

"Because you said in your book that if two or more people got together and prayed about a problem, they'd get results. I've got a business problem, and I need results. I need 'em right away!"

"Well," said Norman, "I'll be glad to pray with you right

over the phone. And I think we'll get results. But I can't guarantee what they'll be."

So he did pray, and the man listened, thanked him, and hung up.

Two or three weeks went by without further word, so at last Norman called the man back. "How are things going now?" he asked.

"Fine, fine," was the cheery reply. "Couldn't be better. That prayer business works, all right. I've been using it ever since."

"Why didn't you let me know?" Norman asked. "Why didn't you keep in touch?"

"Why should I?" boomed the tycoon with shattering sincerity. "I don't need *you* any more."

But increasing numbers of people did continue to need Norman, or at least the message he brought them. Their demands on his time and energy mounted steadily. Up to a point, both halves of the Peale team welcomed this increased tempo of living. There was in Ruth a deep-rooted missionary instinct. As for Norman, he had never forgotten the banner he had seen as a young man in Columbus, the banner stretched across Memorial Hall with its stupendous challenge: *The Evangelization of the World for Jesus Christ in this Generation.* He had little patience with those who deplored bigness in religion, who felt that numbers did not count. If the world was to be gained for Christianity, vast numbers of people would have to be reached. He wanted to reach as many as he could. "I have no doubt," he said, "that St. Paul would gladly have used television, if it had been available to him."

Consequently he did not hesitate to take advantage of some of the new platforms that were offered him. In one national magazine he made a plea for religious unity. Sectarianism, he said, was needlessly separating people who held the same ideals and were worshipping the same God. "Their present disunity," he wrote, "is often so ridiculous that it would be funny if it were not so tragic. Not one modern

Protestant out of fifty could tell you in what doctrinal respects Methodists differ from Baptists, or Presbyterians from Congregationalists. What keeps them apart are not well-reasoned convictions on doctrine, but vested interests, false sentiment about sticks and stones, social stratification, and mere apathy!"

Magazines were only one outlet. The success of the book had also been noticed by the newspaper world. "Stuffy" Walters, city editor of the *Chicago Daily News,* serialized it in the front page of the great Midwestern paper. It was the first time a major newspaper had so used a religious book. Walters found that it was a circulation builder. Roger Ferger, publisher of the *Cincinnati Enquirer* and an old friend, suggested to Norman that he write a weekly column and try to have it syndicated nationally. Editorial response was good, and soon, under the title "Confident Living," the column was appearing in newspapers all over the country. It was handled by the Hall Syndicate of New York. The old reporter of the *Findlay Morning Republican* and the *Detroit Journal* had ink on his fingers again.

The reaction of the Peale children to the increasing glare of publicity was not always favorable. At one point they began to manifest a strong disinclination to go to church. It turned out that it wasn't going to church that bothered them, it was sitting in the minister's family pew. "Because if we do, you see," Elizabeth explained glumly, "everybody knows that man up in the pulpit is our father!"

Ruth got around this dilemma by letting the children sit wherever they chose. Elizabeth promptly selected a perch in the balcony just above her father where she could beam encouragingly at him. She soon learned, also, to go back to Norman's office after each sermon and praise him lavishly. Her father was aware that her enthusiasm was sometimes a bit contrived, but he drew warmth and reassurance from it all the same.

It was at about this time that the first Negro applied for membership in the Marble Church. Norman's reaction was entirely favorable; his religion had taught him that all men were sons of God and therefore brothers, regardless of the color of their skins. Nevertheless, he felt obliged to bring the matter to the attention of the church board.

When the request was presented, there was a moment of silence. Then one of the businessmen-elders spoke up. "Hell!" he said forthrightly. "It's a Christian church, isn't it?" There was no further discussion. The application was accepted. Within a few years a dozen or more Negroes joined the congregation. Many now attend services regularly.

Sometime thereafter Norman read that the head of the Pullman Porters' Union had stated bitterly that segregation invariably was practiced in Fifth Avenue churches. He wrote to the man, assuring him that this was not so and inviting him to come and see for himself. He never had a reply.

Back of Norman as preacher at the Marble Church was one of the best organized church staffs in America. He called it "the team," and it operated year after year with a minimum of friction and a maximum of happy efficiency. Though not a particularly good organizer himself, Norman knew people, and he managed to draw around him a loyal, dedicated, and resourceful group. But there was more to it than that. As a wise observer once commented, "The secret of Marble Collegiate Church is not hard to find: Christ is at its center, and its purpose is to help people change lives."

As the pace of Norman's life quickened, there was little time for leisure, but now and then there would be family reunions at Sugar Tree Farm. Nothing pleased old Clifford Peale more than to sit on the broad veranda with his three sons and talk the sun down the sky. Bob was solidly established in Olean, now, with a growing practice. He was always a bit on the defensive where religion was concerned, being hemmed in on three sides by clergymen. But it was Bob, just the same, who looked down from an airliner one night and said to his brother, "Norman, did you ever stop to think that at the heart of every American town is a cross—a cross made by the lights where the two main streets intersect?"

Leonard had his church in Buffalo. He still had more than his share of the shyness and self-distrust that were part of the Peale heritage. But he had a lot of insight, and little self-deception. Somebody once congratulated him on the modesty that seemed to be a family characteristic. "Thanks," said Leonard, "but you know, where we Peales are concerned it's hard to say what's modesty and what's really egotism cloaked with humility." He also had a wry awareness of the importance of the distaff members of the family. "We Peales know what we want, all right," he said once. "But we like to have our wives make our decisions for us. Then if things go wrong, you see, we can pretend it's not our fault!"

The increased demands on his time did not dismay Norman unduly. Idleness had always bored him; he much preferred the satisfactions that came from deadlines met or tasks accomplished. His working methods were not highly organized; his pockets were always stuffed with scrawled memoranda that he had written to himself. But he was not afraid of endless hours of pencil pushing. And behind the scenes there was always Ruth, arranging for secretarial help, planning transportation, seeing that the house ran smoothly.

Sometimes Ruth would hand him a job. When John was entered in Deerfield Academy and his parents took him up to the school to enroll him, she broached a delicate subject. "Have you talked to John?" she asked Norman. "I mean . . . now that he's leaving home don't you think there are things he ought to know?"

"I suppose so," said Norman uncomfortably.

"Well, you're his father," said Ruth. "I think you ought to have a talk with him."

Norman avoided the issue as long as he could, but Ruth was adamant. "Norman," she said finally, "we're leaving in a few minutes. You've *got* to talk to John. It's your duty!"

With a haunted look, Norman drew his son aside but in about thirty seconds he reappeared. "It's all right," he told Ruth happily. "Come on; let's go!"

What John had said was brief and to the point. "I've got it all under control, Dad. Skip it!"

One problem that not even Ruth could solve was posed by the mail. Each week the letters came in by the hundreds; later they were to come literally by the thousands. Screening them, trying to classify and answer them was an endless struggle.

But it was heartening to read them, all the same. Through the great majority ran a thread of pure joy and gratitude; joy at the discovery of a religion that was understandable and geared to human needs; gratitude for being told how to use it in everyday living.

"It's the simplicity of the message that appeals to them," Norman said to Ruth. "Grove Patterson was right: most great ideas are simple—or can be put simply."

The letters came from rich and poor, young and old, colored and white, Catholic, Protestant, and Jew. They were written on every kind of stationery: business, social, pages torn out of a five-cent tablet. They were phrased in every sort of language, from the scholarly to the semi-literate. They were a cross-section of America: worries, hopes, heartaches, laughter, tears, great faith, little faith, everything.

Many of the personal problems tended to fall into recognizable categories, and in an effort to give capsule advice to the maximum number of people Norman wrote out a series of "How to" cards: "How to Meet Sorrow," "How to Forgive," "How to Say Your Prayers," and so on. Each card contained ten "rules" or specific suggestions, some based on religious, some on psychological principles. Like the printed sermons, they were offered through Sermon Publications on a voluntary contribution basis.

Some of Norman's fellow clerics felt that this was carrying simplification too far. And not all of his readers were helped. "I've done everything you've suggested," wrote one girl from Texas, "and tried to connect my life to God's dynamo. Nothing happens. I guess I must be on A.C. and God on D.C."

But for every correspondent who claimed that nothing happened, there were a thousand who maintained that something did.

On his lecture trips, on trains, on planes, he was constantly meeting strangers who, when they learned his identity, hopefully handed him their problems. Often he was able to help them. A man he happened to sit beside at a New Orleans lunch counter confessed that his life was miserable because he was involved in an extramarital affair with a woman in Baton Rouge. The woman, he said, was threatening to tell his wife if he tried to break off the relationship. Norman asked for the woman's telephone number, called her up, and talked to her so sternly that she agreed to let the unhappy Don Juan go.

Probably the most unexpected remark Norman ever encountered came from a man who asked to be introduced to him. "Oh, Dr. Peale," said the man, "I'm so glad to meet you. It gives me the chance to tell you how happy I've been since I lost Christ!"

"Since you *what?*" asked Norman, amazed.

"Since I lost Christ," the man repeated cheerily. "Since I got rid of my religion. It always made me miserable, but now that I've shaken it off, I'm as happy as can be!"

This, naturally, was a challenge that Norman could not resist. He asked for the whole story, found that the man had had a father who believed, literally, in a God of wrath. So awful were the threats and visions of judgment held up before the impressionable child that he lived in constant terror of divine anger and retribution. It wasn't until the father died that the son was able to bring a measure of peace into his mind by rejecting religion altogether.

Once he understood the background, it was not difficult for Norman to introduce the man to the concept of a God of love, and reawaken a spark of interest in spiritual things.

On another occasion, when he was delivering a commencement address at a midwestern college, he told the story of a boy who overcame the effects of polio and by sheer determination became a champion high jumper. In the audience was a woman in a wheelchair, a hypochondriac full of self-pity and paralyzing fears. When the speech was over, her sons started to lift her from the chair in order to carry her down a flight of stairs. "No," she said, "put me down. If that boy could do what he did, I can walk down these stairs." And she walked down, unaided.

This sort of thing happened all the time. Years later, in Rome, a stranger came up to Norman and paid him what he considered his finest compliment. "Dr. Peale," she said, "I just want to thank you—thank you for helping so many of us simple people over the rough spots of life."

His greatest personal satisfaction came from capturing—or recapturing—some errant soul for the church. Sometimes this missionary zeal had unexpected results. On one occasion Norman became acquainted with a man whose chief passion in life was horses and horseracing. His house was full of trophies. There were handsome paintings of thoroughbreds on all the walls. Even the dining room was full of pictures of horses —eating, naturally.

Despite his racetrack proclivities, this gentleman became so interested in religion that he finally asked if he might help conduct a service. Touched by this show of devotion, Norman consented, briefed him carefully on his duties, and told him he could participate the following Sunday.

All went well until, near the end of the service, the eager assistant suddenly forgot his lines. Everything stopped. The congregation sat in hushed expectancy. Norman waited. His convert gave him an anguished look. "What in *hell*," he hissed helplessly, "do we do now?"

The hush in the church would have driven a lesser man back to the paddock. But Norman stuck by his friend, and his friend stuck by his new-found spiritual life until he died, years later, still strong in the faith.

Although his chief concern was getting people involved in the church, sometimes Norman got himself involved in things outside the church. Through the war, and for a few years afterward, he clung to his conviction that a minister had not only the right but the duty to speak out on political affairs, presidential elections, and so on. In 1948 he had favored the nomination of General MacArthur on the Republican ticket. Later he supported his neighbor, Governor Dewey in his unsuccessful campaign against Truman.

But slowly it began to be apparent to him that such partisan activities on the part of a minister were divisive. They alienated people. They reduced the effectiveness of the pastor as spiritual leader of a united congregation, or even as counselor to people in times of trouble.

At one point he was asked to associate himself with an organization, backed by some extremely wealthy men, whose purpose was to encourage conservatism—or rather, ultra-conservatism. Norman was inclined to join, thinking that by so doing he could win the leader of this group to Christ. In this case, a reporter came to a friend of Norman's and told him bluntly that the newspapers were set to blast the organization as reactionary and unwarranted, and that if Norman joined it he would be blasted too.

"I wish you'd tell Dr. Peale," the reporter said grimly, "that if he continues to let himself be used this way he's going to be branded as a spokesman for millionaires and reactionaries—men who are as far to the right as the communists are to the left. I know he doesn't belong in that group. He's a supporter of the United Nations—and they hate it. He favors foreign aid—and they despise it. But people don't stop to analyze these things; they just believe what they read on the biggest label. Tell him all this, will you? It's time somebody did!"

It was high time, and Norman knew it. "I've been wrong," he said to Ruth. "I've done my ministry a lot of harm by getting mixed up in political activities. I'd have stopped long ago, if it hadn't been for some ministers who kept trying to force me to quit. But from now on, I'm through with this sort of organization. I've got my spiritual work, and I'm going to stick to that. Believe me, from this point on, if the country were collapsing, and a committee were formed to save the Republic, I wouldn't join it!"

"Oh, Norman," Ruth laughed, "don't be silly. Of course you would!"

"No, I wouldn't," her husband said bleakly. "And do you know why? Because it would just turn out to be a front for something else!"

His decision to concentrate on his work was welcomed by his publishers. Sales of *A Guide to Confident Living* were the answer to a publisher's daydream. They wanted the author to try again.

Norman was willing to oblige. The mail flooding into his offices strengthened his conviction that the message he was trying to transmit did indeed help all types of people over the rough spots in life. The success of the manuscript he had once thrown in the wastebasket had left his confidence high. His summer vacations left him free from church responsibilities and gave him time to work. He began to rough out another book.

Basically, the message was the same, with the emphasis shifted slightly from religion to psychology. Listening to the cases discussed at staff meetings of the religio-psychiatric clinic, Norman had become more and more impressed with the suggestibility of the human mind. In case after case, he had seen people cured of emotional disorder when the thoughts and attitudes that were poisoning them were replaced by healthier thoughts and attitudes. More often than not, the new thoughts were simply the basic teachings of Christianity: love, kindness, unselfishness, service—positive ideas as opposed to negative ones, constructive concepts as opposed to destructive. It seemed to Norman that, once they were implanted, these positive ideas were stronger than the negative ones; they could drive them out and keep them out.

"As a man thinketh, so is he." The Bible, as usual, was able to illuminate a tremendous truth in a single phrase. Nor was this belief confined to religious writings, by any means. Marcus Aurelius said it: "Our life is what our thoughts make it." Emerson said it: "A man is what he thinks about all day long." Menninger said it: "Attitudes are more important than facts." In his delving into psychiatric literature, Norman came across a sentence that seemed to state the principle even more explicitly: "In physics, the basic factor is force; in psycology, the basic factor is the realizable wish."

The realizable wish . . . it was around this concept that Norman built the new book. The mind, he said, could not directly control the circumstances that surrounded it. But it *did* control the attitude of the individual to such circumstances. The most effective mind-conditioner known to man was religion. Therefore why not make use of religion to change attitudes and ultimately circumstances?

Christianity, he insisted, was more than just a creed to be believed in; it was also a power to be tapped. The power had a pricetag on it; surrender to God's will, surrender to Christ as one's Savior, elimination of all wrongdoing, self-examination for traces of the pride, envy, malice, or hatred that could block the flow of spiritual power. But the power was there; it was available to people. That was what he meant when he said that Christianity worked—when it was worked.

No writing is easy, but the book seemed to progress with less anguish than its predecessor. Near the end some editorial revisions were suggested that threw Norman into a fit of despondency, and for a while the manuscript gathered dust on his study shelf. But in the summer of 1951 he finished the rough draft while "vacationing" in Honolulu. The search for a title was ended when one of his publishers, Myron Boardman, suggested a phrase from the earlier book: *The Power of Positive Thinking*. It went on sale officially on October 13, 1952.

At first the book showed no great promise of becoming a runaway best seller. It was widely and—on the whole—favorably reviewed, and after five or six weeks appeared on the best seller list. But the New York critics, while friendly, were somewhat casual. No one was prepared for what happened next.

What happened was that the book rose steadily to the top of the list and stayed there, month after month. Two years after publication it was still selling from five to eight thousand copies per week and total sales were pushing toward the two million mark. On April 8, 1956, it passed its 179th week on *The New York Times* best-seller list, breaking the all-time record previously held by Lloyd Douglas' *The Robe*. It was translated into fourteen languages, including Afrikaans and Japanese. Letters to the author poured in at the rate of two thousand a week, not just month after month, but year after year. As a publishing phenomenon nothing equalled it except that perennial best seller, the Holy Bible.

No single factor, clearly, could account for such stunning success. The book had a good title, it was strongly backed by the publisher, it had the prior success of *A Guide to Confident Living* to build on. But beyond all that, and in addition to its spiritual message, it was a peculiarly American book. In it were blended all the idealism and the materialism, the latent religious fervor and the intense practicality of the American people. The book was not afraid to be sentimental, but it was also clear, brisk, and succinct. It pointed to heaven, but it was very much down-to-earth. It had something of the peace of a rural church in it—and something of the pulsing roar of Chicago or Detroit.

The timing, too, was good. The country was weary and disheartened by the bloody stalemate in Korea. Politically, the long Democratic tenure was dragging to an end. People wanted optimism, hope, encouragement—a lift. *The Power of Positive Thinking* gave it to them.

Some reviewers sensed this. Writing in his syndicated column, *Reviewing the Books,* Sterling North said, "Unlike literally hundreds of other books, this one offers hope rather than despair, order rather than chaos, and faith rather than nihilism. Most of us pride ourselves on our 'realism,' our skepticism, our cold-blooded, hardheaded materialism. We're tough, unshockable, impatient with dreamers, mystics and teachers of ethics. We are precisely the sort of people, I fear, who would have crucified Christ, or offered Socrates the hemlock. And we are paying for it with great unhappiness.

"It takes courage to write a gentle, helpful book in this era of the sneer and the wisecrack. For that matter it takes some courage to review such a book with anything but a derogatory quip. . . .

"*The Power of Positive Thinking* was not produced as a bid for literary immortality. It is rather wise, friendly, unpretentious guidance offered by a decent man concerned about the widespread and often needless misery of a nation rich in things but poor in spirit."

North predicted that the book would not please "*avant-garde* cynics who prefer Faulkner, Paul Bowles, and other equestrians of the contemporary nightmare." To some extent this was true; there were mild complaints that the book left something to be desired theologically and that the formulas recommended seemed over-simplified. But most of the criticism was good-humored, like the cartoons that kept turning up in *The New Yorker*. The rage of the intellectuals was yet to come.

The effect of all this on the Peales was similar to the impact of the earlier best seller, only more so. As the avalanche of publicity roared down upon them, Norman's speaking invitations jumped to fifty or more a month. He became known as Mr. Positive-Thinking. His face adorned the cover of *Newsweek*. He shared the cover of *LOOK* with Bishop Sheen. Television sought him as an added attraction to established programs. Ruth was urged to reveal in print everything about the man she had married. The children were invited to write articles about life with Daddy.

And then there was the problem of money.

From the beginning of their marriage, Ruth and Norman had tithed faithfully—at least ten percent of their income and usually much more went to church or charity. Secretarial and travel expenses consumed a great deal. For years, Norman's method of dealing with the problem was fairly simple. Whenever he found himself seriously in the red he went on the road and gave lectures until he bailed himself out.

For the most part, he left the management of money to Ruth. He never knew exactly how much he had, or where it was. Once he went into a bank in Pawling, filled out a counter check, and drew out a hundred dollars or so. "You must have an honest face," said Ruth when he mentioned it to her. "You don't have an account in that bank."

Up to 1949, expenses had always kept one jump ahead of family income. Then, abruptly, the unexpected revenues from *A Guide to Confident Living* pushed the Peales into a high tax bracket.

When it became apparent that his book royalties had made him financially independent, Norman began turning over his lecture earnings to the clinic at the church. It was an expensive form of charity, since he often found himself paying taxes on the money thus donated. But it was a necessary one. By this time the clinic had grown into an organization occupying one whole floor of an office building, with a staff of twenty-four ministers, psychiatrists, psychologists and social workers not only interviewing hundreds of cases each year, but also conducting a training program in pastoral counselling for young clergymen. By 1956 its annual budget had jumped to $170,000, and the chief responsibility for raising this money was Norman's. He personally pledged $15,000 of it, but by raising his lecture fee he was usually able to do better than that. In one period of sixteen months, he contributed $44,000.

Compared to the average ministerial income, there was still a lot left, but Norman saw no reason to apologize for this. He had worked hard all his life. The Horatio Alger tradition in which he had been reared held that hard work and honesty would result in material success, and that a man had a right to enjoy the fruits of his labors—or, at least, that his family did. Norman had little interest in money as a medium of exchange, in the tangible things that money could buy. But money as a measure of success, as a yardstick of personal achievement, this was something—given his background—that he did value.

He knew that there were people who felt that a minister of the Gospel had to be poor to be true to his calling, but this was a belief that he did not share. He had never thought it the Lord's will that ministers should live on the borderline of poverty. He had seen too many pastors and their wives exhausted and embittered by inadequate incomes to have much faith in the spiritual benefits of subsistence living. From childhood, furthermore, he had resented the tendency of society to adopt patterns of thought that set ministers apart, dehumanized them, created artificial barriers between them and other men.

An episode in Pawling spotlighted the whole thing very neatly. At a Rotary luncheon that Norman attended, another minister had an errand to run, and borrowed somebody's car.

The car turned out to be a Cadillac, and as the minister drove away in it a man who knew nothing of the circumstances remarked, "Look at that clergyman driving a big Cadillac! Now isn't that a fine state of affairs!"

Up from Norman's childhood rose a searing memory of the grocery brothers criticizing Clifford Peale for buying the disputed Reo. "Listen," he said furiously to the self-appointed critic, "the man driving that car does more good and helps more people in one day than you do in a year! It's not his Cadillac, but what if it were? Why shouldn't he drive a Cadillac? Why shouldn't he drive anything he pleases?"

So incensed was he that he went right out and ordered a Cadillac for himself. Instantly the familiar sequence of reactions set in. He was sticking his neck out. He was inviting criticism. People would say he was a show-off. People would say . . .

He sat gloomily in his study, wondering if he should cancel the order. But he knew himself pretty well by this time. He knew exactly what would happen. The stubborn Ohio streak in him would prevent him from cancelling the order. The car would arrive. He would regard it with terrible qualms. He would leave it untouched in the garage for about two weeks. Then the defiant Peale inside of him would say to the timid Peale, "What's the matter with you? Are you a man or a mouse? You earned this car, you worked long and hard for it, didn't you? This is a free country, isn't it? Are you afraid to drive your own car for fear of what people will say?

Then he would drive it. But he wouldn't fully enjoy driving it, because some people *would* be critical.

He sat there, contemplating his fate. The door opened and John came through the room, tennis racket dangling. He was getting to be a first-class player. "Hi, Dad."

Norman looked somberly at his son. "John," he said, "if you ever decide to go into the ministry, you're an ass!"

CHAPTER XIV

The Man Who Couldn't

Say No

❦

Norman's advice was not taken; John did decide to enter the ministry.

It was a courageous decision; no son wants to be overshadowed by his father. Knowing this, Norman had always been careful never to exert any pressure on the boy. When John told him of his desire to carry on the family tradition, he was touched and delighted.

The college the boy chose was Washington and Lee, down in the lovely Shenandoah Valley. Virginian traditions, Virginian manners appealed to him. Another reason, perhaps, was that his father had not preceded him there. The decision to enter the ministry left John doubly determined to stand on his own feet. Once, asked to speak to a group of people at college, John was introduced with a flourish as the son of the famous orator Norman Vincent Peale. He arose and looked at his audience levelly. "Let's get one thing straight," he said. "Any oratorical resemblance between my father and me is purely coincidental!"

Margaret was the one who elected to carry on the family name at Ohio Wesleyan. She was a quiet, slender girl with a first-class mind who inherited some of the Peale hesitancy and self-distrust. ("The only member of the family," John said once, "who *hasn't* got an inferiority complex is Mother!") On one occasion at college Margaret called up her father in alarm to say she had been offered a job as student advisor to all freshmen. She said she wasn't at all sure that she was equal to such a responsibility.

"Margaret," Norman told her, "I think it's quite possible that the Lord is giving you a chance to show what you *can* do. Ask Him for His help and guidance, and then go ahead fearlessly and do the job!"

Margaret did, and afterwards said that it was the best antidote for shyness that she encountered in her whole college career.

Of the three children, Elizabeth was probably the most outgoing. She loved horses, games, people. Like Margaret, she had considerable musical talent, and learned to play both the harp and the piano. She had some of her father's hyper-sensitivity, but also some of her mother's self-control. Once, an hour or so before a children's concert, Norman heard her rehearsing a piano selection that she was supposed to play. She seemed so nervous, and made so many mistakes, that her father became concerned. "She can't play that thing at all!" he protested to Ruth. "You'd better get her out of the concert. We'll be embarrassed!"

"She's just getting the mistakes out of her system," Ruth said calmly. "You'll see."

When the crucial moment came, Elizabeth played flawlessly.

As the baby of the family, she might have been somewhat spoiled had she not been insulated against this by a quick and merry mind, and a capacity for self-directed humor that was much like her father's. Once, down in Florida, she went with her parents to view a tract of land near Clearwater that Norman had bought. "Maybe we could have a housing development here some day," Norman said. "But we'd have to think of a good name for it. You know, Venetian Shores, or Happy Acres, or something."

Lizzie wrinkled her forehead thoughtfully. "Why not," she said, "call it Peale's Positive Plots?"

One thing that the children increasingly and unanimously objected to was the relentless intrusion of the outside world into family life. Both parents were at fault in this regard. Ruth, with her compulsion to get things done, was probably more immediately culpable than Norman. But many of the things that she was trying to get done, in the last analysis, were things that Norman had let himself be coaxed or pushed into.

All his life he had found it difficult to say no to people. Partly this was a genuine desire to be of service; partly, perhaps, a fear of being disliked. In any case, given the external pressures that followed the publication of *The Power of Positive Thinking,* such compliance contained the seeds of disaster. Overnight, it seemed, a pair of lives already crammed with activities approached the borderline of frenzy. Ruth's genius for organization managed to preserve an outward semblance of calm, and Norman's devoted team of assistants carried as much of the load as it could. By this time, moreover, he had the benefit of the balanced judgement of Gerald Dickler, a friend and attorney whose advice often kept Norman out of hot water. But the pace was murderous all the same.

There was the church: the spiritual center of all Norman's activities. Here the problem of handling the crowds had become steadily more acute. Stimulated by the widespread interest in Norman's books, people jammed every available inch of space. Contrary to custom in most churches, men consistently outnumbered women. Sunday after Sunday, rain or shine, as many as a thousand people might be turned away—and this after two overflow rooms were packed. It was not unusual for arriving worshippers to find long lines stretching from the entrances. It became necessary to supply church members with tickets which gave them prior admission up to twenty minutes before the service began.

In the end, Norman found a solution of sorts in modern electronics. Each Sunday, using closed circuit television that carried his voice and image to auxiliary rooms, he preached two sermons to some 4,000 people. He no longer tried to preach two different sermons, one in the morning and one in the evening. He now preached the same sermon twice, at consecutive services in the morning. But that still meant the creation and delivery of some forty sermons a year.

There was the clinic, now known as The American Foundation of Religion and Psychiatry. Norman was not directly involved in the day-to-day administration or operation. But he was still President and Chairman of the Board, largely responsible for fund-raising and—with Dr. Blanton—for long-range planning and policy.

There was *Guideposts*. This, too, was competently staffed and capable of running itself. William Boal, a highly competent business manager, had come in to administer publication operations. Len LeSourd, now a seasoned editor, directed a staff of skilled assistants. But Norman had to exercise general supervision over every issue. He also contributed an article of his own every month. In 1956, a Braille edition of *Guideposts* was made available to the blind at regular subscription prices. In 1957 Ruth was made co-editor so that she could attend editorial meetings and report to Norman, who seldom could be there.

There was the column, by now the most widely read religious newspaper feature in the world. These columns could be prepared in advance, and often were. But Norman also liked to maintain a topical quality, which meant that he could not work too far ahead of his deadlines.

There were the weekly radio talks. These, too, could be recorded in advance; about once a month Norman went down to the studios and spent two hours recording three or four of these radio sermons. They were broadcast on twenty-six consecutive Sundays, from October 1 to March 31. The National Broadcasting Company estimated the audience for each talk at about five million listeners. In any case, the average number of sermons mailed out on request ran to over a million and a half a year. Dr. S. Franklin Mack, head of the Broadcasting and Film Commission of the National Council of Churches, under whose auspices the radio program was given, regarded Norman as one of the best "communicators" of religion to the people, especially the unchurched.

By this time there was also a television outlet. In 1952 Norman and Ruth agreed to appear together on a program called "What's Your Trouble?" Ad-libbing back and forth, they discussed the problems and difficulties of people who wrote in for advice. All told, they made fifty-one such films. The public liked them, judging from the response. The critics were less enthusiastic. Too static, was the most frequent complaint. Truth was, Norman was not used to sharing a platform. He tended to defer politely to Ruth, and in trying to be a perfect gentleman lost something of his own candlepower.

There were his books. *The Power of Positive Thinking* did not need much pushing. But there were autograph sessions, visits to bookstores, conferences with the publishers—and, of course, requests for yet another book.

There were magazines. Somehow Norman found time to fill specific requests for articles ("Fool Things I've Done," "The Ten Women I Most Admire," "How to Squelch a Bigot," etc.) He contributed an article a year to *Reader's Digest*. In addition to these, beginning in June, 1954, he conducted a question-and-answer page in *LOOK*. No other magazine feature in the history of publishing had such reader-response. As a rule, magazine fan mail tends to be limited; a hundred letters on a given article is unusual. The Peale page in *LOOK* averaged between five and six thousand letters per issue, and sometimes went over ten thousand.

The questions selected for answering were drawn from this mail. Every fortnight Norman would answer a dozen or so, and send them over to *LOOK*. The editors would then select six or eight to use on the page.

Sometimes the topics were controversial. The loudest repercussions came from questions having to do with interfaith marriages (Norman usually counseled great care and caution, but he did not rule them out altogether) and segregation (he opposed racial discrimination as unchristian). At one point, when the pressure of his work was becoming almost intolerable, Norman tried to cancel the *LOOK* page. The editors promptly called a conference to persuade him to continue. They figured he wouldn't be able to say no. They were absolutely right.

This was not mere compliance, however. Norman considered the *LOOK* page to be one of his most helpful and important contributions. For the Christmas issue in 1957 he wrote the first "pull-out" ever used in the magazine. This was an illustrated pamphlet bearing the title: "Jesus of Nazareth—a Dramatic Interpretation of His Life from Bethlehem to Calvary, written especially for young Americans." It was Norman's first use of fictional characters in telling the story of Jesus. The original idea came from *LOOK*'s publisher Gardner Cowles, who had been impressed by the teen-age reader response to Norman's regular page.

Meanwhile Sermon Publications, reorganized as the Foundation for Christian Living, had grown under Ruth's direction into a complex publishing venture. By 1958, a quarter of a million people worldwide were receiving Norman's sermons regularly, and the number was destined to go much higher.

These sermons were tape-recorded in the Marble Church just as Norman delivered them; then they were edited and printed under Ruth's supervision. Words spoken extemporaneously sometimes need tightening to retain their impact in print, and she became a self-taught expert at this. The Foundation also offered long-playing records with the sermons and background music from the church itself. Somewhere along the line, Norman found time to prepare ten booklets designed to help people in meeting life's difficulties. Like the sermons and the How-To cards, these were made available by the Foundation on a voluntary contribution basis. In seven years, over five million of them were distributed. One designed for young people called "How to Be Young and Enjoy It" coincided with growing public concern over the rising tide of juvenile delinquency. It met with unprecedented demand. In the first six months, 750,000 copies were distributed.

The cost of preparing and distributing the Youth booklet alone was in the neighborhood of $75,000. Most of this was defrayed by voluntary contributions, although profits from the Foundation's sales of books and records helped. In 1953 a new building was erected at Pawling to house the operation; in 1956 it was greatly enlarged. A bold gesture, but as Ruth said, "This thing has been running on faith from the beginning; I don't see any reason to lower our sights now."

The Foundation took a great deal of Ruth's time. During these years she was also a Vice-President of The National Council of Churches, perhaps the highest office a laywoman can hold in the religious field. She was also Vice-Chairman of the Finance Committee and Vice-Chairman of the Broadcasting and Film Commission of the National Council of the Churches of Christ, President of Sorosis Club, and Chairman of Religion of the New York State Federation of Women's Clubs. In addition she was Vice-President of the Board of Domestic Missions of the Reformed Church in America, and later became President, the first woman to hold such an office. In 1953 her old university, Syracuse, gave her an honorary Doctor of Laws degree, and in 1956 she became a trustee.

So she was not exactly idle.

As for Norman, the most time-consuming of all his activities was his lecture program. It wasn't so much a question of preparation as of geography. By 1953 he was speaking some seventy-five or eighty times a winter to audiences of all sorts and sizes. On a Tuesday he might address a bankers' convention in Tulsa. On Thursday he might speak to 50,000 people assembled in the Cotton Bowl at Dallas. On Friday night it might be a National Realtor's Meeting in Chicago. He might cross the country from East to West, or from North to South, but always, like a sort of spiritual homing pigeon, he had to be back in his Fifth Avenue pulpit on Sunday morning.

In these incessant travels, most of Norman's hotel reservations were made for him by Frank Kridel, one of his deacons and a New York hotel manager. Kridel was a dyed-in-the-wool fire buff, an honorary member of the Fire Chief's Association, and consequently, Norman often found himself met, not with a red carpet, but with a red Fire Chief's car at an airport or railroad station.

Norman's attitude toward these endless journeys was ambivalent. He invariably disliked the thought of going, but usually enjoyed himself once he got there. At least, he enjoyed making the speech. The preliminary meetings with strangers, the receptions, the social activities—these he tended to regard as unavoidable evils. An audience of five thousand didn't bother him much, but a social gathering of fifteen or fifty could make him feel awkward and ill-at-ease.

It was hard to pinpoint the reason for this. Perhaps it had something to do with the fact that he could always focus on a single individual, or on a large audience that had, for the moment, its own corporate personality. But at a smaller gathering, where he had to keep shifting his attention rapidly, he felt out of touch.

He was well aware of this quirk in his own nature. Once, scheduled to speak at a large convention in Washington, he suffered through the usual pre-banquet reception, then arose after dinner and made a first-class speech. After the banquet there was another reception, about the same size as the first and with more or less the same people. And here, somewhat to his surprise, Norman found himself laughing, telling stories, being quite one of the boys.

"And you know," he said to Ruth afterwards, "I suddenly realized what was happening. I was still making a speech! I was talking to a group that I considered an audience, and I was perfectly happy. But as soon as I realized that, I felt the icy fingers beginning to reach for me again, and I thought, 'Gosh, I'd better start getting out of here!' So I did!"

These recurrent activities in themselves demanded an expenditure of energy that would have exhausted almost anybody, but there were specialized items as well. In 1954, for example, Norman was "profiled" on Ralph Edwards' television program, "This Is Your Life." Since the subject was supposed to be kept in the dark until the final moment, Ruth had to participate in an elaborate campaign of deception. Norman was lured to the theatre on the pretext that Dale Evans—Roy Rogers' wife and an old friend of the Peales'—was to be the innocent victim. His children and both his brothers flew out to the Coast to be on hand. It was a pleasant evening that seemed to make everyone happy except for the member of the production staff who had hoped for more of a tear-jerker. "Why," he said indignantly afterwards, "they laughed all the time. I didn't hear a single sob!"

Edward R. Murrow visited the Peales' Fifth Avenue apartment with his T.V. "Person to Person" television show. The panel of "What's My Line?" identified him as the mystery celebrity in four tries. He was a frequent guest on many other programs.

There were other propositions to which Norman could not say no. A friend of his was the head of a large greeting card company. When this friend proposed that Norman write brief messages to go on Easter or Christmas cards, and be paid accordingly, Norman saw no reason to decline. He likewise allowed himself to be sponsored by a facial tissue manufacturer on a radio program. Through these activities he earned some $40,000—all of which was given to religious work. Even so, a public relations adviser might have counselled against such moves on the grounds that Norman was getting too close to the invisible line that separated legitimate extensions of the pulpit from commercialization of a reputation that was supposed to be based on matters of the spirit. In earlier days Ruth and Norman might have been more aware of this danger. But by now their life was revolving at such a dizzy pace that quite often there was not enough time to think things through. There was also the growing danger that in trying to do more than was humanly possible, Norman would end by spreading himself too thin. This danger was concealed from them by Norman's conviction that repetition was essential to getting across any message, and by Ruth's missionary urge to spread the message as far as possible. But it was increasingly there.

Eventually Norman dropped the sponsored radio show, but continued his relationship with the greeting card company. He felt the cards gave him a new medium through which to reach people with his message—and to him this was the important thing.

Some of Norman's "involvements" were more hilarious than harmful. Finding him in an unguarded moment, a friend suggested that when he departed this life, he ought not to be buried in an ordinary grave. As a famous minister, as Mr. Positive-Thinking, he ought to have a tomb—a mausoleum, in fact. The person promoting this idea just happened to have a fine marble mausoleum—slightly secondhand, but still imposing—that needed an occupant, or at least a buyer. He talked long and persuasively. The result was that when Norman came back from a trip abroad, there was the mausoleum with the name PEALE chiseled with chilling finality over the marble door.

At once there was great agitation among the many fragmented personalities that dwelt inside Norman. One of these personalities was rather impressed with the notion of a simple Ohio country lad finally coming to rest in a great marble structure that would defy the ravaging fingers of time. But another inner voice spoke up sharply. "Who do you think you are?" demanded this voice with asperity. "Your parents are buried in simple Ohio graves, aren't they? And your grandfather? And his father? Where'd you get the notion that you are better than those people? Are you getting a swelled head, or something?"

The thing was settled by a third aspect of NVP, an impish character who often has the last word anyway. The owner of all these personalities was inspecting the tomb, both pleased and appalled, and finally poked his head inside. There along the wall ran the solemn shelves on which the coffins of departed Peales were to rest for all time. Whereupon the third voice spoke softly into his ear. "Norman," it said, "do you—of all people—really want to spend eternity on the shelf?"

So far nothing conclusive has been done about this, but chances are that sooner or later one marble mausoleum will be offered for resale. Good condition. Slightly used. Cheap!

There was one area, though, where Norman proved himself triumphantly capable of saying no. This area was the dinner table, and his victory came about as a result of an appearance on television. He accepted an invitation to appear as guest star on Steve Allen's show. The program went well, and Norman was quite pleased with himself until he came home and asked his favorite critic, Elizabeth, for her opinion.

"Well, Daddy," said Elizabeth, "the show was fine, but you looked too fat."

"Fat?" cried Norman in stricken tones. "What do you mean —fat?"

"Just what I said. Your jacket looked too tight. The button was straining—right there." And she poked him unfeelingly in the tummy.

"Now, Lizzie," her father said feebly. "You know that television camera angles sometimes make things look distorted."

"That was no camera angle," Elizabeth said positively. "That was you!"

So began the great dieting campaign. Butter, potatoes, sugar, desserts—all disappeared. Cottage cheese became a matter of grave import. Conversations began to have a certain monotony. ("Boy," said Margaret afterward, "did we get tired of hearing what Daddy didn't have for lunch!") The family physician was pleased, and said that for every pound Norman shed he would contribute ten dollars to the Marble Church. With this added spiritual incentive the pounds began to melt away. Ten. Twenty. Twenty-five. Thirty . . . By this time our hero's trousers hung in folds, and his coat flapped like a circus tent, but he would let no one alter them—they were too useful for display purposes.

It finally took a word from John—two words, to be exact—to halt the dizzy spiral. Norman came to breakfast one morning beaming with self-satisfaction. "You know," he said proudly, "I'm down to a hundred and fifty. That's the lowest I've been in years. Why, if I get any thinner, I'll begin to look downright insignificant!"

He paused happily, waiting to be contradicted. John nodded, poker-faced, "That's right," he said.

There was a short, poignant silence. Then Norman reached for the butter dish. The diet wasn't exactly over. But its back was broken.

During all this time, nothing in the mounting pressure and publicity altered Norman's conception of himself as a dedicated minister of the Gospel doing his best with whatever means he could find to further the Lord's work. Basically and primarily he regarded himself as minister of Marble Collegiate Church—everything else was secondary.

Now and then, in his comings and goings across the land, he would find himself giving talks in Columbus, Cleveland or Cincinnati. Usually he would meet old classmates from Ohio

Wesleyan, and they would sit up late at night burnishing the bright college memories. Once he went back to Bowersville and stood in the small downstairs room where he had been born, tasting the faint, bitter-sweet nostalgia of those who try to go back to the past and find it gone—and yet not quite gone.

Once or twice, too, he came again to Lynchburg, where he and Bob had spent so many happy days as children. Here the sense of the past was so strong as to be almost overpowering. He could see it all so plainly—the family setting out from Cincinnati to spend Christmas with Grandpa and Grandma Peale, riding the B & O as far as Blanchester, then changing cars for the little branch line that ran to Lynchburg. The two-car local would chuff importantly through the snow-covered countryside—there always seemed to be snow at Christmastime in those days. The red plush seats would vibrate steadily, overhead the oil-lamps would swing from their chains, the big good-natured conductor would constantly consult the stem-winding watch attached to the massive gold watch-chain spread across his brass-buttoned vest.

They would arrive, quivering with anticipation. They would trudge through the squeaking snow to the white frame house. Five-year-old Norman would be allowed to stand on tiptoe to twirl the handle of the old-fashioned doorbell. The ring would go chiming through the house, the eager footsteps would come running, the door would swing open to warmth and love and welcome, to the smell of roasting turkey, to the ruby glow of coal in the old base burner, to the knowledge that soon there would be Christmas gifts and Christmas carols. . . .

It was all still there, untouched, unchanged beneath the transparent overlay of time. On one visit, Norman went up and rang the bell and introduced himself to the lady who now lived in the house—Mrs. Grace Williams. He told her about some of his memories. Later, when he was speaking in Dayton, his cousin Philip Henderson handed him a bulky package. In it was the old door bell, a gift from Mrs. Williams.

He took it home with him and kept it in his bedroom. And sometimes, when the pressures in Manhattan made things seem a little unreal, he would turn the handle gently, and listen to the reassuring, far-off music of the past.

So the months fled past. If there were signs of a gathering storm, they passed unnoticed in the daily rush of activities. Inside the family, things were going well. Norman's influence and activities were at a peak. Ruth was busy and happy. Margaret was getting ready to graduate from Ohio-Wesleyan —Phi Beta Kappa, no less. She blossomed out as an author: *Family Circle Magazine* ran her article "Life with Daddy." John was starting his career at Washington and Lee.

Elizabeth, too, was getting to be a big girl now. It was time, really, for her to be going away to boarding school. Consequently four schools were carefully selected and application was made to each of them. Elizabeth's marks at Friends Seminary in Manhattan were excellent; it was evident that she would be accepted at one boarding school or another.

But as the fatal deadline approached, enthusiasm cooled rapidly among all members of the Peale family. Everyone still agreed that Elizabeth ought to go away to school, have the companionshiop of children her own age, and not be a solitary child in a family that consisted, most of the time, of two frenziedly busy adults.

In a final solemn talk, Norman undertook to explain this to Elizabeth. She listened dutifully, with downcast eyes. "I know that's all true, Daddy," she said at length. "But after all, if a child loves its parents, and its p-parents love the child, and if . . . well, if a child has a h-happy home . . ." Her voice climbed to a despairing squeak . . . "Don't you think the best place for that child is *in* it?"

A large tear ran down her nose and splashed on the carpet. Everyone wept. The applications were withdrawn. Lizzie stayed home.

CHAPTER XV

The Rage

of the Intellectuals

❧

Most of the reviews that greeted *The Power of Positive Thinking* on its publication in the fall of 1952 were favorable, but not all.

Writing in *The New York Times,* the pastor of a church in Gulfport, Mississippi, stated his objection calmly enough. "Mr. Peale says that he does not minimize or ignore hardships and tragedies. In spite of this statement, these problems seem too easily solved, the success a bit too automatic and immediate, the answers a little too pat, and the underlying theology a shade too utilitarian."

In the *Staten Island Advance,* Winfield Burggraff offered a further criticism: "I said above that the reading of this book will inspire hope, and I believe that it will. At the same time, there is danger that for some it may end in despair. Insofar as the book leaves the impression that by positive thinking you can create your own world ("Expect the Best and Get It" is one chapter heading), and that whatever failures you experience, or ill heath, are all due to lack of correct thinking on your part, it is misleading. The world outside of us is not created by our thoughts, nor is its reality dependent upon our thoughts. That is an error of extreme idealism and of pantheism. The world in which we live is crammed full of tough facts, many of them unyielding facts, which no amount of positive thinking can change. And to leave the impression that we can have things the way we want them, is not a true impression to make. It is entirely foreign to the thinking of the Bible, and to human experience."

These objections, valid or not, might have been forgotten if the book had sold only a few thousand copies. But as it led the best seller list month after month, and as the glare of publicity centered on its author, it was inevitable that the criticism that always seems to follow any spectacular success should also gather momentum.

The impetus came, or seemed to come, from the small magazines of opinion, secular or religious. In 1954 there were rumblings in *The Saturday Review, The Christian Century, Religion in Life,* and elsewhere. But the heavy barrage began in 1955.

In January, *The Reporter* carried an article titled "Some Negative Thinking About Norman Vincent Peale," by William L. Miller, then a professor of religion at Smith College. Unlike some of his fellow critics, Professor Miller could write clearly and with a mordant humor. He had read, he said, all the Peale books. "As a result of reading Dr. Peale's one point in every simple, easy book, chapter and paragraph, I am so full of 'confidence concepts,' 'faith attitudes,' and 'energy producing thoughts,' of 'thought-conditioners' and 'spirit-lifters . . .' that I have the Confidence, Faith, Vigor, Belief, Energy, Efficiency, and Power to write an article criticizing Dr. Peale. Believe me, Dr. Peale, without you I never could have done it."

Actually Professor Miller was so energized that he wrote

virtually the same article twice, once for *The Pastor*, in September 1954, and again for *The Reporter*, in January 1955. The central contention of both was that Peale's books and sermons departed from traditional Christianity by encouraging individual selfishness and denying man's moral helplessness without the grace of God.

Just how Miller missed the minister's emphasis on self-surrender and moral rectitude as prerequisites to any "benefits" from religion was a mystery, but miss them he did. He jumped to other conclusions. "Evil and sin and limitation are to be denied because to admit them would not be positive thinking." Or, again, "One does not admit evil, or guilt, or sin, since that would be 'negative.' The optimism of a secularized middleclass American pervades this message."

The reference to class was interesting, and there were echoes of this elsewhere. Underneath much of the criticism seemed to run deep annoyance with Norman for not displaying more of an itch for fundamental social change. His basic sin, it appeared at times, lay not in oversimplifying religion, or even psychiatry, but in liking the United States of America pretty much the way it was.

If this was a sin, then he certainly was guilty of it—and had been ever since he absorbed the ideas and traditions that had surrounded him as a child in rural Ohio.

The truth was, when such critics had a point, they weakened their case by the shrillness and sarcasm with which they launched their attack. The smaller the magazine, it often seemed, the more ferocious the phraseology and the more profound the conviction of the critic that he alone knew just who God was and how He wanted to be worshipped. Some of the articles were so bitter that the anger seemed out of all proportion to the topic under discussion. It was as if the writers found in Norman a villain who through the years had personally reduced the size of their congregations or thwarted their dreams of some Utopian social order.

The readiness of some people to accept uncritically the notion that Norman had only a single theme was traceable, in part at least, to the title of his great best seller. Positive thinking and Peale had become virtually synonymous. The fact that over the years his sermons had covered a wide range of topics was forgotten. It was true enough that by this time he was, to some extent, a Sunday preacher and a weekday psychologist. But this was a distinction that few if any of the critics bothered to make. His whole ministry was being judged by one facet of it.

Gradually criticism latent in the seminaries and divinity schools worked its way up to the top. At a dinner given in New York by the National Council of Churches, Dr. Liston Pope, Dean of the Yale Divinity School, attacked religious programs on radio and television with searing references to what he called "the peace-of-mind cults." Norman was not at the dinner, but Ruth was. She sat at the head table, and a friend who watched her listen to Pope's speech told her afterward that her face was a study—in impassivity.

Norman was in Chicago, filling a speaking engagement, when reporters swooped down on him, clamoring for a reaction to Pope's remarks. At the time, Norman did not even know what Pope had said. When informed, he looked troubled and replied that the head of a great divinity school must be a sincere, intelligent and honest man, and that perhaps he had better re-examine his own message and methods. If he found that he was deviating in any way from the Gospels as he understood them, Norman told the newsmen, he would do his best to correct the error.

Although his basic sincerity and humility supported him, the rising storm of controversy had left Norman shaken. In a way, Ruth's determination through the years to insulate him as much as possible from criticism or hostility had to some extent weakened his ability to take it—or at least had left him unprepared for such a dose of it. He had always had a respect amounting to awe for the classical scholar, the profound theologian. When he found these ecclesiastical howitzers trained on him, his distress was very real.

That many scholars held him in high regard had been demonstrated throughout the years by the honorary degrees that had been conferred on him. But it was easy to forget these distinctions as the winds of criticism blew louder.

To some extent, the whole uproar was an amplification of a criticism he had once encountered after a talk in Wilmington, Delaware, when a man came up to him and wanted to know why he had made no reference to the Blood of the Lamb. Norman had countered by asking just what the man meant by the Blood of the Lamb. The man said he didn't know, but that all preachers *he* had ever heard talked about it—at least, all the good ones had—and so he didn't see why Norman didn't talk about it too.

"Look," Norman had said in exasperation, "I know what is meant by the Blood of the Lamb, even if you don't. The reason I don't use the old religious terminology is that most of my listeners wouldn't understand it any more than you do. There wouldn't be much point in my getting up there and talking to them in French or German, would there? I try to use language and ideas that every person in my audience can understand."

It was the ancient conflict between the popularizer and the pundit, with the exasperation of the intellectual reinforced, as always, by his inability to command an audience commensurate with what he conceived to be the importance of his views.

All this time the people paid little heed to the critics. Wherever Norman spoke, in auditorium or banquet hall or church, they flocked to listen to him. On one occasion in Los Angeles he was invited by Dr. J. Richard Sneed to fill the pulpit of the great First Methodist Church, largest in the country. The service was scheduled for 10:45 A.M. By ten o'clock, every one of the 3400 seats was occupied, and hundreds of "late comers" were being turned away. The crowds in the street outside were advised by loudspeaker that a second service would be held an hour later. They stayed and filled the church a second time.

Where the critics were concerned Norman was willing to concede that perhaps he had made mistakes of emphasis. "Maybe I *have* made it all sound too easy," he said. "That certainly wasn't my intention, because Christianity isn't easy; it's so tough that nobody lives up to it fully. I always tried to emphasize that fact. And maybe I *have* stressed the tangible, visible rewards of faith too much. But here again, it wasn't because I was trying to appeal to selfishness. It was because I've seen fantastic transformations take place in people who, through self-surrender and the agony of spiritual change, find themselves and become integrated personalities. I've seen these things happen over and over again. I wanted everyone to know about them, to experiment and find out for themselves."

He made these concessions, and he never struck back at his detractors. But he stuck to his guns where his overall ministry was concerned. Discussing the Liston Pope episode with a reporter, he said, "I did review the things I had said and done, the sermons I had preached, the books I had written. I found room for improvement in my performance, but I could find no evidence that what I've been doing and saying for the last 25 years is wrong, or could harm anyone. My message is based on my understanding of our Lord's teaching. My methods may seem over-popular to some of the intellectuals of Protestantism, but I feel sometimes that they are unable to communicate with ordinary churchgoing people largely because they reject such methods.

"When I first began preaching sermons, years ago, I sometimes chose abstract or scholarly themes. Whenever I did, I would see on the faces of my congregation either bewilderment or boredom, or both.

"Whenever I read the New Testament, moreover, it seemed obvious to me that our Lord had been faced with much the same problem—the problem of communicating His ideas to large groups of people. When He wanted to make a point about the brotherhood of men, He didn't talk abstractly; He told a story; a specific story about a certain man who went down from Jerusalem to Jericho and fell among thieves and was finally rescued by the good Samaritan.

"There also seemed to be many references to the importance of simplicity, the need to become like a little child if you were to grasp the deepest truths of living.

"So I began talking in terms that I thought ordinary, everyday people like myself would understand. As a matter of fact, I began preaching most of my sermons *at* myself. I've been doing it ever since.

"People ask me, sometimes, to define my theological position, or tell them exactly where I stand on this point or that. I always try to oblige them, but I don't feel that the exact nature of my theology is the important thing. I believe that my credentials as a minister of Jesus Christ are to be found, not so much in my beliefs about Him, as in the extent to which I am helping people to accept Him as their friend, healer, guide and Savior.

"The privilege of reaching great numbers of people with this message is a gift the Lord has given me and I have used it to the utmost of my ability."

Ruth was concerned about him. In the summer of 1954 they had made a trip to the Holy Land and had had a carefree, happy time. Making plans for the summer of 1955, she decided to persuade him to take a cruise from England to the North Cape and then spend several weeks in Switzerland. Norman hated hot weather. Such an itinerary made it almost certain that he would have none. It would take him away from the atmosphere of discord that was plaguing him and sapping his vitality. Finally, it might give him the time and seclusion needed to work on a new book.

Ruth considered the writing of the book extremely important. She knew that her husband had developed a mental block where another book was concerned. She felt, probably rightly, that this loss of certainty was the result of the criticism. It seemed to her that it was essential for Norman to face and overcome the problem. If somehow he could force himself to hammer out a manuscript, she believed that his old buoyancy and optimism would be restored. It was with this in mind that she made plans for the summer.

Meanwhile, as the controversy continued to rage, Norman was not without strong and loyal defenders. Inside the church, there were those who argued that it was absurd to criticize a popular preacher for not being a profound theologian. In Pittsburgh, Dr. Samuel M. Shoemaker preached a sermon entitled "Spiritual Snobs" in which he said, referring to Norman, "No one knows the tens of thousands of discouraged, shut-away little people who have heard something from him that has given them hope. I know highly educated people who have been missed for years by the scholarly pronouncements of ordinary churchmen, but who have found a working faith through Norman Peale. . . . He talks to millions where scholars talk to handfuls."

A minister once complained to Dr. Shoemaker, "Peale preaches to the galleries."

"He's the only parson I know who has full galleries to preach to," Sam Shoemaker answered with a chuckle.

Dan Poling came to Norman's defense in an editorial in *The Christian Herald* in which he remarked dryly—with regard to tremendous theologians—that once he had heard Reinhold Niebuhr say that he had difficulty in understanding himself.

"To the question, 'What makes Peale tick?' there is a

quick answer," Poling said, "though being quick it is not complete. It was said of Jesus that the common people heard Him gladly. They heard him gladly because they could understand him, because he spoke in the vernacular—the Aramaic, the language of the streets and highways. And this man Peale both lives and talks right down to the grass roots of everyday life, where the common people and all others live and move and have their troubled beings.

"Henry Ward Beecher once said that the successful preacher preaches out of the hearts and hungers of his congregation. Dr. Peale does that, and always out of his own heart and life as well. The Gospel he preaches is hard. He never softens it. But what he does do, and do superlatively, is help make men and women somehow adequate for their occasions.

"Somehow he never fails to convey the conviction, to leave the impression that he is God's man with a message for you, a message that has been seasoned and enriched by the experiences of his own life."

There were laymen willing to stand up and be counted for Norman, too. J. Edgar Hoover spoke of the spiritual strength and peace of mind that the minister's writings had brought him. Norman's old boss, Grove Patterson, also had a few blunt words to say.

"All editors are hardboiled, and know hardboiled things all the way up from eggs. Peale preaches the hardest toughest Gospel I know. One of his followers said to him just the other day, 'You certainly do make religion hard for me. You make me clean up my life.'

"These critics in the pulpits and the magazines leave out, as far as I have heard them or read them, the crux—the very fundamental—of the Peale message. Over and over again he demands spiritual conviction, the confession of sins, the plea for forgiveness, the sacrifice of evil habits, the surrender of the whole man to God and the service of one's fellows. Along with this, he demands the abandonment of negative thinking, the elimination of fear.

"It seems to me that Norman Vincent Peale is to be measured by the definite results of his speaking and writing. The 'Peale controversy' fades into something pretty unimportant when one reads almost any one of those thousands of letters received at the church or the broadcasting studio or the publisher's office. The lives of uncounted thousands of men and women have been changed by the Peale preaching.

"Theologically, I may be unlearned, but I know a religion that works."

Where some psychiatrists were concerned, one objection seemed to be that if emotionally disturbed people tried to rely on "positive thinking," and found that it failed, they might well become worse. Perhaps this was true in some cases, although it was hard to prove—the disturbed people might have become more disturbed in any event. Another charge was that Norman's writings tended to prevent people who needed psychiatric help from seeking it. This was a strange accusation to bring against the man who had brought a whole clinic into his church, who had done more than any other clergyman to gain acceptance in church circles for psychiatry. But it was prevalent in medical circles.

Smiley Blanton, who by now had worked with Norman for almost twenty years, had little patience with his critical colleagues. "Dr. Peale," he said flatly, "is a great pioneer. He was one of the first men—if not the first—to combine the new science of human behavior known as depth psychology with the principles of religion. As a result, he has been able to help more people than either religion or depth psychology could help, acting alone.

"Many people lack normal self-love. This self-criticism, self-depreciation, and belittling of one's abilities is one of the commonest problems that we psychiatrists have to deal with. Dr.

Peale is able in a very remarkable way to restore to people normal self-love, confidence, faith and courage. There are some people who are not helped by his message. But there is no reason why a technique valid for some should be condemned because it doesn't benefit everybody."

The Peales sailed for England in June, stayed there a few days, then embarked on the gleaming white "Stella Polaris" for the cruise to the North Cape, above the Arctic Circle. With them went a dictaphone and a typewriter. "Maybe," said Norman, all his humor not lost, "if I work from sunrise to sunset I'll be able to get the book going. The sun doesn't set at all up there, does it?"

They worked. Norman had brought with him a mass of papers—sermons he had preached, newspaper columns he had written, lecture notes, radio outlines. He and Ruth would agree on a chapter heading. He would read all the pertinent or related material until he was saturated with it. Then he would dictate into the machine and later Ruth would transcribe it.

The first results left a good deal to be desired. The copy ran long; the ring of assurance and authority was lacking. Ruth cut, edited; and Norman revised. He grew weary and disgusted. She would not let him give up.

The cruise ended with much still to be done. They went to Switzerland, where they had rented a house not far from Lucerne, high on the shoulder of the Burgenstock. There the children were to join them.

From the start, Norman loved Switzerland. Like the psalmist, he lifted up his eyes and drew strength from the mountains. He admired the cleanliness and frugality of the people. He felt as if he had found a refuge from the pressures and problems that bedeviled him at home.

Work on the book continued. It was a restatement and reemphasis of Norman's basic conviction that religious faith could drive out fear and by so doing could renew vitality and release unsuspected qualities in people. Positive thinking was buttressed by stress on positive action, vitality in doing something about defeat, something dynamic and creative.

He had never understood why this philosophy had been labeled humanistic or selfish. A reporter once asked him a question about his "self-help books." "They're not self-help books!" protested Norman. "They're God-help books!" On another occasion someone handed him a list of questions designed to test his orthodoxy from a theological point of view. When asked to check the ones that he believed in, Norman took out a pencil and thoughtfully checked them all. "If you believe all these things," said the interviewer, "why don't you preach them?" Norman was genuinely astonished. "Why," he said, "I do!"

In the new book, he put more emphasis on the cautionary note. "Aliveness and a sense of dynamic being," he wrote, "do not come easily. Values of this importance cannot be achieved without spiritual 'blood, sweat, and tears,' to use Churchill's famous phrase. It is hard to change a wrong mental cast developed over many years. Sometimes a person may have such a tremendous spiritual experience that he is changed very quickly and dramatically. But, for the most part, we must painstakingly work and practice our way to vital well-being."

Such statements were valid, and perhaps needed. But unconsciously he was trying to adapt his work to the complaints of his critics, and he knew that this was drawing vitality out of the presentation. Later, after the book was published, he admitted his mistake. "Next time I write a book," he said to Ruth, "I'll pay no heed to the critics. I'll say what I want to say—and let them rave!"

The days went by; the stack of manuscript grew. And Ruth was right—as the task that had seemed so overwhelming diminished, Norman's natural optimism returned. At night they would stand out on the great curve of the mountain and listen to the sound of cow bells far across the valley. In the daytime the view alone was enough to lift the heart.

On Sundays they usually attended a Church of England service in Lucerne. But the road was narrow and tortuous, and one Sunday the children suggested that they have a service at home. They would conduct it themselves, they said—their parents could be the congregation for a change.

And so precisely at eleven o'clock they ushered Ruth and Norman out onto the terrace of the chalet. They had prepared a table with a spotless cloth. On it was a vase of mountain flowers. A Bible lay open. There were two chairs for the congregation. All around them rose the stupendous cathedral of the Alps. Ahead of them, mile after mile, stretched a vast panorama of lakes, villages, forests, and the great snowclad sweep of the Finsterhorn, the Jungfrau, the Eiger. The air was like crystal. The sunlight was warm and golden.

One of the girls read the lesson from the Old Testament; the other read the lesson from the New. Then John preached the sermon. He told about the beautiful country that lay around them, how God was in those hills. He talked about the Swiss people—their sturdiness, simplicity, honesty, piety.

"Take their great national shrines," he said, "a meadow, a path, a rock. In the Thirteenth Century they established the Swiss Confederation on the Meadow of Rütli; that was the beginning of freedom for the Swiss, one of the cornerstones on which America ultimately was built. Then there is the path where William Tell slew the tyrant Gessler, and the rock where Tell swam ashore when they tried to take him prisoner.

"Listen," John said, and from eight miles away they could hear the church bells of Lucerne, thin and sweet in the luminous air. "For hundreds of years, those bells have been telling people that Christ lives, that faith overcomes all difficulties."

Then he prayed. "Lord, help us to feel Your presence here today. Lord, help us to be good. Lord, fill us with faith. . . ."

Watching his son's earnest young face, Norman felt his eyes burn with tears. What was criticism or disapproval compared to a privilege like this? These were the things that counted, that would endure. From such moments, he knew, he drew his own endurance and strength.

He was to need both. Three weeks later he stepped off the boat in New York to receive the news that his father was dying and to be confronted with a new symposium of criticism that brought him to the point of writing out his resignation as a minister of the church.

CHAPTER XVI

The Man in the Dark
Blue Suit

❦§❦

All that summer in Switzerland, working doggedly on the book, he had been concerned about his father's health. All the way home, in September, he found his anxiety growing stronger. As soon as the ship docked he telephoned the little town in Pennsylvania where Clifford and his second wife were living, and learned that his misgivings were justified.

"Dad's pretty low, Norman," his brother said—no layman's opinion, since Bob was a physician. "If you want to be sure of seeing him again, you'd better come right away. Dad's a fighter, and he loves life. But when you're eighty-five and have had a couple of strokes. . . . Well, better not delay; you might regret it."

"I won't," he said, grateful that he was not too late, that there was still time. "I'll take the train tonight; be there first thing in the morning."

So he had only a few hours in New York. But that was time enough for somebody to show him the magazine article.

They showed it to him, no doubt, because they knew he would see it anyway, sooner or later. Or possibly because they assumed he was hardened to criticism by this time. But somehow—perhaps because it was such a brutal contrast to the peace and serenity of Switzerland, perhaps because his concern for his father left him peculiarly vulnerable—the criticism went through him like a poisoned spear.

He tried to conceal his reaction, but Ruth knew. A good wife always knows. "Now Norman," she said, calmly, quietly, "don't let this get you down. It's just one more example of criticism based on misinformation. Or no information. Put it out of your mind, and go on out to Harrison Valley and see your father."

Well, he had tried to take her advice. He had tried to forget it, to put it out of his mind. But he knew that it was walking right along with him as he moved down the ramp that led to the train.

It was close to midnight, now, but the air was heavy, humid, exhausted. And why not, he thought wearily, with eight million frantic people breathing it all day, with cars and trucks and taxis pouring monoxide into it, with factories and power stations and incinerators adding their noxious vapors. . . . The trouble with you, he told himself wryly, is that you're spoiled. People who have to work in this concrete jungle should never go to Switzerland. When they come back, the contrast is too depressing.

He moved on down the ramp with the other passengers. Not a conspicuous figure; rather the reverse. Middle-aged now, medium height, steel-rimmed glasses, sandy hair getting pretty thin on top and a little gray around the edges. In his dark blue suit and dark blue tie he looked more like a businessman than a minister. What was it some writer had said? Like a small-town banker, that was it. Well, there were far worse things than small-town bankers.

The bag he carried in his right hand was getting heavy. The

one in his left hand was light enough; it contained clothes for an overnight trip, little more. But the right hand one was crammed with books, papers, letters, clippings, magazines, and a jumble of cardboard folders that were the despair of his secretaries. "Wait, Daddy," Elizabeth had squealed on one occasion when he was making a particularly hasty departure, "you've forgotten your brains!" Sure enough, his bag of papers was still in the hall. Ever since, it had been known in the family as "Daddy's brains."

He switched his "brains" to his other hand. Ruth always urged him to be sure to get a porter, and he always said he would. But tonight he had been too preoccupied. Besides, some faint voice from the past, some echo of the rigid economy taught him in childhood, always spoke up sternly in the back of his mind, asking if it were really right to pay for a service that you could perform just as well yourself. It was odd, he thought, as he came to the Pullman and gratefully surrendered the bags; the habit of economy ought to be one of the easiest to break—once you could afford to do so. But it wasn't.

He followed the porter to his bedroom. It was cool and quiet; the berth was made up. Ordinarily he liked the privacy of trains, the opportunity they afforded to work without interruption. Trains had always been his faithful servants; so, for that matter, had planes. They had carried him to every state in the Union, and for years they had given him almost complete privacy. Television had changed all that, television and the endless repetition of his picture in newspapers and magazines. Now a trip where no one recognized him was a thing of the past. Well, in a way he liked the recognition, needed the little glow of warmth that came from a word of appreciation or praise. I get a lot of that, he thought. More than I deserve, really; more than enough for any man. Why doesn't it balance the criticism, then? Why doesn't one cancel out the other?

Slowly, almost reluctantly, he opened his work bag and took out the magazine. The editors had tried to be fair, to

present both sides of what they called "the stormiest controversy in American religion today." But the biggest guns,
it seemed, were in the section of the article called *The Case
Against Easy Religion.* And the main target of the big guns
was himself.

Like a man biting down on an aching tooth, he made himself read the charges again. And again he felt something
wince and shrivel inside of him. How could Ruth expect him
to ignore these charges, to forget them, to shrug them off?
These men were no small-time publicity-seekers. They were
some of the best minds, the most respected leaders in Protestantism.

There were their words. There were their photographs. A
bishop of the Methodist Church—the denomination into
which he had been born, the church of his childhood—this
bishop, interviewed in the nation's capital, had said: "I seriously question whether his message is a Christian message. . . .
That kind of preaching is making Christianity a cult of success."

The dean of a great divinity school said, "There is nothing
humble or pious in the view this cult takes of God. The
formulas and the constant reiteration of such themes as 'You
and God can do anything' are very nearly blasphemous."

As he read, almost imperceptibly the train had begun to
move. He sat down on the edge of the berth, feeling the faint
vibration increase. This *cult,* his critics called it. That was a
loaded word, wasn't it? A word with unpleasant connotations,
deliberately chosen to degrade and deride. And *blasphemous.* Was it possible for anyone to preach the Gospel as he
understood it, with prayer and sincerity . . . was it possible
thus to preach and be called blasphemous? He shook his head
slowly. Evidently it was.

He read on. Now the president of the United Lutheran
Church in America was giving his views. He, too, used such
phrases as "this current cult" and "parody of religion." "There

is nothing more sinister," he said, "than the instrumentalization of religion—the use of God to accomplish a special
aim. . . ."

The man in the dark blue suit stopped reading and stared
at his reflection in the mirror. Do I really preach that, he asked
himself; have I ever said anything like that, or even implied
it? How could I? I know that God can't be used in any selfish
way. I know He can't be exploited. He gives us strength and
power when we let Him, when we approach Him humbly and
reverently and with faith, but He can't be used. Did I ever say
He could? This man seems to think I did, and he must be an
honorable man . . . *Instrumentalization,* he said to himself,
there's a word for you! Seven syllables, no less . . .

Abruptly a spark of anger lanced through him. What did
these—these cloud-dwellers—know about people and what
helped or hurt them? What did they know about the struggles
and sorrows and failures and yearnings of ordinary, harassed,
bedeviled human beings, groping for happiness and the chance
to become, somehow, better people than they knew themselves
to be? Surely, surely some of this criticism was being leveled
because he, Norman Veincent Peale, had chosen to be a little
different, because he didn't always look or sound like the
solemn, traditional concept of a preacher.

What has happened to Protestantism, he asked himself, what
has become of the great think-and-let-think tradition? Does
everyone have to act and speak as the self-appointed leaders
decree? Does everyone have to conform, submit . . .

He checked the train of thought. This was resentment, this
was injured pride. It was the sort of emotional thinking that
he was always warning others against. Getting angry, getting
his feelings hurt would not change the grim, inescapable
fact that some of the top men in his own calling considered
him a menace to his church, his congregation, and presuma-
bly to mankind at large.

And if this were so, he thought wearily, who was he to

argue with them, or to hold contrary views? It was all very well for Ruth to brush it all aside. Ruth was his wife, and a more loyal, steadfast, helpful one never breathed. But a wife's testimony was suspect, even in a court of law. Nothing that Ruth said or did could alter the considered judgment of these men. And if they considered him a baleful influence, as obviously they did, there was only one course of action that would satisfy and silence them. Only one.

He tossed the magazine onto the berth. The pretty girl on the cover smiled at him steadily, vacuously. The train was gathering speed, now; beneath him the wheels clicked out their mounting rhythm.

He stood up, shrugged off his jacket, loosened his tie. Thirty-three years in the ministry. A long time. A long, long time. After thirty-three years, the harness became so well-worn, so familiar, that living without it was almost inconceivable.

And yet, what was the use of staying in any profession if the price was conformity, was in this case the deliberate abandonment of techniques and methods that he knew to be effective in reaching people with the message, the simple and tremendous message, that the acceptance of Jesus Christ was the means of transferring the peace and power of an eternal God to weak, benighted, confused mortal men? The techniques worked, when the conditions were met. He had seen it happen, over and over again. He had seen it happen, and he had tried to tell people about it, not in theological terms, but in the plain workaday language of daily life. You were offering the old wine, he said to himself wearily, but you put it in new bottles—that was your crime.

That was your crime, echoed the hurrying wheels, *that was your crime.*

Slowly, painfully, a decision crystalized. He would have to leave the church. It would be hard, but it was the right thing to do. He would leave, but he could still speak, still write outside the church. He would not be silent; he would shift his base, that was all. The message would go on; he would see to that. From his bag of papers he took out pad and pencil, the tools with which he did all his writing on trains. Braced against his knee, the pad quivered with a tremor that made writing difficult, but he was used to this.

Slowly, deliberately, he wrote out his resignation as pastor of the Marble Collegiate Church and as a minister of the Reformed Church in America. He tried to keep it factual and restrained. He stated his conviction that his beliefs and preaching were in harmony with the Gospels, that he had always tried to give a Christ-centered message, that he had never believed —or taught—that the individual could raise himself by his own spiritual bootstraps. But, he went on, he could no longer ignore the fact that some of the best minds in the clergy felt— and felt sincerely—that he was bringing reproach, if not actual discredit, upon his own calling.

This being the case, he wrote, he felt that he had only two alternatives. The first was to change his message and his methods. This he could not do for the simple reason that he believed in both. The second was to remove himself as a source of controversy and a target for criticism. This he was willing to do. Hence his resignation, to take effect immediately.

He added a few words of affection for his congregation, his appreciation of their loyalty and support. Then he put the pencil down, feeling a little sick. He read what he had written, the monitor in his mind automatically suggesting changes that would improve phraseology here, clarify meaning there. But he did not try to make any revisions. He folded the paper and thrust it into the plastic pocket that hung near his pillow. For once, this was no literary endeavor. Besides, the meaning was clear enough.

Resignation: the word had a flat, ugly, negative sound. I've preached positive thinking all my life, he thought. I've preached it to millions of people all over the world. I've been able to communicate with ordinary, everyday people, the ones the scholars never touch. What will they think if I leave the church? Other men have been attacked and yet carried on, trusting their own instincts, believing in their own convictions. . . .

Abruptly he sat down on the berth and rested his forehead on his hand and prayed. It was a prayer of struggle and inner anguish. He tried to empty out all hurt and resentment. He tried to pray for his critics, and finally succeeded. When he raised his head, he smiled a little wryly. They said he was the apostle of easy religion. Well, praying for your detractors wasn't easy. But it was one of the demands his religion made.

Automatically, he went through the routine of going to bed on an American train. Shoes in the locker for the porter—he always derived a childlike pleasure from shoes shined to a mirror finish. Suit hung up. Wallet under the pillow—an old and somewhat foolish precaution, this. Another heritage, no doubt, from his cautious Ohio ancestors.

The magazine that had tormented him all day still lay by the pillow. He put it in the bag with his other papers. Out of sight, out of mind—maybe. He climbed into bed, reached up, switched out the light. The thought came to him of his father, lying weak and semi-paralyzed in his stepmother's little house at Harrison Valley. He closed his eyes and said a prayer for his father, asking the Lord to give him patience and serenity. He also prayed for his loved ones; for Ruth, for the three children. . . .

He tried, then, to go to sleep. But sleep did not come. Lying there in the vibrating darkness, he prayed again, asking the Lord to strengthen him, to help him face the consequences of the decision he had made, to keep all resentment and bitterness out of his heart. Sometimes, when he prayed thus, he was rewarded with a surge of confidence, of reassurance. Sometimes the answer was a deep sense of peace and well-being. But now this did not happen.

As he had recommended so often to other people, he made a

deliberate effort to empty his mind of the thoughts that were tormenting him. He knew that the human brain could consciously hold only one idea at a time, and so he made himself summon up a succession of memories of the past summer in Switzerland—the lake at Lucerne, calm and unruffled; the sound of cowbells in the meadows behind the house at Burgenstock; the Alps at sunset, rising like God's own decision against the flaming sky. As long as he could, he clung to these peaceful images. But all the time, behind them, he was aware of an emptiness, a soreness, a dull ache that would not let itself be banished.

Once he put out his hand and touched the folded paper that contained his resignation. There it was—real, tangible, somehow final. It's done, he said to himself, settled, finished. There's nothing more you can do. Take Saint Paul's advice: having done all, stand. Or better still, having done all, go to sleep.

But sleep was a long time coming. He lay there, staring into the darkness, while under his head the hurrying wheels chanted their iron litany.

His brothers met him at Elmira in the morning: Bob, stocky and bull-shouldered and blunt, the image of their father; Leonard, self-deprecating and shy. It was hard, sometimes, to convince Leonard of his own merits.

Driving southwest through the hazy September morning, Bob warned his older brother not to be shocked by their father's condition. "Dad has had several strokes," he said. "His mind is clear, but he's pretty weak—can't speak above a whisper. You have to lean close to hear what he says. He could go on like this for quite a while, but it's unlikely." He shook his head. "It's quite a strain on Mary."

Mary Peale, their stepmother, was waiting at the door of her little house. White-haired, blue-eyed, she had met and married their father five years earlier. Before that she had had an energetic and useful career as a social worker and—after her first clergyman-husband died—an ordained Baptist minister. Norman knew her to be a woman of great strength of character. He and Leonard had officiated at their father's wedding. It had been a wonderfully happy occasion for the widow and widower, both lonely but both still in love with life, who had agreed to spend their remaining years together.

Now she said, "Your father's longing to see you, Norman. He wants to hear all about Ruth and the children and Switzerland and the new book. . . ." She smiled a little. "Believe me, he's still interested in everything!"

He walked down the hall, stood for a moment summoning up all his reserves of cheerfulness and optimism. He wanted to make sure that no echo of the unhappiness in his own mind should reach his father's consciousness. He prayed briefly that this might be so. Then he opened the door and went in.

The room was bright with morning sunlight. Near the window, in a wheelchair, his father was waiting. Clifford Peale had never been a tall man, but he had been a handsome one, strongly built, with a dark brown mustache and merry blue eyes. Now the once powerful form was wasted, and the mustache was snow white. His eyes had not lost their keenness, or their humor, but his laugh—the wonderful, distinctive, throaty chuckle that his family loved—was only a shadow of itself. "Norman," he said, "it's grand to see you. How's everything?"

"Fine, Dad. Just wonderful!" He was pleased with the conviction he managed to get into his voice. "Got the book finished, all but the final polishing. It nearly finished me, this one. But Ruth got me through, as usual. Kept my nose to the grindstone. To the dictaphone, rather. But tell me—how are you?"

For an hour he sat beside his father, describing the North Cape cruise they had taken in the early part of the summer, telling about the house in Switzerland, the visits to Italy. The old man listened eagerly, but it was apparent that his strength was limited. At last Mary came in and insisted that he lie down. "Norman won't fly away," she said. "He'll be here all day, until late this evening. You get some rest now. Norman, you can sit out under the trees with Leonard and Bob."

Out on the lawn with his brothers he felt that he could discard the mask of gaiety. "It hurts me to see Dad like that," he said. "Not able to join in discussions the way he used to, barely able to speak. It's . . . it's . . ."

"It's the law of life," Bob said. "Dad's fifteen years over the Biblical allotment now. When you live that long, the machinery starts wearing out, that's all."

"I know," Norman said. "But he's always been so active, so vigorous, so . . . alive. And his mind is as sharp as ever."

Leonard nodded. "He always said he wanted to live to be a hundred, remember?"

"He won't make it," Bob said, "but he's had a good life, a useful life. Not many men have served with distinction both as doctor of medicine and doctor of divinity. He was a success in two fields, admired and respected. What more could a man ask?"

Norman pushed his glasses up on his forehead. "Nothing," he said. "Nothing at all."

Bob looked at him. "What's the matter, Norman? What's on your mind? It's not just seeing Dad like this. It's something else. What is it?"

He hesitated, torn between the human desire to share a burden and the awareness that they would not approve of the decision he had reached. But, in the end, he told them. "My mind's made up," he said. "I don't want Dad to know; it would just upset him. But it's reached the point where I have to conform, or I have to get out. I can't do the former, so I've got to do the latter. That's all there is to it."

They disagreed, as he knew they would. Leonard said he owed his loyalty to the millions who believed in him, not to the handful who criticized.

"I know that," he said grimly. "I'll do what I can to reach and help them—outside of the church."

Bob said that he was unduly upset, that the mood of depression and defeatism would pass. "Besides," he added, "up in my neck of the woods I know lots of ministers, sincere, hard-working pastors who truly believe in you. If you resign, won't you be letting them down?"

Norman shrugged wearily. "Perhaps," he said, "but I just don't see how I can go on. Oh, I know I've been discouraged before. But there's something different about it this time. Something final."

They would not agree but, for the time, they stopped trying to sway him. "You'll talk to Ruth, won't you?" Leonard asked. "Before you do anything with that resignation, I mean?"

"Of course," he said. "I've never made a decision of any consequence yet without doing two things—praying about it, and talking it over with Ruth."

"Well," Leonard said, "she'll agree with us. You'll see."

The rest of the day passed quickly. When he was with his father, he kept up his pretense of being gay, buoyant, unconcerned. They talked of many things. At last Mary came in to say that it was time for Norman to go.

His father had been discussing astronomy, a science that had always fascinated him. He had been reading some newspaper article on the subject, he said, just the day before. "And you know," he whispered, "this writer seemed to think that Heaven might be somewhere in the Milky Way!" The blue eyes twinkled with a flash of the old humor. "Better take a look when you go out tonight, Norman. Maybe you'll see it before I do!"

"I'll do that, Dad," Norman stooped to kiss his father's cheek. "And I'll bring Ruth to see you soon."

They were the last words they spoke to each other. Five days later, his father was dead.

The news reached him in New Hampshire, where he and Ruth were staying at the Mountain View House. He had gone there to catch up on some work. There were newspaper columns to write, sermons to plan, a stack of *Guideposts* manuscripts to go through, a batch of *LOOK* questions to answer, the last minute revisions for the new book. Ordinarily he liked the sense of pressure, and the feeling of achievement that came from meeting such demands. But not this time. He worked, as he always did, hour after hour with dogged persistence. But he was haunted by a feeling of vacillation, of indecision, of inadequacy.

He had not changed his mind about resigning from the church. He still felt that it was the logical, the selfless thing to do. But Ruth had persuaded him not to send in the resignation right away. It was too drastic a step to be taken quickly, she said. He should wait a few days, at least. Then, she said, if he still felt it was the right thing to do, she would not try to stand in his way.

When Mary telephoned to say that his father was gone, he and Ruth got in the car and drove through the blue-and-gold weather until they came to Harrison Valley. The little house looked just the same—quiet, peaceful. But he knew it would never be the same for Mary, or for any of them.

There were many telegrams and messages. In eighty-five years a man makes contact with life at many points and leaves his mark on many people. Among all the words of condolence and sympathy, Norman was most touched by something the attending physician said. "What a great gentleman he was; there aren't many like him any more. I was with him all through this last illness, and I never heard him complain. I was with him when he died, too. And the light of reason was in his eyes until I closed them."

The light of reason . . . his father would have liked that.

He thought of this later when he and Ruth stood beside his father's open casket in the little library off the living room.

Death, he firmly believed, was only a transition, a dark door opening to radiance inconceivable. And yet there was always this sense of loss, of abandonment, in those who were left behind.

His father had been so alive, so full of the joy of living. He remembered the winter night when, as a young man in Syracuse, he had been driving his father home and the snow had begun to fall—great lazy flakes at first, then faster and faster until the fields were white and the windshield was frosted and the road disappeared. And he, Norman, had growled his displeasure at this, muttering about driving hazards and whatnot. And suddenly his father had said, "What's the matter with you, boy? Don't you know that it's wonderful to be out in the snow at night? Look at that whiteness! Listen to that silence! Why, it's a miracle! Here we are in the middle of a miracle, and you don't like it!"

Strange, the way things came echoing out of the past. As for the future, in one way he was grateful that his father was gone. His decision to resign from the church would have broken the old man's heart.

"Norman," said a voice behind them, "your father left a message for you."

He turned and saw his stepmother, Mary, standing behind them. Her eyes were shadowed with fatigue, but her voice was steady, calm.

"A message?" he repeated. "What sort of message?"

She turned away and stared out of the window, and he saw that she had a scrap of handkerchief clutched tightly in one hand. "A message he asked me to give you. This is the first chance I've had."

Silence sang in the room. At last Ruth said, "What was it, Mary?"

She turned and faced them. "It was after you left, last week. He kept getting weaker all the time. But finally he called me over and asked me to lean down close, so that I could hear him.

His voice was very feeble. He looked up at me and he said, 'Something's wrong with Norman.' I tried to tell him there was nothing wrong, but he wouldn't listen. He said, 'Something's wrong with Norman. I know him, I can read him like a book, and something's bothering him. And I know what it is. Some of these criticisms are getting to him, they're getting under his skin. He's hurt and discouraged; I've never seen him so down. Now there's something I want you to tell him, from me. Remember it carefully, because I may not get a chance to tell him myself. . . .'"

Mary's voice shook a little; she took a deep breath and went on: "He said, 'Tell Norman I've read every word he's ever written. I've read it all, and I've heard him preach for years, and his message is right. It's in harmony with the basic truths of Christianity and the teachings of Jesus. Tell him I know his message is designed for everyday people, not for scholars, and that I consider him one of the most effective teachers of Christianity in the world today.' And then your father said . . . he said . . ." The tears were running down Mary's face; she no longer tried to stop them. "He said, 'Tell Norman I said they were just a bunch of jackasses, and to pay them no heed —just put his trust in Jesus Christ, and never quit! The Peales never quit. It would break my heart if he should ever quit!'"

She turned away and pressed the crumpled handkerchief to her eyes. In the silence, the clock on the mantel ticked. Norman said, against the tightness in his throat, "Thanks, Mary." He touched Ruth's arm, and they moved away together.

In the adjoining room, he took from his pocket the draft of his letter of resignation. He handed it to Ruth. "Here," he said. "Tear it up."

She tore it into small pieces, dropped the fragments into a wastepaper basket.

He watched them flutter down, out of sight. He said, slowly,

"Dad knew I needed some courage. He's given it to me, just by believing in me."

"He never stopped believing in you," Ruth said. "He believed in you from the beginning, from the very beginning, from the day you were born."

CHAPTER XVII

Full Stride

❦

With Norman's confidence and peace of mind restored, the next two years flashed by quickly.

There was the publication of the book that had cost him and Ruth so much effort: *Stay Alive All Your Life*. In the first year, a hundred and forty thousand copies were sold. Another best seller.

There was another summer in Switzerland, where Norman's affection for that country deepened. "I don't suppose," he said to Ruth, "that the powers that be ever turn to ministers of the gospel for diplomatic appointments. But I can't help envying the American ambassador to Switzerland. What a satisfying job that must be!"

The following summer there had been a memorable trip to the Far East. Ruth had had to talk her husband into it, ignoring his wistful hints that Switzerland would be cool, Switzerland would be beautiful, Switzerland would be nearer, and so on. "Norman," she had said, "the world is shrinking year by year. The Orient is going to play an enormous part in the future. We ought to know more about it. I know you think you don't want to go, but when we come back you'll be glad we went!"

Early in July they left San Francisco, taking John and Margaret with them. They went to Japan, to Hong Kong, to Taiwan, to the Philippines. And Ruth's prediction came true: it was an unforgettable experience.

Everywhere Norman spoke to large audiences. In Japan he spent two hours answering—through an interpreter—questions of Japanese businessmen that ranged from parapsychology to comparisons of Christian and Buddhist ethics. As a roving Rotarian, he spoke to Rotary Clubs all through the Orient. In the Philippines he preached to a congregation of two thousand in the church where his mother, a missionary executive, had conducted services years before. On Taiwan, he preached in the private chapel of Chiang Kai-shek to the Generalissimo and Madame Chiang. His sermon topic that day was "Faith Will Give You Courage!"

Throughout the trip they had been impressed, not only with the warmth of their welcome everywhere, but with the deep hunger they sensed on the part of Asiatic people for more contact, more knowledge, more understanding of the American way of life.

Home again, Norman had found his congregation and friends from everywhere waiting to celebrate his twenty-fifth anniversary as minister of Marble Collegiate Church. He tried to hold the festivities to a minimum, but it was a memorable occasion. Leonard came down from Buffalo and John came up from Virginia to share the pulpit with him. Brother Bob sat with Ruth in the Pastor's pew, Margaret on one side, Elizabeth on the other, and listened proudly as Norman reviewed the twenty-five crowded and eventful years.

Telegrams and letters poured in; from the President of the United States and the Vice President, from both living former presidents, from governors, senators, college presidents, ministers, captains of industry, television and movie stars. From everywhere people sent words of love and admiration. Herbert Hoover summed up all the messages in a single sentence: "You have given great leadership and inspiration to the spiritual forces of our country and to all mankind."

J. Edgar Hoover, Director of the F.B.I., said, "More than any man in the world, Dr. Peale has used every means of communication to reach people, and has taken more beachheads on men's souls."

Compliments and praise from the great and the near-great were welcome, but Norman cherished more the touching tributes that came from ordinary, everyday people everywhere. Day after day the letters poured in, each one saying, in effect, *Thank you. Thank you for helping me to cease my dishonesty, control my anger, live with pain, bear my sorrow, know something about God ...*

A housewife wrote from Tulsa:

I am a woman forty-two years old who has led one of the most frustrated lives imaginable. There probably isn't anything known to womankind that hasn't happened to me at one time or another. I have been married three times and have four children, all girls.

I am from a fairly well-to-do family. My mother died when I was born, and after seven years my father remarried. From that time on, I hated my stepmother, and it was mutual. I always felt not wanted, and to a certain degree I wasn't. It's a horrible existence without a mother's love. In fact, I was suffering from a lack of affection that later grew into an aggravated case of self-pity.

My last marriage, which has lasted for eleven years, was going on the rocks, when a miracle happened to me. I came across your book, *The Power of Positive Thinking*. Dr. Peale, that book changed my life. I have read it three times, reread it, cherished it. After digesting your book, I became alive for the first time in my life. I have begged God's forgiveness for all my sins, and feel He has forgiven me. We have joined the small church in our community, and I have never been so happy or fulfilled as I now am. My husband is a new man, and my children are gloriously happy. Sometimes I'm so shaken with emotion I could cry (I could now). I ask myself, what is this thing that has happened to me, why should I be the recipient of all these blessings when before there was nothing? I always loved God, but I never knew Him. Now I do, and I want the whole world to know it—most of all you! What a wonderful world this is. Bless you.

I have written this down as it came from my heart. Again, I want to thank you for helping me find my way to God. My heart is full of joy, now, and I'm afraid the only way I can repay you is to pray for you, but that I will do.

A doctor wrote from California:

My life story is somewhat different from most you have written about in your books. My childhood was unhappy beyond the power of most people to comprehend. God was painted as a tyrant who spent his time checking the sins of small boys so that He could burn them in everlasting fire. I remained a Christian because I was too frightened to do otherwise.

My mother wanted me to stay home and work in the steel mills. It would be, she said, a good enough occupation for me. Due to the unhappiness and unkindness I had suffered, I felt that everyone was entirely selfish and only interested in some trick to further their own ends. Now I realize that most people did not feel that way, but near the end of my high school course I decided to "show" these people that I was not the dirt under their feet. I decided to become a surgeon.

Believe me, when men decide to make something of themselves for these reasons, they run out of gas sooner or later. I did. I was doing well professionally, but I was dying, mentally. It was my wonderful wife who brought your book home when my mind was grasping for a straw of light or hope. Through the pages of this book, I began to see a merciful, kind, interested, long-suffering, good, and loving God. I understood myself well enough from years of self-dissection, but God I could not see as an interested Being—interested in me, that is.

But then it dawned on me that if the Constellation of Hercules was 35,000 light years away, then God must just be *too great* to forget me. Perhaps you can understand the weights that have rolled off my soul. There were no great unforgiven sins prior to this experience—just a feeling that no one cared, and especially not God.

How much happier I have been nobody can ever realize. May God richly bless you for the great good your written words are doing.

Sometimes the letters were full of humor, conscious or unconscious. A minister friend of Norman's passed along a sample that he had received from one of his parishioners:

I have become intensely interested in the articles and books of Norman Vincent Peale. I like his method, and I describe it as a scientific approach to religion. Having read his book, *The Power of Positive Thinking*, I was fascinated by his chapter on "Making Christ Your Business Partner."

It so happened that my wife and I were making a business trip to New York City, and on the train I told her of the plan outlined in this book. I said that I was going to try it out to see its possibilities.

The following night one of the manufacturers gave a cocktail party which was a very elaborate affair, and when we got back to our hotel room, I was pretty well looped. My wife said, "What would your Partner think of you now?" Of course, I had to admit that He would be somewhat ashamed of me.

The next night, as we were going out for dinner, I turned off all the lights in our hotel room. When my wife asked me why, I replied that I did not think Christ would encourage extravagance, and that even though no one usually bothers to save hotel light bills, I thought it was the considerate thing to do.

We dined at a lovely French restaurant, and started our dinner with a martini. We then ordered a duckling and a bottle of wine with our meal, and it was a delightful affair. But in the taxi on the way back to the hotel I said to my wife, "I don't believe the waiter charged me enough for our dinner. The bill was only $8.50, and surely with the wine and so on it must have been higher than that."

"Well," said my wife, "what would your Partner do in a case like this?"

I said, "Just what I intend to do. I'm going back to pay the difference."

As you know, all taxi drivers hear every word of every conversation. This driver turned around and said, "Are you nuts, or a country hick? People don't do things like that in New York."

I told him that we had had a wonderful meal, and that I would feel better if we paid the fair price.

He said, "I never heard of such a thing. These New York restaurant owners are highway robbers. I should think you'd feel very good to outsmart them."

I said that that wasn't a very Christian attitude and that I was going back to square the account. So I did go back. The hat-check girl recognized me and said, "What's wrong? Why are you back?" When I told her, she said, "Are you kidding?" I assured her I was not kidding, and asked for my waiter. He had gone home, but another waiter checked and found there *had* been a mistake—I owed $14.90 not $8.50.

So I paid it, and the waiter was most impressed and said my waiter would be very grateful.

I guess he was, because about three months later, when we had dinner in the same restaurant, he recognized me and came up to thank me. He said, "You see, when mistakes like this are made, we have to make up the difference ourselves. It so happens that I have a very sick wife, and two small children, and that difference in money meant a great deal to me."

Now then, I think this a perfect example of what a little simple kindness can mean. I'll bet that taxi driver, hat-check girl, and the two waiters went home and told their families of this incident. Naturally, I felt so good about it that I was more than compensated for my honesty, and I am wondering if our world wouldn't be a happier place if more people thought of these little kindnesses. To me, that is religion.

It so happened that that week in New York I was able to test this theory several times, and I now do it many, many times in my daily life, and I am happy to say that in almost every case it works out wonderfully well. I remember your telling me that you had been on a committee with Dr. Peale, and what a regular guy you thought he was. So I thought you might like to hear this little story. . . .

Many appeals for help were touching in their urgency. They came from people of all ages, in all categories. Some were children:

I am a fourteen-year-old girl. My mother has a malignant cancer and has only a few months to live. She has been faithful and good spirited in every way about her tragic fate. She had been bed-fast for about a year and a half, and in the process of things has had to have a leg amputated.

Dr. Peale, I am afraid and constantly worried about the time of her death. I don't know what I shall do, or what kind of person I'll be when it's all over. I have been through more, of course, than I ever dreamed I would. I suppose the Lord did this all to teach us a greatly needed thing. Please excuse my mistakes, sir, but at this point, my hand grows terribly shaky. I hope God will put words into my mind, as to how to say what I mean. Please help me to overcome this fear and dread. I try to keep telling myself that when the good Lord takes my mother, it will be for the best, and she'll live forever with Him, but I still can't rid myself of the empty, longing feeling I'll have when her time comes. . . .

Norman answered the letter as soon as it came to his desk:

Your fine brave letter is before me, and it calls forth in me a prayer that my thoughts will be helpful to you.

You are worried about the time of your mother's passing on into her new experience. We are apt to dread what we do not understand, but we have the promise of Jesus that there is no death as we think of it—only eternal life changing from one form to another. In God's plan, each soul lives in a physical body for a period, then lays it aside and goes into the new life. It is like putting aside a worn garment when it is no longer wanted. It is God's plan, and God is good, so have no fear for your mother—God's love surrounds her.

As for you, Barbara, your letter shows you to be a thoughtful, unselfish, loving mature young lady, a blessing to your parents. You will be lonely—yes, but you will receive understanding and strength to carry you through the difficult days.

You will be in my thoughts and prayers in the coming weeks. Have no fear—"All things work together for good to those who love God". . . .

Letters such as these were usually prompted by Norman's books, but there was also ample evidence that his speaking engagements had a similar impact. Although he rarely used religious terminology in his talks to businessmen, the basic message was there—and the message got through. One cold winter night in Cleveland Norman was addressing a convention of salesmen. Walking down Euclid Avenue on his way to the theater where the meeting was to be held, he happened to see a banner stretched across the street advertising a certain motor oil. It said, "A Clean Engine Delivers Power." Seizing on the obvious analogy, Norman used it in his talk to emphasize the importance of right living if a person wanted to reach his full potential.

After the talk a young salesman came up to Norman exuberantly. "Boy," he said, "did you get through to me! That business about a clean engine delivering power—you were talking right at me. My life, I'm ashamed to say, has been nothing to be proud of in certain areas. Hearing you tonight made me realize that. You didn't mention Jesus Christ in your talk, but I knew you had Him in mind. Sitting there, I asked Him to come into my life and get rid of the grime and filth, and I know He's done it. From now on I'm going to have a clean engine. Thank you!"

Norman considered such episodes extremely significant, because no other minister was making this kind of effort, certainly not on a national scale. For that reason he accepted as many speaking invitations as his crowded schedule would permit, although for every one he accepted he had to turn down at least three.*

On one occasion in the fall of 1958, Norman shared the speaker's platform with the President of the United States. The occasion was the graduating ceremonies in Washington of the National Academy of the Federal Bureau of Investigation. Ruth was in the audience, watching proudly.

---

*The astonishing range of Norman's audiences is indicated in this partial list of sponsors. A complete list would almost be a *Who's Who* of American Industry.

AMERICAN BANKERS ASSOCIATION

NATIONAL INSTITUTE OF DRY CLEANING

NATIONAL RETAIL HARDWARE ASSOCIATION

NATIONAL INSTITUTE OF LOCKER & FREEZER PROVISIONERS

UNITED STATES NAVAL ACADEMY

NATIONAL ASSOCIATION OF MANUFACTURERS

AUTOMOTIVE SERVICE INDUSTRY ASSOCIATION

FEDERAL BUREAU OF INVESTIGATION ACADEMY

UNITED STATES CHAMBER OF COMMERCE

NATIONAL AUTOMOBILE DEALERS ASSOCIATION

NATIONAL ASSOCIATION OF ELEVATOR CONTRACTORS

Like most Americans, Norman was a great admirer of President Eisenhower. A lifelong Republican himself, he felt that the spirit and principles of the G.O.P. were good for the country, and that the honesty and simplicity of the old soldier made him a great leader. He believed, furthermore, that in Richard Nixon the country had a fine Vice President. During the presidential campaign of 1952 the young senator from California had attended a service at Marble Collegiate Church with his family. Greeting him in his office afterward, Norman had expressed pleasure at making his acquaintance. "Oh," said Senator Nixon with a laugh, "I've known you for a long time, Dr. Peale, even though you don't know me. When I was a young naval officer stationed here at the end of the war, Pat and I used to come to hear you preach all the time."

It was an acquaintanceship that was to grow into deep friendship.

That morning in Washington, after the speeches were over, President Eisenhower and Norman sat and talked for perhaps fifteen minutes while diplomas were being awarded to the law-enforcement officers. Afterwards in the car, setting out for Virginia to visit John at Washington and Lee, Norman was still excited.

"He's a wonderful person," he said to Ruth. "I forgot all

HOLIDAY INNS OF AMERICA

ROTARY INTERNATIONAL

NATIONAL POTATO CHIP INSTITUTE

NATIONAL ASSOCIATION OF CEMETERIES

NATIONAL SELECTED MORTICIANS

NATIONAL ASSOCIATION OF RETAIL DRUGGISTS

KENTUCKY FRIED CHICKEN FRANCHISEES

NATIONAL ASSOCIATION OF PURCHASING AGENTS

OHIO STATE FAIR

SALES & MARKETING EXECUTIVES OF WINNEPEG

AMERICAN FOUNDRYMEN'S ASSOCIATION

INTERNATIONAL ASSOCIATION OF ASSESSING OFFICERS

NATIONAL ASSOCIATION OF REAL ESTATE BOARDS

MARY KAY COSMETICS

NATIONAL PAPER BOX MANUFACTURERS' ASSOCIATION

about his being President. He was just another human being, doing the best he can to carry a tremendous load. He doesn't try to carry it all by himself, either. He told me that when he goes to bed at night, he says, 'Lord, I've done the best I could today. Now I wish You'd take charge for a while.'"

"I imagine," said Ruth, "his parents taught him to do that."

"I'm sure they did. He said his mother was one of the most devout people he ever knew. And he told me something she once said to him, something he never forgot. When Ike was a small boy he and his brothers were playing the old-fashioned game of Flinch with his mother. He didn't think much of the luck he was having, and he kept complaining about it. He went on grumbling until his mother said to him, 'Dwight, stop that complaining. You'll find out some day that life is a lot like this game. God deals the cards. It's up to you to play 'em!'"

Ruth smiled a little. "You ought to be able to build a sermon around that."

They were approaching the Lincoln Memorial now, the classic columns white in the clear November sunlight. "Let's drive around the circle," Norman suggested, "and pay our respects to old Abe."

They drove around and parked for a moment where they could look up the terraced steps and see the outline of the great brooding figure within. "What a man he was," Norman said. "All those defeats, all those trials, all those setbacks, and he never quit. It scares me when I think how close I came a couple of years ago to doing just that."

"You didn't though," Ruth said quietly.

"No," her husband said, "thanks to Dad I didn't. Now everything is going well. All the signals seem to be Go. All the signs are pointing up. Maybe everything will be plain sailing from now on."

"I hope you're right," Ruth said.

But Norman wasn't right. He was wrong. One more hard crisis lay just ahead.

CHAPTER XVIII

The Turbulent Sixties

◆§◊◆

Any soul-wrenching experience brings with it the opportunity to grow. Norman had always believed this and had always preached it. He also believed that since he had faithfully practiced in his own life the principles of mental discipline and emotional control that he recommended to others, nothing could upset him very much. In this he was mistaken. Certain developments in the autumn of 1960 did upset him badly—and finding himself so vulnerable upset him still more.

That summer he and Ruth were abroad as usual, traveling in Europe and the Holy Land. In Switzerland he had been pressured by a prominent American clergyman to attend a meeting in Lausanne to discuss the issues in the up-coming American presidential campaign. Later, in London, he found in his mail an invitation, instigated by this same clergyman, to attend a meeting of ministers and laymen in Washington to consider the question of separation of church and state. Like most Americans, Norman considered this a valid principle, but the topic held no burning interest for him. If he hadn't had other business in Washington, he would not have attended the meeting at all.

As it was, he did attend one or two of the sessions. At one session he was asked to chair the meeting. Reluctant, as usual, to refuse any apparently reasonable request, Norman consented—and thereby caused himself to be described as "head of the group," which had absolutely no basis in fact. And, when the going got tough, all others, particularly the clergyman who urged him to participate, were to fade away and leave him to face a storm of criticism alone.

Having been out of the country all summer and arriving in New York just the day before this meeting, Norman did not realize that as the presidential campaign of 1960 heated up, the religious affiliations of the two candidates—an issue of great importance in many people's minds—had been studiously ignored by the press and other media. Even to say that the issue existed was taboo. The result was an unnatural silence beneath which lay an ominous vacuum, or rather an ominous mixture of highly volatile political gases, which needed only a single spark to cause a violent explosion.

Lengthy meetings always bored Norman, and this one was no exception. He left to handle personal matters. When he returned, he was shown a statement that had been drawn up in his absence emphasizing the importance of keeping church and state separate, raising the question of whether this principle could be maintained in case of a Democratic victory, and deploring the silence that had surrounded the issue. The statement did not attempt to tell anyone how to think. It simply recommended the consideration of the question to each person's conscience. Norman's colleagues at the meeting told him that it was to be handed to the press. While troubled by the political connotation, naively he made no objection.

A whirlwind of controversy instantly arose. In the furor, Norman found himself completely alone. Other Protestant clergymen, some of them nationally prominent, had instigated and organized the meeting. Now they were nowhere to be found. The clergyman from the Switzerland meeting later came to Norman's office in New York and apologized for his silence, but by that time Norman had become the target of all the criticism. Actually the statement did force the issue into the open, and ultimately it led to a healthy clarification of the Democratic candidate's position. But the backlash at the time was like the kick of a mule.

Greatly distressed, Norman tried to cancel all his speaking engagements and for the second time in his life wrote out his resignation as pastor of Marble Collegiate Church. Most of his friends remained completely loyal. Out of forty speaking dates that were scheduled, thirty-eight organizations insisted that he appear. The Elders and Deacons of Marble Church refused even to consider his resignation. The first time he appeared in his pulpit after the Washington meeting, the whole congregation rose and stood silently as a token of affection and loyalty, a gesture which heartened him more than any other single thing.

Gradually the storm subsided and—memories being short—it soon faded from people's minds. But for Norman the scars went deep. He kept on preaching his optimistic sermons and writing his up-beat books, newspaper columns and magazine articles, but close friends noted an unaccustomed streak of pessimism in him, as if his discovery that a free society could not always tolerate free discussion had shaken, at least momentarily, his faith in the fairness of people in America.

And indeed, during the turbulent Sixties, faith in America was not always easy to maintain. There were the explosions of racial hatred and violence. There was the appalling and apparently uncontrollable rise in crime. There were the terrible assassinations that shook the nation. There was the steady escalation of the most unpopular war in American history. There was the growing menace of drug abuse. There was the wave of pornography—historically a grim sign of decadence—that seemed to inundate the whole country: theatres, movies, literature, everything. There was the rise of anti-religious activism, with self-appointed zealots working, sometimes successfully, to ban school prayers or bar any reference to the Deity in public ceremonies.

All in all, it was a troubled decade, with confusion and disenchantment dominating the national scene. Returning from his summer travels abroad, Norman was often dismayed by the tension and anger and divisiveness that seemed to prevail at home. He was also troubled by the trend toward social activism in the church. He felt that the church should be aware of and concern itself with social injustice, but not at the expense of its traditional role of winning individual souls to Christ. "If these ultra-liberals don't stop supporting militant and radical groups," he said to Ruth, "if they don't stop draining warmth and vitality and emotion out of religion, we're going to lose the whole ball game."

But if the state of the nation during the 1960's left something to be desired, the private lives of Ruth and Norman continued to be exciting and fulfilling. The first half of the decade saw all three of their children happily married, and in the second half grandchildren were arriving, if not in droves, at least in satisfactory numbers.

Margaret married Paul F. Everett, a dynamic young minister, and went to live in Pittsburgh. They have two children, Jennifer Ruth and Christopher.

John Peale, working for his doctorate in philosophy and teaching at the same time, married Lydia Woods, who presented him with three new additions to the Peale clan: Laura Stafford, Charles Clifford (named after his great-grandfather), and Sarah Lacy. In the fall of 1965 Elizabeth, who after graduating from Mount Holyoke College had worked as a researcher for the *Reader's Digest*, married John M. Allen, a Senior Editor of that magazine. Since Ruth and Norman had bought another home at Pawling, New York John and Elizabeth purchased Sugar Tree Farm on Quaker Hill and soon had two little girls of their own growing up there: energetic, out-going Rebecca Belknap and the somewhat more sedate Katheryn Ruth.

One other pleasant event during these years was the appearance of a motion picture, *One Man's Way*, based on a biography of Norman that had appeared in 1958. Don Murray, who played the part of the young minister, came to Marble Collegiate Church to hear Norman preach and to study his delivery and mannerisms first-hand. Eventually television rights were sold, and the movie appeared in many re-runs across the nation.

During these years Norman's health remained excellent. At one point his gall bladder became troublesome and had to be removed. But there were no complications, and he bounced back quickly after a short stay in the hospital.

Norman's work-load was tremendous. Between 1960 and 1970 he published three more books: *The Tough-Minded Optimist; Sin, Sex and Self-Control; Enthusiasm Makes the Difference*. His newspaper column and radio broadcasts continued to reach millions. His speaking schedule to national business conventions and community public meetings was as crowded as ever.

Norman felt that two of the most significant aspects of his ministry were *Guideposts* and the *Foundation for Christian Living*. In 1970, celebrating its 25th anniversary, *Guideposts* moved into an ultra-modern, $2,000,000 publishing center in Carmel, N. Y. Len LeSourd was still at the helm editorially; on the business end, Bill Boal had retired as general manager and James Leffel had succeeded him. Leonard Peale, Norman's younger brother, had joined the staff as Director of Special Projects. By now circulation was approaching the two million mark, and there were five overseas editions (Chinese, Korean, Thai, Latin-American, and British). In a time when other well-established magazines were in deep financial trouble or disappearing altogether, the dynamic interfaith magazine *Guideposts* continued to grow and prosper, proving Norman's contention that the best road to success is to "find a need and fill it."

The magazine's contents faithfully reflected major changes in the religious climate of the country, especially the reawakening of interest in charismatic forms of worship and the so-called "Jesus revolution" of the late 1960's. But the chief emphasis remained, as always, on the dramatic, personal story of faith at work in ordinary people's lives. Books, records, films, Christmas booklets and television programs broadened still further the magazine's remarkable outreach. As it moved into its second quarter-century, the demand for its message seemed as strong as when it first appeared in leaflet form just after the second World War.

A letter from a housewife in Scottsdale, Arizona, was typical of hundreds received by the editors each year:

"My husband and I started getting *Guideposts* some years ago. Our marriage was in trouble from the start—22 years ago—and was on the verge of divorce countless times. Finally we were divorced a year ago, but both of us were as miserable as ever. One day, reading one of your Spiritual Workshops, I began to feel that I hadn't been praying right. I had saved about 50 issues of *Guideposts*. I got them all out and started reading them again. It took months, but somehow things began to happen in our lives. It affected my husband too, although by now he was living in Indiana—2,000 miles from me. I began praying for him. Last July we met in Chicago and knew how much we really cared. We were remarried on August 25 and have both vowed to keep God at the center of our lives—something we didn't do before. Now you know how much your *Guideposts* helps people."

The growth of the Foundation for Christian Living (an organization entirely separate from *Guideposts*) was just as spectacular as the expansion of *Guideposts*, and in a way even more remarkable since it depended entirely on voluntary contributions. From the start Ruth, who masterminded it all the way, had thought of it as an opportunity for people who could not attend church—shut-ins, invalids, people in hospitals or prisons—to "go to church by mail." But the demand for Norman's sermons came from every type of person, young and old, rich and poor, churchgoers and non-churchgoers all over the world.

By the early 1970's, under the day-to-day direction of Myron L. Boardman, a former publishing executive (the man, in fact, who suggested the title for *The Power of Positive Thinking*), the Foundation's vital statistics had reached astounding proportions. Each month the sermons were reaching a "silent congregation" of more than half a million people in 110 different countries.* Each year the Foundation was sending out some twenty million pieces of mail. It was receiving letters at the rate of more than 2,000 per day. Some of the letters sought advice, others asked for prayers, some simply enclosed contributions as a wordless token of gratitude. The payroll grew to more than ninety persons. A $500,000 building program virtually doubled the amount of office space available—and still was barely enough.

Expenses mounted steadily—but so did contributions. "Three things have made this Foundation possible," Norman once said to a friend. "First, Ruth's faith and vision at the outset. Next, the unbelievable generosity and unselfishness of people who have received Christ in their lives and want other people to share that joy. For us it proved the principle that if you do a constructive service which you believe God wants done, He will see to it that the bills are paid. And finally the devotion and dedication of the Foundation's staff. I know the Lord must approve of what we're doing when He sends us people like Myron Boardman, Oliver Porter, Edwin Ganong, Rocco Murano

---

*To add someone to FCL's mailing list at no charge, simply send the name and address to: Foundation for Christian Living, Pawling, N.Y. 12564.

and all the others. They're simply terrific. The job they do is unique. There's nothing else like it in the history of publishing —or religion!"

In addition to all his other commitments, Norman somehow found time near the end of the turbulent Sixties to act as head of his own denomination; he was President of the General Synod in 1969–70. He was also President of the Protestant Council of the City of New York, an organization of some 1800 churches. He held this post for four years—longer than any predecessor.

The year 1968 brought a happy occasion that once more pushed Norman into the spotlight of national attention. In the autumn of that year, when the presidential campaign pitting Richard Nixon against Hubert Humphrey was at its height, he received a visit from two young people, Julie Nixon and David Eisenhower. "Dr. Peale," said Julie, "we want you to do something for us."

"Of course," said Norman cheerfully. "What?"

"Marry us," they both said at once.

"Marry you?" cried Norman. "Certainly. I'll marry you any time, anywhere! This is wonderful! Who knows about it?"

"Nobody," they said, "except our parents. And now you."

"Where will the wedding be? In the White House?"

"No," Julie said, "right here in this old church. I've loved it ever since I was a little girl. And David loves it too."

Julie went on to make it clear that she considered marriage a sacred relationship and a wedding a religious ceremony. Determined not to have her own turned into a public spectacle, she asked Norman to keep their plans secret until the time came for a formal announcement.

Norman promised that he would, and he did, but neither he nor Ruth foresaw the pressure that would be exerted by all the media. The engagement of these young people, members of two of America's best known families, was finally announced, but not the date of the wedding or the place. Speculation at once reached a feverish intensity. Where would the wedding be? Who would conduct the ceremony?

For the next six weeks Norman could not answer his own phone—Ruth and his secretaries had to screen all calls for him. Inquisitive reporters badgered his office day and night. False rumors were everywhere. One morning, when Ruth and Norman were in Phoenix, Arizona, they turned on a popular TV breakfast show and heard to their amazement and amusement that *Women's Wear Daily* had broken the story: the Nixon-Eisenhower wedding was to take place in the Cathedral of St. John the Divine.

This "scoop" was soon proved false, but even after the correct plans were announced the pressure persisted. Reporters swarmed around like bees, demanding endless details, none of which Ruth was at liberty to divulge. To placate them she finally held a press conference, conducted a tour of Marble Collegiate Church, and gave facts about its long and distinguished history. This hardly satisfied the reporters. "Mrs. Peale," one of them said resignedly, "you can talk more and give less information than anyone I ever listened to!" Others tried to involve her in a discussion of what sort of marriage counseling Norman might be giving to the young couple. When that failed, a persistent news-hen said, "What would *you* do, Mrs. Peale, if a certain young couple brought a marital problem to you?" "I'd refer them to my husband," replied Ruth serenely.

One Sunday when the President-elect and his family, along with Julie's fiancé, attended the early service at Marble Collegiate Church, Julie, who had brought her own Bible, asked if she might talk to Norman between the services about various details of the ceremony. She wanted to use the Quaker "thee" in certain passages, and she had also picked out her favorite Psalms, the 100th and the 121st. She and David were closeted so long with Norman that her father—waiting with his wife and Ruth in the outer office—began to fear she might delay the second service. He was about to knock on the inner office door, but his wife dissuaded him. "Relax Dick," she said. "Remember, you're only the father of the bride."

"I know," said the next President of the United States with a sigh. "I tell you, I can cope with the inauguration all right, but to get through this wedding is something else!"

Elaborate security precautions had to be taken before the rehearsal, which lasted over two hours, and before the wedding itself. Secret Service men were everywhere. Closed circuit television coverage was arranged so that David's grandfather, former President Eisenhower, could watch from the hospital bed in Washington where he was confined. Since the ceremony was held on Sunday, December 22, at 4 p.m., the church was beautifully decorated with Christmas wreaths and greenery and banks of poinsettias. The wreath behind the altar was almost fourteen feet in diameter. The entire Nixon family attended the morning worship service. Everything went off perfectly, and for the Peales the day was doubly exciting because their daughter Elizabeth and her husband John Allen brought their first child to the church to be baptized by Norman: Rebecca Belknap Allen.

By this time, Richard Milhous Nixon had been elected to the presidency. A few months after Julie's wedding, Ruth and Norman were invited to the White House. While they were there, a suggestion was made that led Norman into one of the most exciting and memorable experiences of his life . . . a Presidential assignment in Vietnam.

CHAPTER XIX

Mission to Vietnam

❧

"Norman," said the 37th President of the United States, "I have a job for you."

It was a rainy Sunday in June, 1969. President Nixon had been in office only a few months. One of the innovations he had made at the White House was to have simple, non-denominational religious services on Sunday mornings to which about 300 guests were invited. On this day—Father's Day, 1969—Norman had been asked to preach.

He had hesitated briefly, reluctant to leave his own pulpit and his own congregation. But a request from the White House is almost like a royal command. "Besides," Ruth had said loyally, "the President has so many problems that we should help provide a worship service if he wishes one." So Norman sent word to the White House that he would be honored to be there.

He and Ruth had flown to Washington the night before. A White House limousine met them and took them to their hotel. At 10:30 the next morning another government car drove them to the White House. There an aide conducted them to the First Family's living quarters on the second floor, where the President and Mrs. Nixon greeted them and chatted for a few minutes over coffee. Then the President led the way down to the East Room of the White House where the service was to be held. Here, at the appropriate time, he introduced Norman, who preached a fifteen minute sermon, "Be Glad You Have Problems," to an appreciative audience.

After the service there was a reception where the President and Mrs. Nixon shook hands with everyone. Ruth and Norman, also in the receiving line, were impressed with the diversity of the guests: Supreme Court Justices and Cabinet Ministers, members of the White House staff, secretaries and telephone operators, some with their children. The President seemed to know them all by name and had a pleasant word for each. One old gentleman told him in a quavering voice that the last time he had been at a White House reception as a small boy he had shaken hands with Teddy Roosevelt. "What impressed you most?" President Nixon wanted to know. "His beautiful striped trousers," replied the guest promptly. The President looked down at his own sober dark suit and laughed. "Times have changed," he said.

After the reception, Ruth and Norman were invited to a family lunch in the private dining room on the second floor of the White House. Both the President's daughters, Tricia and Julie, were there, also Julie's husband David Eisenhower, his mother Mrs. John Eisenhower and her daughter Barbara. A fire was laid and the President, who loves open fires, asked an attendant to light it. Conversation was animated, the young people joining eagerly in discussions that ranged across the whole spectrum of national and foreign affairs. And it was in connection with one of these topics that the President suddenly told Norman that he had a job for him.

Although he hadn't the faintest notion of what his host might be going to say, Norman replied that he would be happy to do anything he could.

"What I'd like you to do," the President said, "is go to Vietnam. Talk to our troops there, boys in the field, boys on some of our naval vessels, boys in the hospitals. Give them the same inspirational message that you give Sunday after Sunday in Marble Collegiate Church. Cheer them up, make them feel that the people back home haven't forgotten them, really care about them and appreciate what they're doing. Do you think you could find time for an assignment like that?"

For a moment, a wave of conflicting emotions swept over Norman. He was touched and flattered that the President should think so highly of him and of his ability to reach and help people. He had missed the excitement and privilege of serving his country as a military chaplain in World War II. He knew that any assignment in a war zone carried an element of danger. How would he stand up to the experience of flying over jungles full of hostile guerilla fighters or visiting outposts under fire? For perhaps a second he hesitated. Then he pushed all doubt out of his mind and told the President calmly that he and Ruth were already planning a round-the-world trip and he would be glad to stop over in Vietnam and do whatever such an assignment required.

"Good," said the President. "I'll set it up with our military people. You'll hear from the Secretary of Defense. And I think you'll find it a memorable experience."

It was, indeed. First, Ruth and Norman flew to Japan, where Norman followed his usual pattern of international speaking engagements. Next they went to Taiwan, where President Chiang Kai-shek and Madame Chiang had invited them to stay at their summer palace high up in the mountains. There, at a formal dinner in their honor, Norman happened to ask Madame Chiang how her husband managed to stay so youthful looking and alert despite his great age. "He does it by prayer and meditation," Madame Chiang replied. "He devotes thirty minutes to prayer three times a day."

Next morning, Norman happened to wake up very early. He went to the window and looked out into the chilly mist. What he saw made him call Ruth to join him. Across a court-yard on a balcony a tall robed figure was pacing slowly up and down, followed by a great dog. It was Chiang Kai-shek at his morning devotions, drawing strength and inspiration from his deep Christian faith.

From Taiwan the Peales flew on to Hong Kong, greatest bargain city in the world for shoppers. Then on to Bangkok, where Ruth was to wait while Norman carried out his Vietnam assignment. The next four and a half days were the most crowded and in many ways the most meaningful of his life.

An Army chaplain, Col. Hans E. Sandrock, was assigned to him as chief aide and guide. A small military jet airplane picked them up in Bangkok and flew them to Saigon, where Norman received the first of several military briefings. Then he was whisked to a guest house known as "The White House" where visiting VIP's were given comfortable accomodations. Throughout much of his stay in Vietnam, Norman wore olive drab Army fatigues with "Rev. Peale" lettered above one jacket pocket and the single word "Pastor" above the other.

In the summer of 1969 American military presence in Viet-nam was at its height under the command of General Creighton Abrams. After reading endless accounts in the American press of destruction and devastation in South Vietnam, Norman was prepared to find Saigon practically in ruins. He was amazed to find almost no signs of war at all. It was a busy, crowded city that reminded him of New Orleans with its wrought-iron balconies and handsome residences behind tall iron fences.

Hundreds of bicyclists pedaled through the streets. Shops offered every type of merchandise. Norman was struck by the beauty of the women with their dark eyes and lustrous hair, many wearing a long white garment over black slacks that reached to their ankles and created a very graceful effect. He asked his guide if such women had any contact with the American troops. "Probably not," said Sandy Sandrock. "These are very conservative, highly moral people who live their own lives within their own culture."

As a representative of the President, Norman was given a three-star security rating. This meant that every time he flew in an Army helicopter, three other 'copters went along as protection. He first noticed this on a visit to an American pacification team at an outlying village, where he found a lively game of baseball in progress between a mixed group of Americans and Vietnamese. A black sergeant from North Carolina interpreted a speech of welcome made by the Vietnamese head man of the village. Then he showed Norman what he and his men were doing for the villagers in terms of sanitation, health and education. "Most of our people over here," the Sergeant said, "aren't fighting—they're building. When I finally get out of the Army, I plan to come back here and make helping these people my life's work."

At a dinner given for Norman by General Abrams, the same emphasis was stressed. "You'd never know it from reading the *New York Times*," one high-ranking officer said, "but our presence here is really building a new civilization. All the media back home seem to report is the negative side of this war. I wish they'd talk once in a while about the hospitals and schools that our troops have sponsored!"

Norman was impressed by General Abrams, a man of firm opinions, but also with a gentler side that revealed itself in his love of classical music and fondness for serious books. At the dinner he spoke out strongly against the pornography that seemed to be engulfing the United States, and especially against the degradation of the American stage—sentiments that Norman heartily endorsed.

Norman was equally impressed with Ambassador Ellsworth Bunker, who also entertained him at his residence, a fine old house that once had belonged to a prominent French family.

Again the high ceilings and revolving fans reminded Norman of New Orleans. The table was set in the garden, with flares flickering against the tropical shubbery. White-coated Vietnamese servants moved quietly to and fro. The guests—all male —included several Vietnamese senators. Knowing of the constant danger of assassination attempts, Norman asked his host how he could be sure the Viet Cong might not try to infiltrate the Embassy staff. "I take all reasonable precautions," said the courtly, white-haired Ambassador. "Beyond that, I live without fear."

In that peaceful setting the war seemed far away. It seemed much closer when Norman visited the wounded in various hospitals. Many beds were empty—a sight to gladden the heart —but many were occupied. On entering a ward, Norman would ask his military companions to remain behind, because he wanted to visit these boys as a simple civilian pastor and talk to them without any protocol or constraint. He would stand by a bed and ask the occupant, "What's your name, son? What happened to you? How are you feeling?" Always the answers were cheerful, optimistic, up-beat. They felt fine; they felt great; they wanted to get back to their outfit; they wanted to finish the job. Norman saw hundreds of men and spoke with dozens. Not one complained. Not one criticized the Army. Not one was anti-establishment. "I can hardly believe all this," he said to one hospital chaplain. "How do you account for all these negative reports that are printed in the States or carried on T.V.?" The chaplain shrugged. "I once asked a reporter why he wrote such slanted copy," he said. "The man told me that if he didn't he would lose his job."

One such reporter asked Norman what his "investigations" had revealed so far. "I'm not here as an investigator," Norman told him quietly. "I'm here as a pastor to help anyone who needs my help, that's all." The man looked disappointed and moved away.

A highlight of Norman's Vietnamese adventure was a visit to

the great aircraft carrier *Kitty Hawk*, on combat station off the coast. Norman flew first to the huge American airbase at Danang, then transferred to a small Navy jet capable of landing on the flat-top's deck. The plane was piloted by the admiral's own pilot, the admiral himself being on board the *Kitty Hawk*. Norman could hardly have been in better hands. As they strapped him into a complicated harness and fitted him with a Mae West life jacket, he asked perhaps a bit apprehensively just what all these precautions meant. "Oh," said the pilot, "there's nothing to landing on a carrier. There are five arresting cables stretched across the flight deck. Even if we miss the last one, we can always go around again." Norman then observed his protecting helicopters. The pilot said, "They are just in case we go into the drink."

"Does anyone ever fall in the drink?" Norman wanted to know.

"Hardly ever," said the pilot. "And chances are a helicopter will be able to fish you out if you do."

Not entirely reassured, Norman watched a tiny speck on the horizon grow into a mighty floating airdrome carrying upwards of 5,000 fighting men. Large as it was, the landing area looked alarmingly small against the vastness of the sea. Skillfully the pilot made his approach. Wheels touched the deck. There was a terrific jolt as one of the cables caught the hook. To Norman's considerable relief, they were down—intact.

Waiting in white uniforms were the captain and some of his officers. Since at sea the captain remained constantly on the bridge, he had made his quarters available to Norman, complete with mess-boy ready to bring him anything he wanted. Dinner that night was in the admiral's quarters. After dinner Norman was to address the crew.

They assembled, hundreds of them, in the foc's'le, a huge area between decks. There were sailors perched on cranes, on windlasses, on stanchions. Under the sun-heated metal, even at night it was fearfully hot. While he waited to be introduced,

Norman watched the admiral's crisp uniform turn into a sodden, shapeless mass of cloth. He could feel the sweat trickling down his own back. When he did stand up to speak, and essayed a gesture or two, he found himself swishing perspiration in all directions.

But he forgot his discomfort when he began to speak. He told his listeners that he had asked the President what message he wanted to send to the men fighting this unpopular war so far from home. "The President said to me, 'You tell them that their country loves them, and their President loves them—yes, tell them that God loves them." At the end, the applause was tremendous, and dozens of the men crowded around Norman, wanting to shake his hand.

Later that night he went up on the bridge and watched as combat planes took off and others, their missions completed, came winging back like homing pigeons. At one point the captain was informed that a plane was overdue, and Norman felt the tension that gripped the whole ship until the welcome word came that the missing plane had been spotted by radar.

He had little sleep, because all night long it sounded as if huge chains were being dragged about the metal deck just over his head. Up early for goodbyes, he found that taking off from a carrier is even more hair-raising than landing on one. "They catapult you off," he told Ruth later. "That's fine, but nobody told me that the plane then begins to sink before it picks up speed. It seemed to me that we sank forever before we began to climb again!" It was during this take-off that he noticed the lips of one of his chaplain friends moving silently. "Were you praying?" Norman asked him later. "Sure," said the chaplain promptly. "Weren't you?"

Most unforgettable of all Norman's experiences in Vietnam was the service he conducted for the Seventh Marine Regiment on Hill 55 far up in the combat zone. The Marines had seen hard fighting and had suffered heavy casualties. The service was to be a memorial to the men who had died.

First he flew to the headquarters of the Third Marine Amphibious Force, where he was welcomed by Major General Ormond R. Simpson, commander of the 1st Marine Division. Then he and the General flew on to Camp Muir on Hill 55, the home of the Seventh Marines. There in a shack he was introduced to several Marine chaplains, each of whom described his job to the visitor from New York. One said casually that one of his duties was ministering to an outpost twenty miles away—just a squad of men, but to get there he had to walk the whole distance through mine fields and under fire, never knowing if the next step might be his last.

"Did you volunteer for this duty?" Norman asked.

"Yes," said the chaplain. "I volunteered."

"Why?"

"Because I became a minister to serve the Lord Jesus Christ and His children wherever they might be."

"What denomination are you?"

"Catholic."

"Are you happy in this work?"

The chaplain smiled. "I wouldn't be anywhere else for anything in the world!"

Later Norman said to Ruth, "I really felt unworthy in the presence of such men. They're tremendous—just tremendous."

They left the shack finally and went up a hill—Hill 55. At the top a simple altar had been set up between the flags of the United States and Vietnam. It was hot, but a breeze fluttered the flags. Seated on the ground were perhaps 700 Marines in combat gear, many with their rifles. All around were sandbagged fortifications. In front of the altar was an M-16 rifle, inverted, with its bayonet thrust into a single sand-bag. On top of the rifle was a helmet, symbolic of those who had died in combat.

From the hilltop the ridges and rivers of the region were plainly visible. "That's the infiltration route over there," General Simpson said, pointing across the valley where bombers were at work, the sound of the exploding bombs clearly audible. He went on to indicate different areas that the troops had named: Dodge City, Arizona Territory, Oklahoma Hills, Pipestone Canyon.

The service began. A military band played. The soldiers sang the old majestic hymns: *Nearer My God to Thee,* and *My Faith Looks Up to Thee.* A chaplain read from the Scriptures and offered a prayer. Sitting beside the General, Norman was so deeply moved that he wondered if he would be equal to his assignment. In a moment of doubt and hesitation he turned to the General. "What do you want me to say to them?" he whispered.

The General was staring at the ground. "Why ask me?" he replied. "Some of the men of this regiment have died. Others will die. All are in great danger. This may be the last time some will ever hear the name of Jesus Christ or receive a Christian message. Tell them about patriotism. Tell them that their country is worth dying for. Tell them that freedom is worth any price. Say anything you want."

As he always did before speaking, Norman prayed silently for help and guidance. Then he stood up and faced the tired, patient faces of the Seventh Marines. He spoke first about the sombre hills and valleys and canyons around them and the names they had given them. Some day, he told them, some of those names might be enshrined in American history alongside such names as Lexington and Bunker Hill, Bull Run and Gettysburg, Chateau Thierry and Belleau Woods, Guadalcanal and Iwo Jima . . . all the places where American men have loved their country so much that they were willing to give their lives for it.

Next he spoke to them of their fallen comrades. "You knew those men," he said. "They didn't want to die. They hoped, each one of them, to go home some day, to walk the tree-lined streets of some quiet American town, to see their parents and their sweethearts and their wives again. Now they have sacrificed all that, but their sacrifice is testimony to a dream. The dream is that we're going to build on earth some day a state of affairs that Jesus called the kingdom of God, where men will live together in love and peace and harmony regardless of racial origin or national background or any difference."

As he spoke, the lines of a poem came into his mind. On his way to the service on Hill 55 he thought the poem might be suitable, but he had been unable to remember all the words. Now, suddenly and effortlessly the words came to him, written by an Englishwoman half a century ago and half a world away, but appropriate still:

"I saw the spires of Oxford
    As I was passing by,
The gray spires of Oxford
    Against a pearl gray sky.
My heart was with the Oxford men,
    Who went abroad to die.

The years go fast in Oxford,
    The golden years and gay,
The hoary Colleges look down
    On careless boys at play.
But when the bugles sounded war,
    They put their games away.

. . .

God rest you happy, gentlemen,
    Who laid your good lives down,
Who took the khaki and the gun
    Instead of cap and gown.
God bring you to a fairer place
    Than even Oxford town.

A deep hush had fallen on Hill 55. There was no sound except for the snapping of the flags and the dull explosions of the bombs far across the valley. In that silence Norman felt closer to his audience and closer to some ultimate reality than ever before in his life. "In the solemnity of this moment," he said, "we must face the fact that you are the ones who are called upon to endure the stress of battle. You are the ones who must bear the heat and burden of the day. May the good God, your Heavenly Father, and your Savior Jesus Christ watch over you and protect you and keep you from harm. But if, in the uncertainties of battle, the moment comes when you too are called to go forward with your fallen comrades, may you meet it bravely, and know that your soul is clean at the last, and that another life is just beginning. And may we who are older and cannot fight the battles everlastingly keep faith with you, so that together we shall turn not only our own beloved country but the whole world into a place of peace and good will.

"As for those who have died here, we can say about them the greatest thing that can be said about any mortal man: 'Greater love hath no man than this, that he lay down his life for his friend.' "

He walked back to his seat through a profound silence. Nobody stirred. When he looked at the General, he saw tears on that tough Marine warrior's face. A black soldier with a magnificent voice stood up and sang, "*How Great Thou Art.*" A squad of riflemen fired a volley. A bugler played "Taps." The service was over.

There was no time to linger; the hilltop was too exposed; the officers did not like to keep the men so concentrated; they had to get back to their posts. Within a week, although Norman could not know it, many of these men including a battalion commander would be dead.

He shook hands with all the officers. He climbed into the helicopter whose rotors were revolving and strapped himself into his seat. But then on impulse he unfastened the belt, stood up, and went to an open hatch in the rear where he had an unobstructed view. Just below him the General and the 700 men and officers of the Seventh Marines were drawn up at attention, saluting him. He felt his throat tighten. Not knowing exactly how he should respond, he raised his hand and waved. Instantly the rigid lines dissolved and fourteen hundred hands waved goodbye in return.

He watched until they were out of sight. Then he went back to his seat, put his face in his hands, and wept like a child.

CHAPTER XX

The View from the

Top of the Hill

❧

As the hectic Twentieth Century moved into its eighth decade, Norman could look around him with considerable optimism and satisfaction. God was in His heaven—and if everything was not entirely right with the world, things were looking considerably better. In the White House his friend Richard Nixon was winding down the war. His own ministry was reaching more people than ever. The obsession with social action seemed to be diminishing in the churches. All over the country young people were reaching out on their own and finding a relationship with Christ that left them filled with a soaring sense of joy. The national climate of anger and recrimination that had prevailed for so long seemed to be disappearing.

The pessimism that had shadowed Norman's thinking during the mid-Sixties had also vanished. "This country went through some tough trials," he told his friends. "But that's life's way of renewing things. It takes a strong wind to blow away dead leaves and knock down dead branches but then, if the tree is sound, it will put forth new growth."

His critics and detractors seemed to have faded away. "I guess I've outlived them," he said with a grin. "In a way I miss them; it's stimulating to be shot at. Actually, the trouble with those fellows was that they were preaching a sterile religion, too theoretical, too abstract. Mine is so simple. All I've tried to do is tell people that their lives can be bigger, better, finer, greater and happier through a positive faith in Jesus Christ. Christianity works—when it's worked. That's the whole message. That's all I've been trying to say all these years."

He kept on saying it every Sunday morning from the pulpit of the Marble Collegiate Church, although by now he was past the age when many ministers retire. "You know," he said to Ruth one Sunday, "when I was up there in the pulpit this morning, orating as usual, all of a sudden I thought: I'm getting awfully tired of the sound of my own voice!"

She had to repress a smile. "It went right on, though, didn't it?"

"Sure it did," said Norman. "It had to, poor thing. But sometimes I wonder what it would be like to have a little house somewhere and just take it easy. No more pressure. No more preaching. No more lecture tours. Do a little writing perhaps . . ." He looked sideways at her to judge the effect of this idyll. The suppressed smile was visible now. "Ha!" said Norman briskly. "I'd probably go crazy, wouldn't I?"

Ruth laughed out loud. "You certainly would," she said. "What's more, you'd probably drive me crazy too!"

The first year of the decade brought a great loss to Norman; his brother Bob died. Like many physicians, Bob was more concerned about other people's health than his own. He steadfastly refused to lighten his heavy work-load, and eventually the strain proved too much for him.

A few days after Bob's death Norman had one of the remarkable psychic experiences that sometimes come to sensitive or spiritually attuned people. In a sermon preached on Easter Sunday, 1971, he told his congregation about it.

"On November 30, 1970," he said, "my younger brother, Bob, died. He was a doctor of medicine, with a very scientific mind. Naturally in our lifetime we talked a great deal about sickness and death, because that was his business—and mine too, when you get right down to it. He was not as demonstrative, perhaps, as I am, but his faith was the same.

"Bob's office is near the Foundation for Christian Living building in Pawling, New York. Between the Foundation's building and Bob's office is an open plaza. On the 4th day of December, 1970, a Friday morning, we were having a prayer service in the auditorium of the Foundation. All our fellow workers were gathered there. Somebody was introducing me to make some remarks.

"It was a glorious winter morning; sunlight was pouring through the windows. I was not thinking about Bob consciously at all; I was thinking of what I was about to say in my talk. But all of a sudden, I saw him—I saw Bob. He seemed to be walking rather rapidly across the plaza toward his office. Now I couldn't physically see the plaza because there was a wall separating me from it, in fact there were two walls of concrete block with no windows on that side of the auditorium. All the same, I saw him clearly and distinctly, He looked to be about forty years of age, a handsome man in the full health of middle life. And there was a wonderful smile on his face. He saluted me in the old, familiar gesture, and this is what I understood him to say: 'Forget it, Norman; it's all all right.' And then the whole scene faded.

"They introduced me to give my remarks, but I was so emotionally overwhelmed that I could not speak. I told the people that some day I would tell them why. I once read a book in which the writer made the point that although we cannot see through the blades of an electric fan when they are stationary, we can see through the whole radius of the fan when the blades are revolving at high speed. In this case I had experienced something like this phenomenon which enabled me to see through physical barriers and limitations and experience my brother's presence."

Norman was convinced that his brother had been allowed momentarily to get through to him, to reassure him that all was well with him, that death was just a transition. Ruth, who was sitting beside him when he had the experience, felt just the same way.

Ruth had started out the decade by joining Norman as a writer of books, and indeed a writer of best sellers. Some years previously she had written an article for *Reader's Digest* called "The Adventure of Being a Wife." In it she defended the much-maligned institution of marriage and expressed her conviction that being a wife was the most challenging and demanding career any woman could have, and the most difficult. Norman's publishers, Prentice-Hall, asked her if she would expand the article into a full-length book. Ruth had doubts about her ability to do this, but Norman encouraged her to try. She had helped him with all his books, he said; now it was time for her to attempt one on her own. The job took her almost a year, but results were gratifying. By the end of 1971, more than 150,000 copies of the book were in print, three book clubs had distributed it, and many magazines had published extracts from it.

Norman was so proud that he frequently referred to Ruth's book in his talks, claiming enthusiastically that it was better than any of his own. He even managed to sustain his enthusiasm when once or twice listeners came up afterward and earnestly agreed with him.

When her book was published, Ruth had many invitations to appear on television programs. One was the David Frost show, where she found herself on a panel with three other women who were stridently hostile to the institution of marriage and to most of the values that Ruth had advocated in her book.

Outnumbered and certainly out-shouted, Ruth maintained her poise and defended her beliefs. "Although," she said later, "I remember wondering how on earth I got myself into such a situation."

Afterward, the program mail flooded in, praising Ruth's dignity and composure under fire. And there was a surprising sequel to the episode. One of Ruth's most vocal antagonists on the panel was a black girl whose militant ideas included a vast contempt for matrimony. Months later, appearing again as a guest on the same show, the same girl announced that she was getting married. "You?" cried David Frost, astonished. "Married?" "Yes," said his panelist cheerfully. "When we had that discussion with Mrs. Peale, I was so impressed with how she acted and what she said and how happy she seemed that I decided she must be right and the rest of us must be wrong. So I'm getting married!"

Ruth's book produced a deluge of fan mail. Many writers had problems and she spent much time trying to give advice and encouragement to those correspondents. Norman's mail, too, continued to be as varied and fascinating as ever. One quaintly spelled letter that reached him at the Foundation for Christian Living from a nine-year-old named Susan was particularly touching:

Dear Dr. Norman Viencent Peal:

I have this proplem that I would like you to send me some booklets on. My mother is on dope and I am living with my Grandmother. My mother never married. We don't get to see her very often. That's my sister and I. And could you put her on your pray list. I go to church every Sunday. I am only nine years old so I don't really understand.

Norman answered quickly, praising her courage, sending her some literature, and promising to keep her in his prayers. "Understanding the unhappy things in our lives," he wrote, "is very hard to do, no matter how old we are. I don't understand many times myself. I try always to remember, though, that the bad things don't come from God, but from His enemy, who wants us to blame God for them and give up hope." He ended his letter: "So each night, Susan, when you go to sleep, give the day back to God's hands. Each morning when you wake up, take a lovely new day from Him and 'put it on' the way you would a new dress. Expect nice things from the day (be sure to look for them) and you will have many happy dreams come true."

Three years later he heard from the child again. Now Susan was twelve. Everything—except perhaps her spelling—was much better. Her sister was happily married. Her mother, completely changed, was no longer on dope. "I want to thank you," she wrote, "for your prayer that was said for her and I can fell asuared that it was heard. Let me end this letter with my thanks to you again."

Delighted with this turn of events, Norman wrote back congratulating her "for the wonderful way God has worked in your life and in your mother's life." He added: "You may be interested to know that your first letter so impressed me that soon after receiving it, I read it when I preached in the White House. The President and Mrs. Nixon, and particularly Julie, were deeply touched by it. I thought you would be interested to know that."

In December, 1971, the First Family visited New York. On Sunday morning they came to Marble Collegiate Church to hear Norman preach, greeted him and Ruth affectionately at the church steps as they arrived and visited in Norman's study. Young David Eisenhower particularly liked an anecdote Norman used in his sermon about Abraham Lincoln in illustrating the basic stability and solidity of the nation. According to the story, Lincoln was visiting an old farmer and his wife somewhere in Illinois. It was in August, the time of year when the earth passes through the swarm of particles in space that causes a rain of shooting stars. Looking out of the window late at night, old Hiram observed this phenomenon and became convinced that it was the end of the world. In a panic, he woke up his wife. "Call Abe!" was the wife's first thought. "He'll know what to do!"

So Hiram woke up Abe and told him what he had seen. Gaunt and lanky in his nightshirt, Abe went to the window, poked his head out, and watched the falling stars for a few moments. Then he drew his head in. "It's all right, Hiram," he said reassuringly. "The great constellations still stand!"

Young David was so impressed with the sermon that he wrote Norman a long letter expressing the hope that he could live up to his own great heritage and do something worthwhile for his country.

David was not the only member of the family who wrote to Norman. A few days later a handwritten note came from the President—most unusual, because he rarely if ever communicates in that manner:

Dear Norman,

It was not until I returned to the White House that I learned from Julie of the special things that you did to make our visit to Marble Collegiate such a memorable one.

The photograph in the program was taken on the wedding day three years ago. And the organist played the same music as we left the sanctuary as he did on that day.

As Julie said, "Only the Peales would have been so thoughtful."

Your prayer for the family was moving, your sermon eloquent, and above all your friendship cherished beyond description.

I only wish we could come more often!

From all the Nixons to all the Peales our very best wishes for Christmas and the new year.

R.N.

Norman replied, thanking the President and assuring him

that his letter would always be a treasured heirloom in the Peale family.

More and more the global aspects of Norman's ministry were coming to the fore. For years he had been one of America's most popular convention speakers—he once estimated that he had given close to 2,000 speeches in every State of the Union except Alaska. But now requests were coming in from foreign lands as well. Partly this was a response to his books, published in thirty-three languages all over the world, and the dissemination of his sermons by the Foundation for Christian Living. But the basic reason, Norman felt, was that people were much the same everywhere, with the same problems, the same hopes and fears and dreams. "People want to hear about positive thinking and positive living," he said, "because they know instinctively that there is a deep correlation between these ideas and a positive religious faith. They need that faith, they want that faith, and positive thinking helps them find it. It's not I; it's the message!"

Dramatic proof of this came on a trip he and Ruth took to Australia in the spring of 1971. Rotary International had asked Norman to be the main speaker at a convention of 17,300 Rotarians and their wives from practically every country under the sun. As soon as his acceptance was announced, he was besieged by invitations from Australian ministers to preach in their churches. He and Ruth arrived in Sydney on a Saturday night, having stopped briefly at Pago-Pago in American Samoa where Norman also gave a talk. The next morning he preached two sermons to overflow crowds in St. Stephen's Presbyterian Church. The same night he spoke to an enthusiastic audience that filled a large theatre. He preached again on Wednesday at a noonday service. Again the church was packed. At night he addressed a vast congregation in the great St. Andrews Anglican Cathedral.

The climax came on the last day of the Rotary convention when Norman was the featured speaker at the final session.

There were six thousand people in one hall, five thousand in another, and the overflow filled the street outside. Norman's speech was titled, "Positive Thinkers Get Positive Results." When he finished, his listeners leaped to their feet and gave him a terrific ovation. "It's amazing," the grateful and gratified Norman said to Ruth. "The concept of positive thinking has gone right around the world!"

He loved the excitement of speaking to responsive audiences. "I'm like an old fire-horse," he said once, "who hears the bell. I get a great kick out of watching the crowd gather, feeling the tension build up inside me, knowing the thrill that comes when you really get through to them." But all the acclamation left him unchanged. People were often amazed by his self-deprecating modesty. "He's the easiest man in the world to work for," one of his assistants said. "He never pressures you. He just leaves you to do the job, and so of course you knock yourself out trying to do it."

Although getting a bit older, Norman managed to retain the youthful, almost impish quality that his friends had always found so endearing. On one speaking trip to Nevada, for example, he and Ruth found themselves in Las Vegas. In this gambling capital of the nation, slot machines were everywhere —even in the airport. While waiting for their plane to depart, Norman bought a newspaper for ten cents and made a telephone call for another dime. This left him with a nickel change from a quarter.

Across the lobby other departing passengers were feeding money into the one-armed bandits. "You know," Norman said suddenly, "I think I'll put this nickel into one of those machines and see what happens."

"What will happen," Ruth said, "is that you'll lose your money. Besides, it's gambling."

"It's only a nickel," Norman protested. "After all these years of rectitude, don't you think it would be all right?"

"It's the principle of the thing," Ruth pointed out calmly.

"Suppose someone should see you and be influenced by you?"

"No one will see me," Norman predicted confidently. "No-body knows me around here." He put his nickel in the nearest machine, seized the lever—and froze as he heard his name being called. "Oh, Dr. Peale," cried one of two beaming ladies who had come up behind him. "You don't know us, but we know you. We've heard you preach at Marble Church many times!"

Norman was so flustered that he didn't even look to see whether his nickel had won anything or not.

"You see," murmured Ruth when the ladies had departed, "your sins will find you out!"

Although he remained astonishingly youthful, Norman's perspective was changing in deeper ways. He was more tolerant of ideas that differed from his own, and of people who held such ideas. "You finally learn to accept people as they are," he told a friend. "That's a philosophy that doesn't come to you overnight. You have to grow into it."

There seemed to be a growing serenity about him, the assurance of a man who has fought hard battles with life, and with himself, and come through them intact. Fears and hesitancies dropped away, including one of the most basic fears of all. Loving life as he did, something in Norman had always shied away from the thought of death. But suddenly that dread was gone.

"It was a remarkable thing," he said, telling Ruth about it. "I was coming out of a hotel after speaking at a banquet. I guess we had been talking about death. And all of a sudden, looking up at the stars, I knew I was no longer afraid of it. All at once it seemed like such a simple thing, such a simple change."

"Don't think I'm ready to depart this life. I love living. I'm thrilled by everything, as much now as when I was a boy..." he paused... "perhaps even more."

Ruth shared this philosophy completely. One night in January 1972, the writer of this book happened to have dinner with the two of them in their apartment on Fifth Avenue. They were planning a trip to East Africa, where they had never been. Norman kept leaping up to bring brochures and guidebooks to the table. They were as excited as a pair of children. Knowing that in November alone they had made three separate trips to California, their guest marveled at their energy and enthusiasm.

"Oh," said Ruth, "one of the great discoveries we've made is that things don't have to slow down as you get older. On the contrary, they can get more exciting, more dynamic, more fulfilling. Good things can get better, big things can get bigger. Look at the Foundation, reaching and helping more and more people. Look at *Guideposts*, more readers every year. Look at us; we have more speaking engagements, more challenges and opportunities now than ever!"

"Yes," said Norman, "there are always great things in the future when you try to serve God and people."

Serving God and people . . . perhaps this is the place to leave them. Joyously doing just that.

AN AFTERWORD

by

Norman Vincent Peale

◈

First of all, never for one minute did I ever expect my biography to be written. That sort of thing I felt was reserved for statesmen and big business tycoons and movie stars—certainly not for preachers. For one thing, I couldn't see that there were in my life enough mountains and valleys or outstanding dramatic incidents as are found in most biographies where the hero becomes President or head of a big business corporation or wins a movie Oscar. True, there has been a lot of excitement in my life and not a little struggle. I have had my share of hard moments and compensating victories, and I have always found life terribly interesting, even fascinating; but I could not imagine anyone finding enough to make of it a full-scale biography.

But this was before I met Arthur Gordon, the author of this volume. He came to see me nearly twenty years ago when I was the center of some rather hostile controversy on the part of a few of the Protestant clergy hierarchy because I had published a book called *The Power of Positive Thinking.* This was written in the unchurchy language of the average person and showed how right thinking and faith could change people's lives and transform their defeats into victories through applied Christianity.

Arthur Gordon became interested in knowing what kind of character I was and interviewed me. Subsequently he wrote an article in a national magazine that presented a fair and dispassionate treatment. My publisher liked Arthur's work and in due course engaged him to undertake a biography.

If there is no other value in the work itself, I shall eternally be grateful that it was written, for it gave me the opportunity to form a friendship with a most remarkable man. For Arthur Gordon is a rare and gifted person, indeed I think a genius as an interpretive writer. Because he has a most disarming and sincere humility, and an honest depreciatory attitude as regards himself, he will no doubt vigorously disclaim these comments; but the fact remains that he is one of the few really great literary craftsmen of our time, a writer of extraordinary gifts.

Arthur is a man of idealistic nature, having deep spiritual motivation. He possesses the ability to enter into the lives of others to an unusual degree. As a guest in the home he is a member of the family, even to helping clear the table. He has the amazing power to know and recall the most minute details relating not only to the subject of his writing but all others in the family, friends, and even passing contacts with many people. This quality of perceptiveness lends amazing accuracy to his character delineations.

During the writing of this manuscript we were together constantly both in New York and our country home at Pawling and traveling to places connected with early days, during which developed an enduring admiration and affection for this creative man and consummate writer. Since this biography was to be published, I was honored indeed that the biographer selected turned out to be Arthur Gordon.

One incident serves to illustrate the astonishing sensitivity and perceptive powers which I have often seen demonstrated by Arthur. In Cincinnati one day we drove up Gilbert Avenue toward Peebles Corner. I described hot summer days in my boyhood riding with my parents up that long grade in an old-fashioned open streetcar in which the seats ran the width of the car, the conductor ringing up fares from an outside running board.

I told him how the condenser panted beneath the floorboards when the car stopped, and tried to describe the smells wafted up in the still, hot summer air.

I felt certain it was a nostalgic experience that could have reality only for those who experienced it, and Arthur's age precluded that. But to my astonishment when I read his manuscript the experience was so sharply and poignantly re-created that I found myself in tears reliving this acute memory of my boyhood.

If this all-too-generous account of one simple life can be of interest and inspiration, I shall be grateful indeed.

NORMAN VINCENT PEALE

ABOUT THE AUTHOR

ARTHUR GORDON lives in Savannah with his English-born wife Pamela and their children who are sixth-generation Georgians. He is a graduate of Yale and attended Oxford University in England as Rhodes Scholar from Georgia.

In 1936 Mr. Gordon joined the Hearst Magazine Company and by 1940 was Managing Editor of *Good Housekeeping*. He served for three years with the Eighth Air Force in World War II, emerging with the rank of lieutenant colonel. From 1946 to 1948 he was Editor-in-Chief of *Cosmopolitan*.

A versatile writer with many books and magazine articles to his credit, Mr. Gordon is a Staff Writer for *Reader's Digest* and a roving editor for *Guideposts*.

In 1955 he wrote an article on Norman Vincent Peale for *Redbook*. The two men have been close friends ever since, and this biography is the result of that friendship.